D1832429

CENSUS OF INDIA 1951

Census of India 1871-1951, 9 Sets In 384 Bindings (9788121258876) Rs. 700000

Census of India 1951, 27 Vols. In 58 Bindings (9788121271196) Rs. 117000

1. India - Report (9788121273169) Rs. 1750 (Vol. I, Pt. 1 - A)
2. India - Appendices to the Census Report (9788121273145) Rs. 2125 (Vol. I, Pt. 1 - B)
3. India - Demographic Tables (9788121273121) Rs. 2075 (Vol. I, Pt. 2-A)
4. India - Economic Tables (General Population) (9788121273107) Rs. 3475 (Vol. I, Pt. 2-B)
5. India - Economic Tables (Rural & Urban Population) (9788121273084) Rs. 2325 (Vol. I, Pt. 2-C)
6. UTTAR PRADESH - Report (9788121273060) Rs. 2640 (Vol. II, Pt. 1-A)
7. UTTAR PRADESH - Subsidiary Tables (9788121273046) Rs. 1375 (Vol. II, Pt. 1-B)
8. UTTAR PRADESH - GENERAL POPULATION TABLES (9788121273022) Rs. 1000 (Vol. II, Pt. 2-A)
9. UTTAR PRADESH - Economic Tables (9788121273008) Rs. 3540 (Vol. II, Pt. 2-B)
10. UTTAR PRADESH - AGE AND SOCIAL TABLES (9788121272988) Rs. 4280 (Vol. II, Pt. 2-C)
11. Madras And Coorg - Report (9788121272964) Rs. 1590 (Vol. III, Pt. 1-A)
12. Madras And Coorg - Tables (9788121272940) Rs. 1940 (Vol. III, Pt. 2-A)
13. Madras And Coorg - Tables (9788121272926) Rs. 1270 (Vol. III, Pt. 2-B)
14. Bombay, Saurashtra And Kutch - Report And Subsidiary Tables (9788121272902) Rs. 1750 (Vol. IV, Pt. 1)
15. Bombay, Saurashtra And Kutch - General Population Tables, Social And Cultural Tables And Summary (9788121272889) Rs. 2050 (Vol. IV, Pt. 2-A)
16. Bombay, Saurashtra And Kutch - Economic Tables And Household And Age (Sample) Tables (9788121272865) Rs. 2320 (Vol. IV, Pt. 2-B)
17. Bihar - Report (9788121272841) Rs. 1785 (Vol. V, Pt. 1)
18. Bihar - Tables (9788121274043) Rs. 3690 (Vol. V, Pt. 2-A)
19. Bihar - (Economic Tables) (9788121272827) Rs. 1680 (Vol. V, Pt. 2-B)
20. West Bengal, Sikkim & Chandernagore - Report and Vital Statistics West Bengal (9788121272803) Rs. 3700 (Vol. VI, Pt 1-A & B)
21. West Bengal, Sikkim & Chandernagore - Report (9788121272780) Rs. 2700 (Vol. VI, Pt. 1-C)
22. West Bengal, Sikkim & Chandernagore - Tables (9788121272766) Rs. 2740 (Vol. VI, Pt 2)
23. Calcutta City (9788121272742) Rs. 2900 (Vol. VI, Pt 3)
24. THE CALCUTTA INDUSTRIAL REGION - Tables (9788121272728) Rs. 2270 (Vol. VI, Pt 4)
25. Madhya Pradesh - Report (9788121272704) Rs. 2370 (Vol. VII, Pt. 1-A)
26. Madhya Pradesh - Subsidiary Tables And Notes Thereon (9788121272681) Rs. 1740 (Vol. VII, Pt. 1-B)
27. Madhya Pradesh - General Population Tables And Summary and Economic Tables (9788121272667) Rs. 2690 (Vol. VII, Pt. 2-A & B)
28. Madhya Pradesh Household And Age (Sample) Tables, And Social And Cultural Tables (9788121272629) Rs. 1740 (Vol. VII, Pt. 2-C)
29. Madhya Pradesh - Maternity Tables (9788121272605) Rs. 900 (Vol. VII, Pt. 2-D)
30. Punjab, Pepsu, Himachal Pradesh, Bilaspur & Delhi - Report (9788121272582) Rs. 3500 (Vol. VIII, Pt. 1-A)
31. Punjab, Pepsu, Himachal Pradesh, Bilaspur & Delhi - Subsidiary Tables (9788121272568) Rs. 1540 (Vol. VIII, Pt. 1-B)
32. Punjab, Pepsu, Himachal Pradesh, Bilaspur & Delhi - General Population, Age & Social Tables (9788121272544) Rs. 2175 (Vol. VIII, Pt. 2-A)
33. Punjab, Pepsu, Himachal Pradesh, Bilaspur & Delhi - Economic Tables (9788121272520) Rs. 1240 (Vol. VIII, Pt. 2-B)
34. Hyderabad - Report (9788121272506) Rs. 2900 (Vol. IX, Pt. 1-A)
35. Hyderabad - Subsidiary Tables (9788121272483) Rs. 1120 (Vol. IX, Pt. 1-B)
36. Hyderabad - Tables (9788121272469) Rs. 1270 (Vol. IX, Pt. 2-A)
37. Hyderabad - Tables (9788121274005) Rs. 1850 (Vol. IX, Pt. 2-B)
38. Rajasthan And Ajmer - Report (9788121272445) Rs. 2200 (Vol. X, Pt. 1-A)
39. Rajasthan And Ajmer - Subsidiary Tables And District Index of Non-Agricultural Occupations (9788121272421) Rs. 2440 (Vol. X, Pt. 1-B)
40. Rajasthan And Ajmer - Appendices (9788121272407) Rs. 1090 (Vol. X, Pt. 1-C)
41. Rajasthan And Ajmer - Tables (9788121272384) Rs. 2350 (Vol. X, Pt. 2-A)
42. Rajasthan And Ajmer - Economic Tables (9788121272360) Rs. 1640 (Vol. X, Pt. 2-B)
43. Orissa - Report (9788121272346) Rs. 2620 (Vol. XI, Pt. 1)
44. Orissa - Tables General Population, Social and Cultural and Land Tables (9788121272322) Rs. 1000 (Vol. XI, Pt. 2-A)
45. Orissa - Tables Tables Relating to Economic Classification, Household and Age (9788121272308) Rs. 1525 (Vol. XI, Pt. 2-B)
46. Assam, Manipur And Tripura - Report (9788121273961) Rs. 2380 (Vol. XII, Pt. 1-A)
47. Assam, Manipur And Tripura - Subsidiary Tables (9788121273947) Rs. 1175 (Vol. XII, Pt. 1-B)
48. Assam, Manipur And Tripura (9788121273909) Rs. 990 (Vol. XII, Pt. 2-A)
49. Assam, Manipur And Tripura - Economic Tables And Household And Age (Sample) Tables (9788121272285) Rs. 1575 (Vol. XII, Pt. 2-B)
50. Travancore-Cochin - Subsidiary Tables and Report and Tables (9788121272261) Rs. 2450 (Vol. XIII, Pt. 1 & 1-A & 2)
51. Mysore - Report (9788121272247) Rs. 2590 (Vol. XIV, Pt. 1)
52. Mysore - Tables (9788121272223) Rs. 1825 (Vol. XIV, Pt. 2)
53. Madhya Bharat & Bhopal - Report and Subsidiary Tables (9788121272209) Rs. 1210 (Vol. XV, Pt. 1-A & B)
54. Madhya Bharat & Bhopal -Tables General Population Tables, House-Hold And Age (Sample) Tables And Social And Cultural Tables (9788121273824) Rs. 1555 (Vol. XV, Pt. 2-A)
55. Madhya Bharat & Bhopal - Economic Tables (9788121273800) Rs. 1055 (Vol. XV, Pt. 2-B)
56. Vindhya Pradesh - Report And Subsidiary Tables (9788121272162) Rs. 1550 (Vol. XVI, Pt. 1)
57. Vindhya Pradesh - General Population, Age, Social And Economic Tables (9788121272148) Rs. 2050 (Vol. XVI, Pt. 2)
58. The Andaman And Nicobar Islands - Report & Tables (9788121272124) Rs. 680 (Vol. XVII, Pt. 1 & 2)

Owing to the antiquity and rarity of this book, certain pages are regrettably absent, and readability is compromised due to the blurring of the original text. If you possess any insights regarding the availability of these missing sections, kindly inform us. Your assistance is crucial in ensuring the completion of this significant work for the benefit of future generations.

CENSUS OF INDIA, 1951

VOLUME - XVII

THE ANDAMAN AND NICOBAR ISLANDS

PART I - REPORT
PART II - TABLES

A. K. GHOSH

GYAN

Published by

Gyan Publishing House
5, Ansari Road
Daryaganj, New Delhi-110002
Phone: 011-47034999, 9811692060
E-mail: books@gyanbooks.com

Distribution Network
gyanbooks.com
India, USA, Canada, UK, Australia

© Publisher

All rights reserved. No part of this work may be reproduced, stored, adapted, or transmitted in any form or by any means, electronic, mechanical, photocopying, micro-filming, recording or othrwise, or translated in any language, without the prior written permission of the copyright owner and the publisher.

ISBN: 978-81-212-7123-3 (Set) 28 Vols. In 52 Bindings

ISBN: 978-81-212-7212-4 (PB) Vol. XVII, Pt. I, II

First Published, 1955

2nd Impression 2024

Printed at: Gyan Press, Delhi.

The book is sold subject to the condition that it shall not, by way of trade or otherwise, be lent, resold, hired out, or otherwise circulated without the prior publisher's written consent.

CENSUS OF INDIA 1951

CENSUS OF INDIA, 1951

VOLUME XVII

THE ANDAMAN
AND
NICOBAR ISLANDS

PART I—REPORT
PART II—TABLES

A. K. GHOSH, I.C.S.,

Chief Commissioner

and

Ex-officio Superintendent of Census Operations,

Andaman & Nicobar Islands

PUBLISHED BY THE MANAGER OF PUBLICATIONS, DELHI

PRINTED BY THE GOVERNMENT OF INDIA PRESS, CALCUTTA, INDIA

1955

CONTENTS

PART I—REPORT

PART II—TABLES

General Population Tables

Economic Tables

Household and Age (Sample) Tables

Social and Cultural Tables

Summary Figures for Districts

PREFACE

THIS REPORT should really have been written by Shri S. K. Gupta, I.A.S., who was Deputy Commissioner of the Andaman and Nicobar Islands from 1948 to 1951, and who as Census Superintendent organized and carried out the census operations up to the stage of enumeration in March 1951. Shri Gupta, unfortunately, was transferred on the completion of his three years in March 1951. He was, therefore, unable to study the detailed figures after tabulation in order to write the report in the form indicated by the Government of India a few days before he made over charge. He did, however, write an introduction to the report. As that is not in the form required by Government, it has been published as Appendix 'A' to this report. The credit of organizing these census operations and carrying them through up to the difficult stage of enumeration is entirely his.

On the departure of Shri Gupta I took over census work. There was no other alternative, as I had been in these Islands then for two years, and as Shri Gupta's successor did not arrive till October, more than six months after he had left the Islands. Being preoccupied with my normal work, I have, unfortunately, not been able to spare very much time for census work. That is why this report has been delayed. I have been able to complete it just in time, on the eve of my own departure. I suggest that as census work is becoming more and more important, and in these Islands becoming more and more complex, a full-time Superintendent should be appointed for the 1961 Census. Although more economical, it is an unsatisfactory arrangement to saddle an officer who already has a full-time job to be part-time Superintendent in addition to his own other work.

It only remains for me to thank all those who have helped to carry this Census to a successful conclusion. I must make particular mention of Bishop John Richardson, M.P., who (himself a Nicobari) organized and ably carried out the census of all the Nicobar Islands under the able guidance of Shri Gupta. Bishop Richardson and his assistant Abednego crossed the seas in small sailing vessels and canoes during February and March 1951, and carried their labour of love to a successful conclusion. I must also mention Shri P. Sundaramurthi, Treasury Officer, who acted as Deputy Superintendent of Census Operations in addition to his other duties throughout, except for a brief period when he was posted elsewhere. My Secretary, Shri K. C. Banerjea, ably carried on the work of Deputy Superintendent during Shri Sundaramurthi's absence. Shri V. Sadasivan has ungrudgingly and without any remuneration given help whenever required in preparing tables and in studying the statistics. Shri V. Gurumurthi as clerk in charge of the Census Department was responsible for the able management of the office side of the work. My Personal Assistant, Shri P. J. Samuel ungrudgingly spared time from his numerous other duties to look after the census papers, and to type the report out of office hours at odd times. Last of all come a host of others, too numerous to mention, without whose willing help these censuses would not be possible—people who, because they work for the love of the work and without any payment, make our censuses so economical.

I am indebted to the writers of the previous Censuses, particularly to Sir Richard Temple, Mr. R. F. Lowis and Mr. M. C. Bonnington for the information contained in their reports. I have freely drawn upon this information in writing my own report.

A. K. GHOSH,
Chief Commissioner
&
Ex-officio Superintendent of Census Operations.

PORT BLAIR,
Dated the 20th July, 1953.

PART I
REPORT

CENSUS OF INDIA, 1951

REPORT

ON THE

ANDAMAN & NICOBAR ISLANDS

INTRODUCTION

It is usual in Census Reports to give detailed information about the history and geography of the area covered. But as information about the Andaman and Nicobar Islands can be found in previous Census Reports (noticeably in those of 1901 by Sir Richard Temple and of 1931 by Mr. M. C. Bonnington) I do not propose to give a detailed description of these Islands. But as conditions here are so unlike anything to be found in the rest of India, it is essential that a brief general description be given so that this report may be self-contained.

2. The Andaman and Nicobar Islands, though they form one administrative unit, and in this and previous Censuses were taken as one district, consist of two separate groups of islands with entirely different populations with their separate problems, and living under very dissimilar conditions. The Andamans consist of a chain of islands stretching from Landfall Island in the north to Little Andaman in the south, in an arc stretching over some 200 miles of sea. About 80 miles to the south of Little Andaman is Car Nicobar, the northernmost of the Nicobar group of islands, continuing in an arc for another 200 miles to Great Nicobar, which is only some 120 miles distant from the northern tip of Sumatra.

3. The Andaman Islands consist of five islands lying so close together as to form for all practical purposes one land mass, with Little Andaman some 40 miles to the south, but connected by a chain of little islands, which form stepping stones across the sea to Great Andamans. From time immemorial the Andaman Islands have been inhabited by a small Negrito people divided into several groups and tribes hostile to each other. Recent anthropological studies, both social and on their blood groups, tend to show that these Negritos are an extremely ancient people, who probably occupied the whole of South-East Asia in pre-historic times. They have cultural connections with the Semang of Malaya and the Aeta of the Philippines, as the recent researches of Professor Cipriani (an anthropologist who during 1951, 1952 and 1953 did valuable work in these Islands) will show. His note on the origin of these peoples may be seen in Appendix 'E'. These people continued in undisputed position of the Andamans (except for sporadic raids by Malays and Chinese who came here in ships to collect slaves) for countless generations until the first recorded attempt to colonize the Andamans was made in 1789, when Captain Archibald Blair, R. N., established a settlement under the orders of the Government of India at what is now known as Port Blair. A few years later this colony was moved to the north, to what is now known as Port Cornwallis. But the colony did not prosper because of malaria; and had ultimately to be closed down in 1796.

4. About sixty years later the question of opening a naval station in the Andamans to protect the crews of ships wrecked off these Islands was again mooted. While this was under discussion, and papers and despatches were travelling between London and Calcutta, the people of India made their first major attempt to throw out their alien conquerors in 1857. The ruthless suppression of the Mutiny resulted in problem of finding accommodation for a vast number of prisoners; and it was decided to send these men to the Andamans. The old settlement at Port Blair was revived; and the first batch of convicts arrived in 1858. The newcomers came into conflict with the original inhabitants, who naturally resented the coming of these strangers into their country; and there were several affrays between the aboriginals and the new settlers. In course of time one group of the aboriginals, the Andamanese, were won over and induced to come into the settlement, where they were not only boarded and lodged free but were given gifts. The result of this kind treatment has been the elimination of this tribe, who have decreased from an estimated four or five thousand in the 1860s to only twentythree in 1951. Such are the effects of the gifts of civilization (tobacco, alcohol, venereal and other diseases) to these primitive peoples! The

17 HOME/54

Jarawas, another group, have fortunately for themselves remained hostile ever since the foundation of the penal settlement—nearly a hundred years ago. Previous Census reports—those of 1901, 1911 and 1921—give details of expeditions led against these people. Such tactics have not endeared us to the Jarawas; and they have remained implacably hostile. It was therefore quite impossible to visit their camps and enumerate them; and only an estimate can be made of their numbers—an estimate based on the information obtained from Forest Officers who have been serving in these Islands for the last 20 or 30 years and know these forests intimately. The Jarawas number perhaps three or four hundred in all to-day. In 1901, Sir Richard Temple estimated their total at about 600. This shows that during the last fifty years this tribe at least has been more or less stationary in numbers—both Sir Richard Temple's figures and mine are only estimates. The third group of aboriginals lived in Little Andaman, and were saved from interference because of their isolation. They as well as the Jarawas continue to be in the same state of civilization as they were perhaps 10,000 years ago. Dr. Cipriani lived with the Onges for three months between February and May 1953, and succeeded in enumerating over 400 of them. He estimates their total number today at about 600. According to him these people are still living in the paleolithic (or the Old Stone) age. The Onges have, unfortunately for them, recently acquired the habit of coming from Little Andaman to Port Blair in their little canoes to obtain tobacoo, sugar and other luxuries not to be found in their native forests. If this continues, they will go the same way as the Andamanese in the course of next hundred years. As the numbers of the aboriginals declined, so the strength of the penal settlement increased, until it reached its zenith at the beginning of this century. It was ultimately abolished in 1945.

5. The people of the Nicobar Islands are entirely different racially from the aboriginals of the Andamans, whom they displaced many hundreds of years ago. They, unlike the Andamanese, are a vigorous and thriving people, who have adapted themselves to their changing conditions, and who are rapidly increasing in numbers now that hospitals and other medical aids have been made available to them. Their origin is a little doubtful: possibly they came from Burma originally. But as we travel to the south an increasing amount of Malayan and Chinese blood is noticeable. The people of all the Nicobar Islands have been enumerated for the first time in this Census—all of them except a few semi-hostile people who live in the interior of Great Nicobar, the Shom-Pens. Shri B. S. Chengapa, Conservator of Forests led an expedition to Great Nicobar in 1952, and travelled extensively over that island for two months. He came into contact with practically all the Shom-Pen settlements; and he estimates their total number to-day at about 200.

6. The decade 1941 to 1950 has been of tremendous importance to the Andaman Islands. It has marked the ending of an epoch with the abolition of the penal settlement in 1945. It witnessed the occupation of the country by an alien force—the Japanese—between March 1942 and October 1945, during which occupation the islands were very short of food because only military stores could be brought in due to the Allied blockade—and these only in submarines. The Allies landed a commando party by submarine in the Andamans, and the Japanese came to know of their presence, though they never succeeded in capturing the men. In order to extort information about these spies the Japanese troops inflicted severe and prolonged torture on many people, particularly people who knew English; and as a result of these tortures an unknown number of men, women and children died. When food was running short the Japanese Commander decided to take drastic steps: ruthlessly eliminate the old and the infirm, and leave only those who could work for the foreign invaders. As a result of this policy many hundreds of people were shot, and many more hundreds drowned in seas. By these and other methods the population of the Andamans was reduced by over 3,000 during the three years and a half the Japanese occupied the Islands. And had the Allies not come in October 1945, bringing with them supplies of food and medicines and clothes, the number of deaths would have been very much greater.

7. With the abolition of the penal settlement in 1945 a free pardon was granted to all convicts; and they as well as ex-convicts were all offered repatriation to their homes in the mother country at Government expense. Nearly 4,000 souls took advantage of this offer, with the result that by 1946 the population of the Islands had fallen below 14,000, whereas in 1941 it was over 21,000. But newcomers have been coming in at an increasing rate to replace these losses. Sporadic efforts have been made between 1949 and 1952 to resettle refugees from East Bengal on the lands abandoned by the repatriated convicts; and over 1,500 people have been so settled during these four years. These 1,500 people have occupied all the old available lands. But as the Andaman Islands are still definitely underpopulated, and have to rely on the mother country both for labour and for food, a proper plan has

been made to settle 20,000 people in these Islands during the next five years; and the first lot of about 400 pioneers under this scheme have already come to the Andamans in May and June 1953. They are but the forerunners of a great stream of immigrants who will more than double the population of the Andamans before the next Census is taken in 1961. As the present intentions are to continue the settlement of people—not all refugees—in these Islands even after the implementation of the first Five Year Scheme, the population of the Andaman Islands will continue to grow steadily until it numbers about a lakh of souls. After that there should be a pause, and a detailed survey made to find out how many people these Islands can support without danger to their very existence. As a glance at the maps (facing pages XLI & L) will show, the Andaman and Nicobar Islands are narrow, and no place is more than 10 or 12 miles from the sea. The country which is very hilly, is at present covered with dense forests. Indiscriminate destruction of these forests, and the conversion of the land into paddy fields may result in such soil erosion that in the course of a few generations the soil built up during millions of years will all be washed into the sea, and nothing but a chain of barren rocks in the sea will be left behind. That this is not an idle nightmare will be evident from a visit to several areas that have been indiscriminately deforested within the last hundred years.

CHAPTER I

General Population

1. Preliminary Remarks—The Andaman and Nicobar Islands, although they form one district both for civil administration and for the Census, consist of two entirely different groups of Islands with entirely different problems. In the Andamans the increase and decrease in population was until 1945 entirely artificial; and is even now far more influenced by outside factors than by natural causes. In the Nicobars, on the other hand, there is little outside interference; and increases and decreases are mainly due to natural causes.

From 1858 until October 1945 the Andaman Islands were a penal settlement; and except for the steadily decreasing number of aboriginals, almost the entire population consisted of convicts and of people who were in these Islands in connection with these convicts—warders, armed forces, administrative personnel, and merchants catering to the above. The strength of the population, therefore, depended entirely on the number of convicts that were sent to these Islands from the mainland. If a large number of convicts were received, up went the population; if, on the other hand, the number of convicts coming in fell below normal, down went the population.

Since the abolition of the penal settlement in 1945 no convicts have, it is true, been sent to these Islands. But artificial factors continue to influence the growth of population: the bringing in of large numbers of labourers from various parts of India on contract to serve in these Islands for one year has artificially inflated the immigration figures; the plan to settle refugees from East Pakistan in the Andamans has resulted in an increase of nearly ten per cent. of the population during the years 1949, 1950 and 1951.

For these reasons the figures for general distribution and density of population, for growth of population, for their movement and natural increase, as well as the livelihood pattern do not have much significance for the future. A change of conditions or a change of policy will immediately bring about large changes in these figures.

2. General distribution and density—The table below gives a comparative statement of the population for the last fifty years:

Year	Andamans	Nicobars
1901	18,138	6,511
1911	17,641	8,818
1921	17,814	9,272
1931	19,223	10,240
1941	21,316	12,452
1951	18,962	12,009

Although between 1901 and 1941 the population of the Nicobar Islands increased steadily, during the last decade it showed a small decrease. The decrease is due to the effects of the last war, when the Nicobar Islands were under the occupation of Japanese Forces, and the people suffered many hardships as a consequence. Another cause of this decrease is the severe epidemic of poliomyelitis that swept the Nicobars during 1947-48.

In the Andamans the population has fluctuated between 1901 and 1941 according as the strength of the penal settlement increased or decreased. But by 1941 the number of free settlers (those who had come of their own free will from the mainland to settle in the Andamans, as well as convicts who had elected to remain in these Islands after they had served their terms, and their children) was becoming an appreciable proportion of the total population; and just before the evacuation of the Islands in March 1942, the population of the Andamans was probably the highest it has ever been.

The Japanese Armed Forces occupied these Islands in March, 1942; and held sway here for over three years and a half, until the Allies occupied the Islands in October, 1945. A rough and ready census was taken on reoccupation by the Rationing authorities; and the population was found to be approximately 18,000. Thus, during this period the population decreased by 3,300, due to shortage of food, as well as because of the torture and the systematic killing by the Japanese Forces—towards the end of their tenure the Japanese evidently decided that the population should be reduced as the food supply was inadequate, since no food could be brought in from outside due to the Allied blockade. They, therefore, set about destroying the aged and the infirm in a systematic manner. Several hundred were shot, while several hundred more were taken out to sea in launches and thrown overboard miles from the nearest land.

When the Allied Forces reoccupied the Andaman Islands, the Government of India issued a proclamation abolishing the penal settlement, remitting all sentences, and offering to repatriate at Government expense all those who wished to return to India. Some 4,200 persons availed of this offer during 1945 and 1946. By the end of the latter year the population of the Andamans had sunk to a little under 14,000—a net reduction of 7,000 (or 33 per cent.) in some five years.

During the ensuing five years the population increased by over 5,000 (an increase of 36 per cent.) due to the influx of some 1,500 refugees, as well as a large number of labourers brought by the Forest and other Departments for work, since convict labour was no longer available.

3. Growth—As I have said before already, the growth of population in the Andamans is mainly due to artificial causes, not natural causes. In the Nicobars, where natural causes have free play, there was a slight set-back during the decade under review because of the war, and because of the sudden appearance of a disease (poliomyelitis) to which the Nicobarese were unaccustomed, and against which they therefore had no immunity.

4. Movement of population—Immigration and emigration are, as has already been stated, artificial, not natural, in so far as the Andaman Islands are concerned. As for the Nicobars, if we consider the islands as a whole, both immigration and emigration are for all practical purposes nil.

The immigration figures for the Andamans have been artificially swelled by the coming and going of labourers from the Chotanagpur Plateau of Bihar and from South India. These labourers, almost always single men, come to the Andamans on contract for one year; and nearly all of them return home after their year's work in these Islands. In addition to these temporary immigrants, between 1949 and 1951 some 1,500 displaced persons from East Bengal arrived in Port Blair, to be settled on lands vacant as a result of deaths during the Japanese regime, and the repartriation of convicts and ex-convicts on the abolition of the penal settlement in 1945.

5. Natural increase, births and deaths—As the Japanese Forces, for some unknown reason destroyed all old records, the figures for births and deaths prior to 1945 are not available. Hence it is impossible to calculate the increase in population due to natural causes—the excess of births over deaths—during this decade. But under normal conditions this increase is higher than in most parts of the rest of India, as figures available since 1946 show.

6. Livelihood pattern—Subsidiary Table I(8) (at page xvi) shows the distribution of the livelihood pattern per 10,000 of the general population. At first sight the figures for Class V (Production other than cultivation) look rather startling at 56·60 per cent. But this is somewhat misleading because in this class has been included the people of the Nicobar Islands. As the main source of livelihood of these people is their coconut plantations, supplemented by produce from small gardens, and as they do not cultivate land for annual crops, they have been classed as planters, not as cultivators. If we omit the Nicobarese, who, though not classed as cultivators, live off the land, the figures in Class V will come down from 56·60 per cent. to about 10 per cent., which is not at all an unreasonable figure.

The four agricultural classes together comprise some 14 per cent. of the general population; and out of this 14 per cent. the vast majority, that is to say about 13 per cent., belongs to the group of cultivators who either wholly or mainly own the land they cultivate. Only 0·5 per cent. are cultivators of land that is not wholly or mainly owned by them and their dependents. That is because in the Andamans there are practically no rent receiving interests: land is held by the cultivator directly under Government.

Private enterprise is still very small in the Andaman Islands; and most undertakings—the exploitation of the forests, the running of the sawmills, the running of the dockyard—are directly managed by Government. This explains the high percentage in Livelihood Class VIII—21 per cent. of the population being dependent for their livelihood on other services and miscellaneous sources.

7. Concluding remarks—The growth of population in the Andaman Islands will for many years to come continue to be largely influenced by outside factors. During the four years from 1949 to 1952 inclusive some 1,861 persons were brought from Bengal to settle in lands available in the South Andamans; and of them 1,527 remained behind, and only 334 have gone back to the mainland. This hap-hazard re-settlement of refugees has now stopped; and we have made plans systematically to deforest some 20,000 acres of land in the Middle Andamans and settle 4,000 families of agriculturists in these lands during the next five years. A beginning has already been made; and the first 100 families (comprising 356 souls) arrived in the Andamans during May and June 1953. On an average of five souls per family, this means that during the next five years some 20,000 persons (half of them refugees from Bengal and the other half volunteers from the rest of India) will be settled in the Andamans, thus more than doubling the population in half a decade. As the present intentions are to make a second Five Year Plan as soon as the first has been implemented, and as it is estimated that the Andaman Islands can support an agricultural population of about a lakh of souls, the natural increase in population will continue to be insignificant in comparison with the artificial for perhaps another generation.

The check in the increase of the Nicobarese population was only temporary. These people, who are healthy and vigorous, and to whom medical aid has been increasingly made available since the end of the war, continue to multiply at a rapid rate—I might almost say at an alarming rate, for they love their homes, and show a marked disinclination to emigrate even to the other islands of the Nicobar group. As a result, Car Nicobar, with an area of 49 sq. miles and a population of 8,374, is already overcrowded. We are, however, planning to induce families to emigrate to the less crowded islands by beginning forest operations in Nancowry, Katchal, Great and Little Nicobar, and opening forest villages there. Surplus families from Car Nicobar will be taken to these forest villages, the men given employment for four or five years, while the other members of their families establish coconut plantations, and then settled permanently in these villages when the plantations can support the people, when the forest operations will be transferred to some other place.

SUBSIDIARY TABLES

Series I

I (1) Area and Population, Actual and Percentage, by Taluk Density

Natural Division and District	Taluk with Density: Under 100 — Area	Under 100 — Population	100-150 — Area	100-150 — Population	150-200 — Area	150-200 — Population	200-300 — Area	200-300 — Population	300-450 — Area	300-450 — Population	450-600 — Area	450-600 — Population	600-750 — Area	600-750 — Population	750 & over — Area	750 & over — Population
(1)	(2)	(3)	(4)	(5)	(6)	(7)	(8)	(9)	(10)	(11)	(12)	(13)	(14)	(15)	(16)	(17)
Bay Islands																
Andaman & Nicobar District	3,215 (square miles)	31	..	..	..	..	..	..	..	..	..	..	..	..	..	..

I (2) Variation and Density of General Population

Natural Division and District	Population: Percentage Increase (+) / Decrease (—) 1941 to 1951	1931 to 1941	1921 to 1931	Density 1951	1941	1931	1921
(1)	(2)	(3)	(4)	(5)	(6)	(7)	(8)
Bay Islands							
Andaman & Nicobar District	—8·3	+14·6	+8·8	10	11	9	9

I (3) Mean Decennial Growth Rates during Three Decades

Natural Division and District	Mean population of decade 1941-50	1931-40	1921-30	Mean population of decade for area under registration of births and deaths 1941-50	1931-40	1921-30	Growth of population during decade 1941-50	1931-40	1921-30	Mean decennial growth rate 1941-50	1931-40	1921-30	Registered births during decade 1941-50	1931-40	1921-30
(1)	(2)	(3)	(4)	(5)	(6)	(7)	(8)	(9)	(10)	(11)	(12)	(13)	(14)	(15)	(16)
Bay Islands															
Andaman & Nicobar District	32,369	31,616	28,275	32,369	31,616	28,275	—2,797	+4,305	+2,377	—8·6	+13·6	+8·4	..	..	..

Series I—contd.

I (3) Mean Decennial Growth Rates during Three Decades—*concld.*

Natural Division and District	Mean decennial birth rate (registered)			Registered deaths during decade			Mean decennial death rate (registered)			Decennial rate of natural increase (registered)			Migration-cum-Registration error		
	1941-50	1931-40	1921-30	1941-50	1931-40	1921-30	1941-50	1931-40	1921-30	1941-50	1931-40	1921-30	1941-50	1931-40	1921-30
(1)	(17)	(18)	(19)	(20)	(21)	(22)	(23)	(24)	(25)	(26)	(27)	(28)	(29)	(30)	(31)
Bay Islands															
Andaman & Nicobar District	..	..	..	..	..	..	..	..	..	..	..	..	..	..	..

NOTE—Columns 14 to 31 cannot be filled up as all the previous census records have been destroyed by the Japanese during their occupation of these Islands.

I (4) Immigration

Natural Division and District where enumerated	Born in								
	District of enumeration			Other districts of same natural division			Other parts of the State		
	Persons	Males	Females	Persons	Males	Females	Persons	Males	Females
(1)	(2)	(3)	(4)	(5)	(6)	(7)	(8)	(9)	(10)
Bay Islands									
Andaman & Nicobar District	**19,323**	**9,964**	**9,359**	..	..	..	..	..	..

Natural Division and District where enumerated	Bron in											
							Beyond India					
	Adjacent States			Other parts of India			Pakistan			Other territories		
	Persons	Males	Females	Persons	Males	Females	Persons	Males	Females	Persons	Males	Female
(1)	(11)	(12)	(13)	(14)	(15)	(16)	(17)	(18)	(19)	(20)	(21)	(22)
Bay Islands												
Andaman & Nicobar District	..	..	..	**10,277**	**8,145**	**2,132**	..	..	..	**1,371**	**946**	**425**

I (5) Emigration

State where born	Enumerated in India									Enumerated outside India			Natural Population		
	State			Adjacent States			other States								
	Persons	Males	Females	Persons	Males	Females	Persons	Males	Females	Persons	Males	Females	Persons	Males	Female
(1)	(2)	(3)	(4)	(5)	(6)	(7)	(8)	(9)	(10)	(11)	(12)	(13)	(14)	(15)	(16)
Andaman & Nicobar Islands	..	..	..	..	..	..	**104**	**76**	**28**	..	..	..	**19,427**	**10,040**	**9,387**

I (6) Migration between the State and other parts of India

State	Immigration			Emigration			Immigration *minus* emigration	
	1951	1931	Variation	1951	1931	Variation	1951	1931
(1)	(2)	(3)	(4)	(5)	(6)	(7)	(8)	(9)
Andaman & Nicobar Islands	**10,277**	**14,255**	**3,978**	**104**	**552**	**448**	**10,173**	**13,703**

Series I—concld.

I (7) Variation in Natural Population

State	1951 Recorded Population	1951 Immigrants	1951 Emigrants	1951 Natural Population (2+4—3)	1931 Recorded Population	1931 Immigrants	1931 Emigrants	1931 Natural Population (6+8—7)	Percentage Increase (+) Decrease (—) (1931-51) in Natural Poputation
(1)	(2)	(3)	(4)	(5)	(6)	(7)	(8)	(9)	(10)
Andaman & Nicobar Islands	**30,971**	**11,648**	**104**	**19,427**	**29,463**	**14,255**	**552**	**15,760**	**+23·3**

I (8) Livelihood Pattern of General Population

Natural Division and District	Per 10,000 of General Population belonging to Livelihood Class I	II	III	IV	V	VI	VII	VIII
(1)	(2)	(3)	(4)	(5)	(6)	(7)	(8)	(9)
Bay Islands								
Andaman & Nicobar District	**1,313**	**53**	**42**	**16**	**5,660**	**464**	**353**	**2,099**

CHAPTER II

Rural Population

1. Preliminary remarks—This is the first time that any distinction has been made in these Islands between rural and urban areas: until the 1941 Census the entire area was treated as rural. For the 1951 Census, only the Headquarters area (that is to say Port Blair) has been treated as urban; and all the rest of the Islands as rural. But even in Port Blair, though it has electric light, running water, tarred roads and a taxi service of a sort, conditions still verge on the rural. And until recently the entire developed area of the Andamans (except for a few temporary forest camps where extraction of timber was going on) was within a few miles of Port Blair. Conditions to-day are changing rapidly, with the proposal to settle in the Middle Andamans in the next five years an agricultural population that will exceed the present total population of the Andaman Islands. Simultaneously, Mayabander is quickly developing as the Headquarters area for the North Andamans; and by 1961 that also will probably be classified as an urban area, for there also forest industries—a sawmill and a plywood factory—are developing, and the amenities of life are being provided gradually.

2. General distribution—The total urban population, the inhabitants of Port Blair, number 8,014 only. All the rest of the people, numbering 22,957, and comprising 74·1 per cent. of the total population, live in villages scattered throughout the Andaman and Nicobar Islands; but are mostly concentrated in the south of the Andamans and in Car Nicobar Island.

3. Growth—As I have said in the first chapter, growth of population in the Andaman Islands, both urban and rural, is governed entirely by outside factors. The entire population of the Nicobar Islands being rural, the remarks made about their growth in the first chapter hold good for this chapter also.

4. Movement—As this is the first time that areas have been classified into urban and rural, no figures can be given showing the movement into or out of urban areas.

5. Natural increase, births and deaths—Unfortunately it is not possible to compare the natural increase during the decade 1941 to 1950 with previous decades, because all records, including those of births and deaths, were destroyed during the Japanese occupation. Moreover, during this period of occupation artificial factors grately enhanced the death rate.

6. Livelihood pattern—The livelihood pattern for the rural population shows somewhat the same trend as for the general population. A high percentage belongs to Class V—Production other than cultivation—because the coconut planters of the Nicobars have been shown in this class.

The entire cultivated area—cultivated for paddy—is in the Andamans; and therefore the agricultural classes are in the Andamans alone.

7. Concluding remarks—Rural population in the Andamans is bound to increase rapidly with the implementation of the plans to colonize the Middle and the North Andamans, which are at present almost uninhabited. When this happens, the population of the Andaman Islands will be predominantly rural. This is as it should be; for the Islands will then be able to produce more food than they require. This is essential for the safety of a community cut off by hundreds of miles of sea from the mother country, as our experiences during the last war showed. Because of the Allied blockade, the Japanese occupying forces were able to import food and other necessities in progressively decreasing quantities during 1944 and 1945—practically bringing in nothing except military stores during the latter year. The people of the Andaman Islands which was deficit in food, and a large part of whose requirements came from the mainland of India before the war, suffered terribly; and thousands died. The total number of deaths in the Nicobar Islands, on the other hand, was perhaps a hundred or two—because the Nicobarese were self-sufficient in food, and continued to live off the produce of their coconut plantations and their

17 HOME/54

gardens during the war, as they had done before. The lesson is there for all to see: a balanced economy is essential if these Islands are to prosper.

SUBSIDIARY TABLES

Series II

II (1) Distribution of Population between Villages

Natural Division and District	Population per Village	Number per 1,000 of General Population in Villages	Number per 1,000 Rural Population in Villages with a population of 5,000 & over	2,000 to 5,000	500 to 2,000	Under 500
(1)	(2)	(3)	(4)	(5)	(6)	(7)
Bay Islands						
Andaman & Nicobar Islands	**122**	**741**	..	..	**238**	**762**

II (4) Livelihood Pattern of Rural Population

Natural Division and District	Per 10,000 Rural Population belonging to Livelihood Classes I	II	III	IV	V	VI	VII	VIII
(1)	(2)	(3)	(4)	(5)	(6)	(7)	(8)	(9)
Bay Islands								
Andaman & Nicobar Islands	**1,694**	**69**	**56**	**16**	**6,551**	**163**	**194**	**1,257**

NOTE—*This is the first time that an attempt has been made to distinguish RURAL and URBAN population and hence, Table II (2)—Variation and Density of Rural Population and Table II(3)—Mean Decennial Growth Rates during Three Decades of Rural Population, cannot be compiled.*

CHAPTER III

Urban Population

As I have already said in Chapter II, this is the first time that a distinction has been made between urban and rural areas in these Islands. Port Blair, with a population of 8,014, has been classified as an urban area—the only urban area in the Andaman and Nicobar Islands—as it is a small provincial town. There are no cities in these Islands, nor are any likely to spring up for many generations to come.

SUBSIDIARY TABLES

Series III

III (1) Distribution of Population between Towns

Natural Division and District	Population per Town	Number in Towns per 1,000 of General Population	Number per 1,000 of Urban Population in Towns with Population of			
			20,000 & over	10,000 to 20,000	5,000 to 10,000	Under 5,000
(1)	(2)	(3)	(4)	(5)	(6)	(7)
Bay Islands						
Andaman & Nicobar Islands	**8,014**	**259**	..	..	**1,000**	..

III (6) Number per 1,000 of the General Population and of each Livelihood Class who live in Towns

Natural Division and District	General Population	Livelihood Class							
		I	II	III	IV	V	VI	VII	VIII
(1)	(2)	(3)	(4)	(5)	(6)	(7)	(8)	(9)	(10)
Bay Islands									
Andaman & Nicobar Islands	**265**	**44**	**42**	**15**	**250**	**142**	**739**	**593**	**556**

III (7) Livelihood Pattern of Urban Population

Natural Division and District	Per 10,000 Urban Population belonging to Livelihood Classes							
	I	II	III	IV	V	VI	VII	VIII
(1)	(2)	(3)	(4)	(5)	(6)	(7)	(8)	(9)
Bay Islands								
Andaman & Nicobar Islands	**221**	**9**	**2**	**15**	**3,107**	**1,325**	**809**	**4,512**

NOTE—*Only during this 1951 Census these Islands were divided into URBAN and RURAL areas and hence, Table III(2)—Variation and Density of Urban Population, Table III(3)—Mean Decennial Growth Rates during Three Decades, Table III(4)—Towns Classified by Population and Table III(5)—Cities—Chief Figures, cannot be compiled.*

CHAPTER IV

Agricultural Classes

1. Preliminary remarks—Out of a total population of 30,971 in the Andaman and Nicobar Islands in 1951, 4,411 have been recorded as agriculturists. That is to say, only 14·2 per cent. of the total population are shown as agriculturists. This figure is misleading, because the entire population of the Nicobar Islands live off the land, even though they have been recorded as plantation owners because they own coconut plantations. If we add the population of the Nicobars to the number of agriculturists in the Andamans, the percentage of people living off the land in the Andaman and Nicobar Islands rises to 16,400, which is 53 per cent. of the total population, and is a reasonable figure.

Other persons also live off the land, but indirectly; people like the large number of labourers employed by the Forest Department for felling, dragging, rafting and shipping timber. But as these men draw monthly wages, and do not live off what they themselves produce from the land, they cannot be classed as agriculturists.

2. Agricultural population—It may not be out of place to remark here that the broad classification of the agricultural population into four groups is unsuited to the conditions prevailing in the Andamans. Land here is allotted to a person on lease for a certain period under certain conditions directly by Government, which ultimately owns all the land. There are practically no intermediate rent receiving classes. Because of this, Class I (Cultivators of land wholly or mainly owned) and Class IV (Non-cultivating owners of land; Agricultural rent receivers, etc.) are non-existent. But to fit the present set-up here within the four classes, the procedure adopted was to classify all those who hold land directly under Government as Class I, those who cultivate land leased by another in Class II, and in Class IV are included those who receive rent in cash or in kind for land leased to them but cultivated by some other person.

3. Active and semi-active workers in cultivation— All self-supporting persons in the three agricultural classes (Classes I to III) are classified as active workers. Self-supporters in non-agricultural classes with cultivation as a secondary means of livelihood, as well as the earning dependants of the three agricultural classes are considered to be semi-active workers. Their numbers given in Subsidiary Table IV (6) (at page xxiii) represent 7·8 per cent. of the total population. The percentage of semi-active workers is 44, as against 55 per cent. of active workers. These figures show that all available manpower has been enlisted for cultivation, due to the fact that there is a shortage of agricultural labour in these Islands, as there is indeed of all kinds of labour. Because of this shortage of labour, and because jobs are easily available in Government run industries (the Forest Department, the Marine Department, the P. W. D., etc.), the percentage of active workers engaged wholly in cultivation is reduced.

4. The proportion of active and semi-active workers to the total population is 1 : 12·8— That is to say, a single agriculturist feeds thirteen persons. This figure might, however, give a wrong impression because many people are engaged in industries; and their wages go to purchase food and other necessities of life from the mainland of India.

5. Progress of Cultivation —Paddy is the main crop in the Andaman Islands, coconut in the Nicobars. In the latter the largest number of people is concentrated in Car Nicobar, where there is very little room for expansion. On the other islands the number is more or less stationary, and so is the area under coconut. It will be necessary for the people of Car Nicobar to emigrate to some of the other less crowded islands, and set up coconut plantations themselves on virgin land there if they are not to perish. We have, unfortunately, as yet no figure of the area under coconut in the Nicobar Islands.

In the Andaman Islands the area under paddy in 1931 was 4,100 acres; and this has increased to 5,600 acres by 1951—even though some 500 acres of good land have been temporarily thrown out of use due to damage to dykes, and inundation of sea water. These lands will again soon be reclaimed by rebuilding the sea walls and repairing the old sluice gates. Even though the area under cultivation has increased, and continue to increase slowly, the production of food is still quite inadequate to feed the population of the Andamans; and more than half the foodgrains needed still continue to be imported from the mainland of India.

But it is hoped to change all this within the next decade, because under the Five-Year Colonization scheme it is planned to bring an additional 20,000 acres under cultivation before the end of this decade. When this happens the Islands will be self-sufficient at least in respect of rice, even though the population will have been doubled within this period.

6. Conclusion—When the present Five-Year Colonization scheme has been completed the Andamans will contain a more balanced population, the agricultural class ceasing to be only some 24 per cent. of the general population, as at present. (I am speaking only of the Andaman Islands just now). By the time the second Five-Year Plan has been implemented the Islands should be surplus not only in food but also in labour. It should then no longer be necessary to import labourers at great expense on a year's contract to work in the forests and in the other departments of Government; and it should be possible to export rice to the motherland in return for the food she has been sending to these Islands ever since the establishment of the penal settlement nearly a hundred years ago.

SUBSIDIARY TABLES

Series IV

IV (1) Agricultural Classes per 1,000 persons of General Population ; number in each class and sub-class of 10,000 persons of All Agricultural Classes ; and comparison with agricultural holdings by size

Natural Division and District	Agricultural Classes per 1,000 persons of General Population	Number per 10,000 persons of All Agricultural Classes: Total — Self-supporting persons	Total — Non-earning dependants	Total — Earning dependants	I—Cultivators of land wholly or mainly owned and their dependants	II—Cultivators of land wholly or mainly unowned and their dependants	III—Cultivating labourers and their dependants	IV—Non-cultivating owners of land; Agricultural rent receivers and their dependants
(1)	(2)	(3)	(4)	(5)	(6)	(7)	(8)	(9)
Bay Islands								
Andaman & Nicobar Islands . .	**142**	**3,122**	**6,395**	**483**	**9,220**	**374**	**297**	**109**

Natural Division and District	Distribution of 1,000 agricultural holdings by size of holding (in acres): 0 to 1	1 to 2	2 to 3	3 to 4	4 to 5	5 to 6	6 to 7	7 to 8	8 to 9	Above 9
(1)	(10)	(11)	(12)	(13)	(14)	(15)	(16)	(17)	(18)	(19)
Bay Islands										
Andaman & Nicobar Islands . .	**10**	**170**	**220**	**335**	**202**	**45**	**12**	**4**	**1**	**1**

IV (2) Livelihood Class I (Cultivators of land wholly or mainly owned and their dependants)

Number per 10,000 persons of Livelihood Class I in each sub-class ; Secondary Means of Livelihood of 10,000 persons of Livelihood Class I

Natural Division and District	Number per 10,000 of Livelihood Class I: Self-supporting persons	Non-earning dependants	Earning dependants	Number per 10,000 of Livelihood Class I whose Secondary Means of Livelihood is: Cultivation of owned land — Self-supporting persons	Cultivation of owned land — Earning dependants	Cultivation of unowned land — Self-supporting persons	Cultivation of unowned land — Earning dependants	Employment as cultivating labourers — Self-supporting persons	Employment as cultivating labourers — Earning dependants
(1)	(2)	(3)	(4)	(5)	(6)	(7)	(8)	(9)	(10)
Bay Islands									
Andaman & Nicobar Islands . .	**2,963**	**6,535**	**502**	..	**54**	..	**194**	..	**108**

Natural Division and District	Number per 10,000 of Livelihood Class I whose Secondary Means of Livelihood is: Rent on Agricultural land — Self-supporting persons	Rent on Agricultural land — Earning dependants	Production other than cultivation — Self-supporting persons	Production other than cultivation — Earning dependants	Commerce — Self-supporting persons	Commerce — Earning dependants	Transport — Self-supporting persons	Transport — Earning dependants	Other services and miscellaneous sources — Self-supporting persons	Other services and miscellaneous sources — Earning dependants
(1)	(11)	(12)	(13)	(14)	(15)	(16)	(17)	(18)	(19)	(20)
Bay Islands										
Andaman & Nicobar Islands . .	**2**	..	**118**	**2**	**219**	**17**	**10**	..	**263**	**125**

Series IV—contd.

IV (3) Livelihood Class II (Cultivators of land wholly or mainly unowned and their dependants)

Number per 10,000 persons of Livelihood Class II in each sub-class ; Secondary Means of Livelihood of 10,000 persons of Livelihood Class II

Natural Division and District	Number per 10,000 of Livelihood Class II			Number per 10,000 of Livelihood Class II whose Secondary Means of Livelihood is					
				Cultivation of owned land		Cultivation of unowned land		Employment as cultivating labourers	
	Self-supporting persons	Non-earning dependants	Earning dependants	Self-supporting persons	Earning dependants	Self-supporting persons	Earning dependants	Self-Supporting persons	Earning dependants
(1)	(2)	(3)	(4)	(5)	(6)	(7)	(8)	(9)	(10)
Bay Islands									
Andaman & Nicobar Islands	**4,121**	**5,515**	**364**	..	..	..	**61**	..	..

Natural Division and District	Number per 10,000 of Livelihood Class II whose Secondary Means of Livelihood is									
	Rent on agricultural land		Production other than cultivation		Commerce		Transport		Other services and miscellaneous sources	
	Self-supporting persons	Earning dependants	Self-supporting persons	Earning dependants	Self-supporting persons	Earning dependants	Self-supporting persons	Earning dependants	Self-supporting persons	Earning dependants
(1)	(11)	(12)	(13)	(14)	(15)	(16)	(17)	(18)	(19)	(20)
Bay Islands										
Andaman & Nicobar Islands	..	**61**	**424**	..	**364**	..	..	..	..	**242**

IV (4) Livelihood Class III (Cultivating labourers and their dependants)

Number per 10,000 persons of Livelihood Class III in each sub-class ; Secondary Means of Livelihood of 10,000 persons of Livelihood Class III

Natural Division and District	Number per 10,000 of Livelihood Class III			Number per 10,000 of Livelihood Class III whose Secondary Means of Livelihood is					
				Cultivation of owned land		Cultivation of unowned land		Employment as cultivating labourers	
	Self-supporting persons	Non-earning dependants	Earning dependants	Self-supporting persons	Earning dependants	Self-supporting persons	Earning dependants	Self-supporting persons	Earning dependants
(1)	(2)	(3)	(4)	(5)	(6)	(7)	(8)	(9)	(10)
Bay Islands									
Andaman & Nicobar Islands	**6,183**	**3,817**	..	..	..	..	..	..	..

Natural Division and District	Number per 10,000 of Livelihood Class III whose Secondary Means of Livelihood is									
	Rent on agricultural land		Production other than cultivation		Commerce		Transport		Other services and miscellaneous sources	
	Self-supporting persons	Earning dependants	Self-supporting persons	Earning dependants	Self-supporting persons	Earning dependants	Self-supporting persons	Earning dependants	Self Supporting persons	Earning dependants
(1)	(11)	(12)	(13)	(14)	(15)	(16)	(17)	(18)	(19)	(20)
Bay Islands										
Andaman & Nicobar Islands	..	..	**458**	..	**305**	..	..	..	**76**	..

Series IV—contd.

IV (5) Livelihood Class IV (Non-cultivating owners of land ; Agricultural rent receivers and their dependants)

Number per 10,000 persons of Livelihood Class IV in each sub-class ; Secondary Means of Livelihood of 10,000 persons of Livelihood Class IV

Natural Division and District	Number per 10,000 of Livelihood Class IV			Number per 10,000 of Livelihood Class IV whose Secondary Means of Livelihood is					
				Cultivation of owned land		Cultivation of unowned land		Employment as cultivating labourers	
	Self-supporting persons	Non-earning dependants	Earning dependants	Self-supporting persons	Earning dependants	Self-supporting persons	Earning dependants	Self-supporting persons	Earning dependants
(1)	(2)	(3)	(4)	(5)	(6)	(7)	(8)	(9)	(10)
Bay Islands									
Andaman & Nicobar Islands	**4,792**	**4,583**	**625**	..	..	..	..	..	..

Natural Division and District	Number per 10,000 of Livelihood Class IV whose Secondary Means of Livelihood is									
	Rent on agricultural land		Production other than cultivation		Commerce		Transport		Other services and miscellaneous sources	
	Self-supporting persons	Earning dependants	Self-supporting persons	Earning dependants	Self-supporting persons	Earning dependants	Self-supporting persons	Earning dependants	Self-supporting persons	Earning dependants
(1)	(11)	(12)	(13)	(14)	(15)	(16)	(17)	(18)	(19)	(20)
Bay Islands										
Andaman & Nicobar Islands	..	..	**417**	..	**209**	**209**	..	..	**1,250**	**417**

IV (6) Active and Semi-active Workers in Cultivation

Natural Division and District	Cultivation				Cultivation of owned land			
	Total	Principal means of livelihood of self-supporting persons	Secondary means of livelihood of self-supporting persons whose principal means of livelihood is other than cultivation	Secondary means of livelihood of earning dependants	Total	Principal means of livelihood of self-supporting persons	Secondary means of livelihood of self-supporting persons whose principal means of livelihood is other than cultivation	Secondary means of livelihood of earning dependants
(1)	(2)	(3)	(4)	(5)	(6)	(7)	(8)	(9)
Bay Islands								
Andaman & Nicobar Islands	**2,422**	**1,354**	**905**	**163**	**2,063**	**1,205**	**826**	**32**

Natural Division and District	Cultivation of unowned land				Employment as cultivating labourers			
	Total	Principal means of livelihood of self-supporting persons	Secondary means of livelihood of self-supporting persons whose principal means of livelihood is other than cultivation	Secondary means of livelihood of earning dependants	Total	Principal means of livelihood of self-supporting persons	Secondary means of livelihood of self-supporting persons whose principal means of livelihood is other than cultivation	Secondary means of livelihood of earning dependants
(1)	(10)	(11)	(12)	(13)	(14)	(15)	(16)	(17)
Bay Islands								
Andaman & Nicobar Islands	**222**	**68**	**71**	**83**	**137**	**81**	**8**	**48**

AGRICULTURAL CLASSES

Series IV—concld.

IV (7) Progress of Cultivation during Three Decades

Natural Division and District	Average net sown (A1) in acres				Average area sown more than once (A2) in acres				Average net area irrigated (A3) in acres				Average area irrigated more than once (A4) in acres			
	1951	1941	1931	1921	1951	1941	1931	1921	1951	1941	1931	1921	1951	1941	1931	1921
(1)	(2)	(3)	(4)	(5)	(6)	(7)	(8)	(9)	(10)	(11)	(12)	(13)	(14)	(15)	(16)	(17)
Bay Islands																
Andaman & Nicobar Islands	3,810*	..	..	..	23*	..	..	..	..	..	..	..	..	..	..	..

*On the basis of records available for 4 crop years from 1947-48 to 1950-51. Previous records have been destroyed by the Japanese during their occupation of these Islands.

The area relates to paddy only as no records of other foodgrains are available.

Columns 10 to 17 cannot be filled up as no irrigation system exists in these Islands.

IV (8) Components of Cultivated Area *per Capita* during Three Decades

Natural Division and District	Unirrigated single-crop cultivation *per Capita* (U.S.C.) (in cents)				Unirrigated double-crop cultivation *per Capita* (U.D.C.) (in cents)				Irrigated single-crop cultivation *per Capita* (I.C.S.) (in cents)				Irrigated double-crop cultivation *per Capita* (I.D.C.) (in cents)			
	1951	1941	1931	1921	1951	1941	1931	1921	1951	1941	1931	1921	1951	1941	1931	1921
(1)	(2)	(3)	(4)	(5)	(6)	(7)	(8)	(9)	(10)	(11)	(12)	(13)	(14)	(15)	(16)	(17)
Bay Islands																
Andaman & Nicobar Islands	12·2	..	..	..	0·08	..	..	..	..	..	..	..	..	..	..	..

IV (9) Land Area *per Capita* (1951); and Trend of cultivation *per Capita* during Three Decades

Natural Division and District	Land Area *per Capita* (1951)		Area of Cultivation *per Capita* (in cents)			
	Total land area *per Capita* (in cents)	Area cultivated and cultivable *per Capita* (in cents)	1951	1941	1931	1921
(1)	(2)	(3)	(4)	(5)	(6)	(7)
Bay Islands						
Andaman & Nicobar Islands	6,643·6	18·8	18·8	*	14	*

* Figures not available.

CHAPTER V

Non-Agricultural Classes

Preliminary remarks—Although the tables show that the non-agricultural classes comprise a vast majority of the population, this is because the people of the Nicobar Islands has (as has repeatedly been pointed out before) been included as non-agriculturists. If the figures for the Nicobars are omitted, we shall obtain a truer picture. Even so, the proportion of non-agriculturists to agriculturists is rather high. That is because until now the land under cultivation in the Andamans is comparatively small ; and a large number of people work in the Government dockyard, in the Government sawmill, and for Government in forests extracting timber.

2. Non-Agricultural population ratios—A great difference will be noticed between agricultural and non-agricultural classes in the ratio of self-supporters and non-earning dependants. This is explained by the fact that many children, and almost all the women in the Nicobar Islands work equally with their fathers and their husbands in the plantations.

3. Employers, Employees and Independent Workers—Out of every 10,000 self-supporters, only 50 are employers, while 7,583 are employees and 2,332 are independent workers. This is explained by the fact that in the Andamans nearly all employment is controlled by the State ; and as yet there is little private enterprise. This will gradually change with the development of these Islands, and the establishment of small scale industries, as is contemplated at present. The large percentage of employees—76·2 per cent. of the total number of self-supporters—include the many people employed in the various Government departments and Government industries, such as the Labour Force, the Public Works Department, the Forest Department, the sawmills and the Government dockyard.

The independent workers are men, earning their living as fishermen, petty shop-keepers, carpenters, and small craftsmen.

4. Primary industries other than cultivation, mining and quarrying—This class represents nearly half of all the industries in these Islands ; and forestry and wood working occupies the first place.

5. Mining and quarrying—These industries do not, for all practical purposes, as yet exist in these Islands.

6. Processing and manufacture of foodstuffs, textile, leather—These industries are also conspicuous by their absence. A few people are engaged in weaving and a few men as tailors. Others prepare vegetable oils (mostly coconut oil) and dairy products, followed by makers of aerated waters and other beverages for sale locally.

7. Processing and manufacture of metals and chemicals—Heavy industries are completely absent from these Islands. The few people shown in Subsidiary Table V(11) (at page xxx) are mostly workers in the Government dockyard, engaged in repairing steel hulled boats and launches. The figures also include a few independent workers in metals like gold and silver, as well as tinsmiths, blacksmiths, etc.

8. Processing and manufacture not specified elsewhere—The vast majority of the few people shown in Subsidiary Table V(12) (at page xxx) are workers in wood—sawyers, carpenters, turners, and joiners—as is to be expected in a place like the Andamans where wood is found in abundance, and all buildings are of timber.

9. Construction and utilities—Most of the people shown in Subsidiary Table V(13) (at page xxx) are workers in public utilities—sweepers and scavengers employed by the Medical Department of this Administration. Others are engaged on the construction and maintenance of roads, bridges and buildings under the P. W. D., while yet others are employed in the local power station run by Government.

10. Commerce—There is very little commerce as such in these Islands: most of the people shown in Subsidiary Table V(14) (at page xxxi) being petty businessmen engaged in retail trade. There being no banking or insurance facilities in the Andamans, practically no people are engaged in these businesses.

11. Concluding remarks—Because of the deviations made in the classification of non-agricultural groups and in industries and services from previous census, it is not possible to make a comparative study of these groups.

All things considered, the enumerators have done a good job of work and have made a reasonably correct appraisal of the various categories. Their work has been facilitated by the fact that in this small community most people know each other, and know what they are doing.

The absence of major industries is very marked, as is also the fact that Government is the largest, and almost the only employer. But within the next decade the position should change considerably ; and a number of small industries should have developed. Moreover, the right to exploit nearly 700 sq. miles of forests in the

17 Home/54

North Andamans was in 1951 leased out for 25 years to a Company. This should lead in due course to the establishment of industries connected with timber in Mayabander, and the employment of a large number of people by this Company there.

SUBSIDIARY TABLES

Series V

V (1) Non-Agricultural Classes per 1,000 persons of General Population ; number in each Class and Sub-Class per 10,000 persons of All Non-Agricultural Classes ; and number of Employers, Employees and Independent Workers per 10,000 Self-supporting persons of All Non-Agricultural Classes

Natural Division and District	Non-Agricultural Classes per 1,000 persons of General Population	Number per 10,000 persons of All Non-Agricultural Classes — Total — Self-supporting persons	Non-earning dependants	Earning dependants	V—Production other than cultivation	VI—Commerce
(1)	(2)	(3)	(4)	(5)	(6)	(7)
Bay Islands						
Andaman & Nicobar Islands	**858**	**3,749**	**3,619**	**2,632**	**6,599**	**541**

Natural Division and District	Number per 10,000 persons of All Non-Agricultural Classes — VII—Transport	VIII—Other services and miscellaneous sources	Number per 10,000 Self-supporting persons of All Non-Agricultural Classes — Employers	Employees	Independent Workers	Others
(1)	(8)	(9)	(10)	(11)	(12)	(13)
Bay Islands						
Andaman & Nicobar Islands	**412**	**2,448**	**50**	**7,583**	**2,332**	**35**

V (2) Livelihood Class V (Production other than cultivation)

Number per 10,000 persons of Livelihood Class V in each Sub-Class ; Number per 10,000 Self-supporting persons of Livelihood Class V who are Employers, Employees and Independent Workers ; Secondary Means of Livelihood of 10,000 persons of Livelihood Class V

Natural Division and District	Number per 10,000 of Livelihood Class V — Self-supporting persons	Non-earning dependants	Earning dependants	Number per 10,000 Self-supporting persons of Livelihood Class V — Employers	Employees	Independent Workers
(1)	(2)	(3)	(4)	(5)	(6)	(7)
Bay Islands						
Andaman & Nicobar Islands	**2,976**	**3,117**	**3,907**	**12**	**7,331**	**2,657**

Number per 10,000 of Livelihood Class V whose Secondary Means of Livelihood is

Natural Division and District	Cultivation of owned land — Self-supporting persons	Cultivation of owned land — Earning dependants	Cultivation of unowned land — Self-supporting persons	Cultivation of unowned land — Earning dependants	Employment as cultivating labourers — Self-supporting persons	Employment as cultivating labourers — Earning dependants	Rent on agricultural land — Self-supporting persons	Rent on agricultural land — Earning dependants
(1)	(8)	(9)	(10)	(11)	(12)	(13)	(14)	(15)
Bay Islands								
Andaman & Nicobar Islands	**377**	**1**	**12**	..	**4**	**2**	**12**	..

Number per 10,000 of Livelihood Class V whose Secondary Means of Livelihood is

Natural Division and District	Production other than cultivation — Self-supporting persons	Production other than cultivation — Earning dependants	Commerce — Self-supporting persons	Commerce — Earning dependants	Transport — Self-supporting persons	Transport — Earning dependants	Other services and miscellaneous sources — Self-supporting persons	Other services and miscellaneous sources — Earning dependants
(1)	(16)	(17)	(18)	(19)	(20)	(21)	(22)	(23)
Bay Islands								
Andamann & Nicobar Islands	**11**	**3,868**	**13**	**12**	..	**6**	**23**	**19**

Series V—contd.

V (3) Livelihood Class VI (Commerce)

Number per 10,000 persons of Livelihood Class VI in each Sub-Class ; number per 10,000 Self-supporting persons of Livelihood Class VI who are Employers, Employees and Independent Workers ; Secondary Means of Livelihood of 10,000 persons of Livelihood Class VI

Natural Division and District	Number per 10,000 of Livelihood Class VI			Number per 10,000 Self-supporting persons of Livelihood Class VI		
	Self-supporting persons	Non-earning dependants	Earning dependants	Employers	Employees	Independent Workers
(1)	(2)	(3)	(4)	(5)	(6)	(7)
Bay Islands						
Andaman & Nicobar Islands	**4,871**	**4,934**	**195**	**544**	**4,621**	**4,835**

Natural Division and District	Number per 10,000 of Livelihood Class VI whose Secondary Means of Livelihood is							
	Cultivation of owned land		Cultivation of unowned land		Employment as cultivating labourers		Rent on agricultural land	
	Self-supporting persons	Earning dependants	Self-supporting persons	Earning dependants	Self-supporting persons	Earning dependants	Self-supporting persons	Earning dependants
(1)	(8)	(9)	(10)	(11)	(12)	(13)	(14)	(15)
Bay Islands								
Andaman & Nicobar Islands	**104**	**7**	**42**	..	..	..	**42**	..

Natural Division and District	Number per 10,000 of Livelihood Class VI whose Secondary Means of Livelihood is							
	Production other than cultivation		Commerce		Transport		Other services and miscellaneous sources	
	Self-supporting persons	Earning dependants	Self-supporting persons	Earning dependants	Self-supporting persons	Earning dependants	Self-supporting persons	Earning dependants
(1)	(16)	(17)	(18)	(19)	(20)	(21)	(22)	(23)
Bay Islands								
Andaman & Nicobar Islands	**480**	**14**	**202**	**104**	**14**	**7**	**77**	**62**

V (4) Livelihood Class VII (Transport)

Number per 10,000 persons of Livelihood Class VII in each Sub-Class ; Number per 10,000 Self-supporting persons of Livelihood Class VII who are Employers, Employees and Indepenient Workers ; Secondary Means of Livelihood of 10,000 persons of Livelihood Class VII

Natural Division and District	Number per 10,000 of Livelihood Class VII			Number per 10,000 Self-supporting persons of Livelihood Class VII		
	Self-supporing persons	Non-earning dependants	Earning dependants	Employers	Employees	Independent Workers
(1)	(2)	(3)	(4)	(5)	(6)	(7)
Bay Islands						
Andaman & Nicobar Islands	**4,840**	**5,014**	**146**	**38**	**9,698**	**264**

Natural Division and District	Number per 10,000 of Livelihood Class VII whose Secondary Means of Livelihood is							
	Cultivation of owned land		Cultivation of unowned land		Employment as cultivating labourers		Rent on agricultural land	
	Self-supporting persons	Earning dependants	Self-supporting persons	Earning dependants	Self-supporting persons	Earning dependants	Self-supporting persons	Earning dependants
(1)	(8)	(9)	(10)	(11)	(12)	(13)	(14)	(15)
Bay Islands								
Andaman & Nicobar Islands	**119**	**18**	**183**	**9**	**9**	..	**37**	**9**

Natural Division and District	Number per 10,000 of Livelihood Class VII whose Secondary Means of Livelihood is							
	Production other than cultivation		Commerce		Transport		Other services and miscellaneous sources	
	Self-supporting persons	Earning dependants	Self-supporting persons	Earning dependants	Self-supporting persons	Earning dependants	Self-supporting persons	Earning dependants
(1)	(16)	(17)	(18)	(19)	(20)	(21)	(22)	(23)
Bay Islands								
Andaman & Nicobar Islands	**146**	..	**46**	**27**	**18**	**9**	**18**	**73**

Series V—contd.

V (5) Livelihood Class VIII (Other services and miscellaneous sources)

Number per 10,000 persons of Livelihood Class VIII in each Sub-Class; number per 10,000 Self-supporting persons of Livelihood Class VIII who are Employers, Employees and Independent Workers; Secondary Means of Livelihood of 10,000 persons of Livelihood Class VIII

Natural Division and District	Number per 10,000 of Livelihood Class VIII			Number per 10,000 Self-supporting persons of Livelihood Class VIII			
	Self-supporting persons	Non-earning dependants	Earning dependants	Employers	Employees	Independent Workers	Others
(1)	(2)	(3)	(4)	(5)	(6)	(7)	(8)
Bay Islands							
Andaman & Nicobar Islands	**5,401**	**4,449**	**150**	**12**	**8,226**	**1,663**	**99**

Natural Division and District	Number per 10,000 of Livelihood Class VIII whose Secondary Means of Livelihood is							
	Cultivation of owned land		Cultivation of unowned land		Employment as cultivating labourers		Rent on agricultural land	
	Self-supporting persons	Earning dependants	Self-supporting persons	Earning dependants	Self-supporting persons	Earning dependants	Self-supporting persons	Earning dependants
(1)	(9)	(10)	(11)	(12)	(13)	(14)	(15)	(16)
Bay Islands								
Andaman & Nicobar Islands	**212**	**9**	**37**	**3**	..	**2**	**74**	**5**

Natural Division and District	Number per 10,000 of Livelihood Class VIII whose Secondary Means of Livelihood is							
	Production other than cultivation		Commerce		Transport		Other services and miscellaneous sources	
	Self-supporting persons	Earning dependants	Self-supporting persons	Earning dependants	Self-supporting persons	Earning dependants	Self-supporting persons	Earning dependants
(1)	(17)	(18)	(19)	(20)	(21)	(22)	(23)	(24)
Bay Islands								
Andaman & Nicobar Islands	**52**	**22**	**34**	**23**	**2**	**3**	**22**	**83**

V (7) Territorial distribution of 10,000 Self-supporting persons of All Industries and Services in the State (by Divisions)

Natural Division and District	All Industries and Services (*Total*)	0—Primary Industries not elsewhere specified	1—Mining and Quarrying	2—Processing and Manufacture: Food-stuffs, Textiles, Leather and Products thereof	3—Processing and Manufacture: Metals, Chemicals and Products thereof
(1)	(2)	(3)	(4)	(5)	(6)
Bay Islands					
Andaman & Nicobar Islands	**9,922**	**4,315**	..	**130**	**490**

Natural Division and District	4—Processing and Manufacture: Not elsewhere specified	5—Construction and Utilities	6—Commerce	7—Transport, Storage and Communications	8—Health, Education and Public Administration	9—Services not elsewhere specified
(1)	(7)	(8)	(9)	(10)	(11)	(12)
Bay Islands						
Andaman & Nicobar Islands	**324**	**221**	**704**	**609**	**1,227**	**1,980**

NOTE—*Table V(6)—Comparison of the Classification of the Population by Livelihood Class at the 1951 and 1931 Censuses, not reproduced.*

Series V—contd.

V (8) Territorial distribution of 10,000 Self-supporting persons in the State, engaged in Primary Industries not elsewhere specified (by Sub-Divisions)

Natural Division and District	Division—0 (*Total*)	0.1—Stock raising	0.2—Rearing of small animals and insects	0.3—Plantation Industries	0.4—Forestry and collection of products not elsewhere specified	0.5—Hunting (including trapping and Game Propagation)	0.6—Fishing
(1)	(2)	(3)	(4)	(5)	(6)	(7)	(8)
Bay Islands							
Andaman & Nicobar Islands	**4,281**	**138**	**5**	**3,109**	**6,674**	**23**	**51**

V (9) Territorial distribution of 10,000 Self-supporting persons in the State, engaged in Mining and Quarrying—(by Sub-Divisions)

Natural Division and District	Division—1 (*Total*)	1.0—Non-metallic mining and quarrying not otherwise classified	1.1—Coal mining	1.2—Iron ore mining	1.3—Metal mining except iron ore mining	1.4—Crude Petroleum and Natural Gas	1.5—Stone-quarrying, clay and sand pits	1.6—Mica	1.7—Salt, saltpetre and saline substances
(1)	(2)	(3)	(4)	(5)	(6)	(7)	(8)	(9)	(10)
Bay Islands									
Andaman & Nicobar Islands	..	..	..	..	..	..	..	..	..

V (10) Territorial distribution of 10,000 Self-supporting persons in the State, engaged in Processing and Manufacture—Food-stuffs, Textiles, Leather and Products thereof (by Sub-Divisions)

Natural Division and District	Division—2 (*Total*)	2.0—Food Industries otherwise unclassified	2.1—Grains and pulses	2.2—Vegetable oil and dairy products	2.3—Sugar Industries
(1)	(2)	(3)	(4)	(5)	(6)
Bay Islands					
Andaman & Nicobar Islands	**129**	**310**	**930**	**1,240**	

Natural Division and District	2.4—Beverages	2.5—Tobacco	2.6—Cotton Textiles	2.7—Wearing apparel (except footwear) and made-up textile goods	2.8—Textile Industries otherwise unclassified	2.9—Leather, leather products and footwear
(1)	(7)	(8)	(9)	(10)	(11)	(12)
Bay Islands						
Andaman & Nicobar Islands	**698**	..	**775**	**5,194**	**465**	**388**

Series V—contd.

V (11) Territorial distribution of 10,000 Self-supporting persons in the State, engaged in Processing and Manufacture—Metals, Chemicals and Products thereof (by Sub-Divisions)

Natural Division and District	Division—3 (*Total*)	3.0—Manufacture of metal products otherwise unclassified	3.1—Iron and Steel (Basic Manufacture)	3.2—Non-Ferrous Metals (Basic Manufacture)	3.3—Transport Equipment
(1)	(2)	(3)	(4)	(5)	(6)
Bay Islands					
Andaman & Nicobar Islands	**486**	**1,296**	**41**	..	**7,017**

Natural Division and District	3.4—Electrical machinery, apparatus, appliances and supplies	3.5—Machinery (other than electrical machinery) including Engineering Workshops	3.6—Basic Industrial Chemicals, Fertilisers and Power Alcohol	3.7—Medical and Pharmaceutical Preparations	3.8—Manufacture of chemical products otherwise unclassified
(1)	(7)	(8)	(9)	(10)	(11)
Bay Islands					
Andaman & Nicobar Islands	..	..	..	..	**1,646**

V (12) Territorial distribution of 10,000 Self-supporting persons in the State, engaged in Processing and Manufacture—Not elsewhere specified (by Sub-Divisions)

Natural Division and District	Division—4 (*Total*)	4.0—Manufacturing Industries otherwise unclassified	4.1—Products of petroleum and coal	4.2—Bricks, tiles and other structural clay products	4.3—Cement, Cement pipes and other cement products
(1)	(2)	(3)	(4)	(5)	(6)
Bay Islands					
Andaman & Nicobar Islands	**321**	**436**	..	..	..

Natural Division and District	4.4—Non-metallic mineral products	4.5—Rubber Products	4.6—Wood and wood products other than furniture and fixtures	4.7—Furniture and Fixtures	4.8—Paper and Paper Products	4.9—Printing and Allied Industries
(1)	(7)	(8)	(9)	(10)	(11)	(12)
Bay Islands						
Andaman & Nicobar Islands	..	..	**9,377**	..	..	**187**

V (13) Territorial distribution of 10,000 Self-supporting persons in the State, engaged in Construction and Utilities (by Sub-Divisions)

Natural Division and District	Division—5 (*Total*)	5.0—Construction and maintenance of works—otherwise unclassified	5.1—Construction and maintenance—Buildings	5.2—Construction and maintenance—Roads, Bridges and other Transport works	5.3—Construction and maintenance—Telegraph and Telephone Lines	5.4—Construction and maintenance operations—Irrigation and other agricultural works	5.5—Works and Services—Electric Power and Gas supply	5.6—Works and Services—Domestic and Industrial water supply	5.7—Sanitary Works and Services—Including scavengers
(1)	(2)	(3)	(4)	(5)	(6)	(7)	(8)	(9)	(10)
Bay Islands									
Andaman & Nicobar Islands	**219**	**137**	**1,324**	**1,552**	..	**183**	**1,370**	..	**5,434**

Series V—contd.

V (14) Territorial distribution of 10,000 Self-supporting persons in the State, engaged in Commerce (by Sub-Divisions)

Natural Division and District	Division—6 (*Total*)	6.0—Retail trade otherwise unclassified	6.1—Retail trade in foodstuffs (including beverages and narcotics)	6.2—Retail trade in fuel (including petrol)	6.3—Retail trade in textile and leather goods
(1)	(2)	(3)	(4)	(5)	(6)
Bay Islands					
Andaman & Nicobar Islands	**699**	**5,279**	**3,476**	**72**	**558**

Natural Division and District	6.4—Wholesale trade in foodstuffs	6.5—Wholesale trade in commodities other than foodstuffs	6.6—Real Estate	6.7—Insurance	6.8—Moneylending, banking and other financial business
(1)	(7)	(8)	(9)	(10)	(11)
Bay Islands					
Andaman & Nicobar Islands	**14**	**200**	**344**		**57**

V (15) Territorial distribution of 10,000 Self-supporting persons in the State, engaged in Transport, Storage and Communications (by Sub-Divisions)

Natural Division and District	Division—7 (*Total*)	7.0—Transport and communications otherwise unclassified and incidental services	7.1—Transport by road	7.2—Transport by water	7.3—Transport by Air
(1)	(2)	(3)	(4)	(5)	(6)
Bay Islands					
Andaman & Nicobar Islands	**604**	..	**1,606**	**6,457**	**696**

Natural Division and District	7.4—Railway Transport	7.5—Storage and Warehousing	7.6—Postal Services	7.7—Telegraph Services	7.8—Telephone Services	7.9—Wireless Services
(1)	(7)	(8)	(9)	(10)	(11)	(12)
Bay Islands						
Andaman & Nicobar Islands	..	..	**215**	..	**99**	**927**

V (16) Territorial distribution of 10,000 Self-supporting persons in the State, engaged in Health, Education and Public Administration (by Sub-Divisions)

Natural Division and District	Division—8 (*Total*)	8.1—Medical and other Health Services	8.2—Educational Services and Research	8.4—Police (other than village watchmen)	8.5—Village officers and servants including village watchmen	8.6—Employees of Municipalities and Local Boards (but not including persons classifiable under any other division or sub-division)	8.7—Employees of State Governments (but not including persons classifiable under any other division or sub-division)	8.3, 8.8 and 8.9—Employees of the Union Government (but not including persons classifiable under any other division or sub-division); and Employees of Non-Indian Governments
(1)	(2)	(3)	(4)	(5)	(6)	(7)	(8)	(9)
Bay Islands								
Andaman & Nicobar Islands	**1,218**	**1,084**	**509**	**3,588**	**378**	..	**4,433**	**8**

Series V—concld.

V (17) Territorial distribution of 10,000 Self-supporting persons in the State, engaged in Services not elsewhere specified (by Sub-Divisions)

Natural Division and District	Division—9 (*Total*)	9.0—Services otherwise unclassified	9.1—Domestic services (but not including services rendered by members of family households to one another)	9.2—Barbers and Beauty Shops	9.3—Laundries and Laundry services
(1)	(2)	(3)	(4)	(5)	(6)
Bay Islands					
Andaman & Nicobar Islands	**1,965**	**8,692**	**738**	**132**	**173**

Natural Division and District	9.4—Hotels, restaurants and eating houses	9.5—Recreation services	9.6—Legal and business services	9.7—Arts, letters and journalism	9.8—Religious, Charitable and Welfare Services
(1)	(7)	(8)	(9)	(10)	(11)
Bay Islands					
Andaman & Nicobar Islands	..	**15**	**66**	**72**	**112**

CHAPTER VI

Families, Sexes and Principal Age Groups

1. Preliminary remarks— In this chapter will be found information about houses and households, sex, civic conditions, and age groups. Comparisons with previous Census figures have been made wherever possible. But unfortunately this has been found to be impossible in many cases because of the lack of data. In discussing civic conditions and the size of households, figures obtained for the sample population were taken.

2. Territorial distribution of houses and households— The decrease in the number of households in the decade 1941-50 is explained by the fact that the Japanese Forces destroyed many houses for military reasons during the three and a half years they occupied the islands. The delay in making good the damage is due to the fact that building materials were not available in adequate quantities in the years immediately following the war.

The shortage of houses is less felt in the rural area, where mud and thatch buildings, are easily erected. In urban areas houses are more permanent, and therefore more difficult to build. The figures indicate this: an average of 1·2 household per house in the rural area and 1·9 for the urban.

3. Size and composition of households—Subsidiary Table VI(2) (at page xxxiv) shows the distribution according to the size of household population taken from the sample of households. The number of persons per household in rural areas is more than double the figure for urban areas. This can be explained by the way of living of the Nicobarese, where a large number of people live in their beehive type communal huts.

4. Sex Ratios—The number of females per thousand males in these Islands during the previous decades is shown in the table below :

1921	303
1931	495
1941	574
1951	625

In the early settlement days (1891) the number was only 167.

This preponderance of males is explained by the artificial conditions prevailing in a convict settlement. Modification of penal conditions in 1926, when convicts were for the first time allowed to bring their families from the mainland, brought about a sudden rise in the ratio of women to men; and this ratio has continued increasing since then. But as conditions in the Andaman Islands still continue to be unnatural, the ratio is not likely to reach parity for some time to come. Even to-day large numbers of labourers are brought to work in the Andamans on contract for a year; and almost without exception these people do not bring their families to the Andamans. But with the implementation of the plan to colonize the Middle and the North Andamans, conditions will change; and in course of time the number of women will equal the men. If I might venture on a forecast, by 1961 the number of females per thousand males should be of the order of 800 because the number of men and women are more or less equal amongst the people who are coming to settle permanently in these Islands as the colonists generally bring their families with them.

5. Marital Status ratios—Subsidiary Table VI(7) (at page xxxvi) shows the marital status of the sexes for 1951, and for previous censuses. No figures for 1941 are available; but for 1931 and 1921 the tables have been completed for the general population from the records available for those decades.

In 1921 the percentage of unmarried persons was less than that of married persons, whereas the reverse is the case in 1951. But in 1921 there were only 303 females per thousand males. This apparent discrepancy is explained by the fact that the persons enumerated in 1921 in the Andamans were mostly convicts, who had perforce left their families behind on the mainland. It is noteworthy that child marriages are absent in these Islands: no male in the group 0-14 is married, and only 0·02 per cent. of the females in this group. The majority of the married people are in the productive age group of 15-34, followed by the people in the age group 35-54. In fact, the people in these two age groups comprise almost the entire married population.

6. Age groups—The table below will show at a glance the number of persons per 10,000 in each age group:

	Per 10,000
0- 1	366
1- 4	1,076
5-14	2,009
15-24	2,269
25-34	1,923
35-44	1,281
45-54	656
55-64	260
65-74	109
75 and over	51

These age groups have been worked out from the sample population. As the 1941 figures are not

17 Home/54

available, and as the age grouping adapted in previous censuses was different, a comparative discussion is not possible.

Nearly 90 per cent. of the total population is below 44, which shows a young and vigorous community. This is as it ought to be in an area earmarked for intensive development within the next decade or two.

7. Conclusion— The decade under review was of great significance for these Islands: it marked the end of one epoch and the beginning of another, because with the abolition of the penal settlement in 1945 the very basis of the existence of the people of the Andamans has changed.

The occupation of the Andaman and Nicobar Islands by the imperial Japanese Forces from March 1942 to October 1945 has also had a very noticeable effect. The Islands were subjected to severe economic, social and psychological disturbances; and the effects of these have not yet worn off nearly eight years later.

The partition of India in 1947 brought in its train the problem of its refugees; and the Andamans has offered a home and a new start in life to a number of these unfortunate people—a number that is a mere drop in the ocean compared to the total number of refugees that have streamed into India during the last six years, but a number that already exceeds 10 per cent. of the popultion of the Andaman Islands. Even so, the Andaman Islands with a density of population of less than 8 to the square mile, are definitely under-populated; and offer scope for further development, and resettlement of more people from the mother country. Until this is done the Islands will not be self-sufficient either in the matter of food or in the matter of labour.

SUBSIDIARY TABLES

Series—VI

VI (1) Persons per 1,000 houses and houses per 100 square miles and comparison with past censuses

Natural Division and District	General Population — Persons per 1,000 houses				Rural Population — Persons per 1,000 houses				Urban Population — Persons per 1,000 houses				Houses per 100 square miles			
	1951	1941	1931	1921	1951	1941	1931	1921	1951	1941	1931	1921	1951	1941	1931	1921
(1)	(2)	(3)	(4)	(5)	(6)	(7)	(8)	(9)	(10)	(11)	(12)	(13)	(14)	(15)	(16)	(17)
Bay Islands																
Andaman & Nicobar Islands	**5,844**	**5,666**	**5,200**	**5,000**	**6,736**	..	..	..	**4,236**	..	..	..	**165**	**180**	**180**	**110**

VI (2) Number of households per 1,000 houses and distribution by size of 1,000 Sample Households of Rural and Urban Population

Natural Division and District	Rural — Households per 1,000 houses	Rural — Household Population — Persons	Males	Females	Small 3 members or less — Number	Persons	Medium 4-6 members — Number	Persons
(1)	(2)	(3)	(4)	(5)	(6)	(7)	(8)	(9)
Bay Islands								
Andaman & Nicobar Islands	**1,193**	**4,380**	**2,446**	**1,934**	**540**	**818**	**270**	**1,365**

Natural Division and District	Rural — Large 7-9 members — Number	Persons	Very large 10 members or more — Number	Persons	Urban — Households per 1,000 houses	Household Population — Persons	Males	Females
(1)	(10)	(11)	(12)	(13)	(14)	(15)	(16)	(17)
Bay Islands								
Andaman & Nicobar Islands	**117**	**985**	**73**	**1,212**	**1,888**	**2,430**	**1,541**	**889**

Natural Division and District	Urban — Small 3 members or less — Number	Persons	Medium 4-6 members — Number	Persons	Large 7-9 members — Number	Persons	Very large 10 members or more — Number	Persons
(1)	(18)	(19)	(20)	(21)	(22)	(23)	(24)	(25)
Bay Islands								
Andaman & Nicobar Islands	**763**	**1,104**	**193**	**970**	**37**	**282**	**7**	**74**

Series VI—contd.

VI (3) Family Composition of 1,000 households of the General Population

Natural Division and District	Sample Household Population			Heads of households and their wives		Sons of heads of households	Daughters of heads of households	Other male relations to heads of households	Other female relations to heads of households
	Persons	Males	Females	Males	Females				
(1)	(2)	(3)	(4)	(5)	(6)	(7)	(8)	(9)	(10)
Bay Islands									
Andaman & Nicobar Islands	**3,412**	**1,997**	**1,415**	**956**	**485**	**555**	**485**	**386**	**368**

VI (4) Females per 1,000 males (General, Rural and Urban Population); and comparison with previous censuses

Natural Division and District	General Population				Rural Population				Urban Population			
	1951	1941	1931	1921	1951	1941	1931	1921	1951	1941	1931	1921
(1)	(2)	(3)	(4)	(5)	(6)	(7)	(8)	(9)	(10)	(11)	(12)	(13)
Bay Islands												
Andaman & Nicobar Islands	**625**	**574**	**495**	**303**	**662**	..	..	..	**530**	..	..	..

VI (5) Females per 1,000 males in Agricultural Classes and Sub-Classes

Natural Division and District	All Agricultural Classes				I—Cultivators of land wholly or mainly owned and their dependants	
	Total	Self-supporting persons	Non-earning dependants	Earning dependants	Total	Self-supporting persons
(1)	(2)	(3)	(4)	(5)	(6)	(7)
Bay Islands						
Andaman & Nicobar Islands	**856**	**125**	**1,939**	**104**	**868**	**111**

Natural Division and District	I—Cultivators of land wholly or mainly owned and their dependants		II—Cultivators of land wholly or mainly unowned and their dependants			
	Non-earning dependants	Earning dependants	Total	Self-supporting persons	Non-earning dependants	Earning dependants
(1)	(8)	(9)	(10)	(11)	(12)	(13)
Bay Islands						
Andaman & Nicobar Islands	**1,934**	**97**	**755**	**172**	**1,844**	**500**

Natural Division and District	III—Cultivating labourers and their dependants				IV—Non-cultivating owners of land; Agricultural rent receivers and their dependants			
	Total	Self-supporting persons	Non-earning dependants	Earning dependants	Total	Self-supporting persons	Non-earning dependants	Earning dependants
(1)	(14)	(15)	(16)	(17)	(18)	(19)	(20)	(21)
Bay Islands								
Andaman & Nicobar Islands	**541**	**141**	**2,571**	..	**1,286**	**1,300**	**1,750**	..

Series VI—contd.

VI (6) Females per 1,000 males in Non-Agricultural Classes and Sub-Classes

Natural Division and District	Non-Agricultural Classes				V—Production other than cultivation			
	Total	Self-supporting persons	Non-earning dependants	Earning dependants	Total	Self-supporting persons	Non-earning dependants	Earning dependants
(1)	(2)	(3)	(4)	(5)	(6)	(7)	(8)	(9)
Bay Islands								
Andaman & Nicobar Islands	**593**	**46**	**1,333**	**1,299**	**648**	**28**	**1,097**	**1,315**

Natural Division and District	VI—Commerce			
	Total	Self-supporting persons	Non-earning dependants	Earning dependants
(1)	(10)	(11)	(12)	(13)
Bay Islands				
Andaman & Nicobar Islands	**537**	**75**	**1,706**	**273**

Natural Division and District	VII—Transport				VIII—Other services and miscellaneous sources			
	Total	Self-supporting persons	Non-earning dependants	Earning dependants	Total	Self-supporting persons	Non-earning dependants	Earning dependants
(1)	(14)	(15)	(16)	(17)	(18)	(19)	(20)	(21)
Bay Islands								
Andaman & Nicobar Islands	**483**	..	**1,726**	**1,286**	**488**	**76**	**1,747**	**865**

VI (7) Marital Status of 1,000 persons of each sex of General Population and comparison with previous censuses

Natural Division and District	Males											
	Unmarried				Married				Widowed			
	1951	1941	1931	1921	1951	1941	1931	1921	1951	1941	1931	1921
(1)	(2)	(3)	(4)	(5)	(6)	(7)	(8)	(9)	(10)	(11)	(12)	(13)
Bay Islands												
Andaman & Nicobar Islands	**564**	..	**448**	**365**	**396**	..	**481**	**549**	**40**	..	**71**	**86**

Natural Division and District	Females											
	Unmarried				Married				Widowed			
	1951	1941	1931	1921	1951	1941	1931	1921	1951	1941	1931	1921
(1)	(14)	(15)	(16)	(17)	(18)	(19)	(20)	(21)	(22)	(23)	(24)	(25)
Bay Islands												
Andaman & Nicobar Islands	**512**	..	**439**	**405**	**394**	..	**490**	**462**	**94**	..	**71**	**133**

VI (8) Age distribution of 1,000 married persons of each sex (and comparison with 1941 census)

Natural Division and District	Males								Females							
	0—14		15—34		35—54		55 and over		0—14		15—34		35—54		55 and over	
	1951	1941	1951	1941	1951	1941	1951	1941	1951	1941	1951	1941	1951	1941	1951	1941
(1)	(2)	(3)	(4)	(5)	(6)	(7)	(8)	(9)	(10)	(11)	(12)	(13)	(14)	(15)	(16)	(17)
Bay Islands																
Andaman & Nicobar Islands	..	..	**481**	..	**455**	..	**64**	..	**2**	..	**678**	..	**290**	..	**30**	..

Series VI—contd.

VI (9) Infants per 10,000 persons

Natural Division and District	Infants per 10,000 persons of: General Population 1951 Persons	General Population 1951 Males	General Population 1951 Females	General Population 1941 Persons	Rural Population Males	Rural Population Females	Urban Population Males	Urban Population Females	Agricultural Classes Males	Agricultural Classes Females	Non-Agricultural Classes Males	Non-Agricultural Classes Females
(1)	(2)	(3)	(4)	(5)	(6)	(7)	(8)	(9)	(10)	(11)	(12)	(13)
Bay Islands												
Andaman & Nicobar Islands	**366**	**147**	**219**	..	**141**	**211**	**164**	**240**	**171**	**256**	**144**	**214**

VI (10) Young Children (aged 1-4) per 10,000 persons

Natural Division and District	Young children per 10,000 persons of: General Population 1951 Persons	General Population 1951 Males	General Population 1951 Females	General Population 1941 Persons	Rural Population Males	Rural Population Females	Urban Population Males	Urban Population Females	Agricultural Classes Males	Agricultural Classes Females	Non-Agricultural Classes Males	Non-Agricultural Classes Females
(1)	(2)	(3)	(4)	(5)	(6)	(7)	(8)	(9)	(10)	(11)	(12)	(13)
Bay Islands												
Andaman & Nicobar Islands	**1,076**	**636**	**440**	..	**567**	**417**	**821**	**505**	**513**	**570**	**652**	**501**

VI (11) Boys and Girls (aged 5-14) per 10,000 persons

Natural Division and District	Boys and girls per 10,000 persons of: General Population 1951 Persons	General Population 1951 Males	General Population 1951 Females	General Population 1941 Persons	Rural Population Males	Rural Population Females	Urban Population Males	Urban Population Females	Agricultural Classes Males	Agricultural Classes Females	Non-Agricultural Classes Males	Non-Agricultural Classes Females
(1)	(2)	(3)	(4)	(5)	(6)	(7)	(8)	(9)	(10)	(11)	(12)	(13)
Bay Islands												
Andaman & Nicobar Islands	**2,009**	**1,059**	**950**	..	**1,166**	**1,040**	**770**	**707**	**1,396**	**1,368**	**1,013**	**893**

VI (12) Young men and women (aged 15-34) per 10,000 persons

Natural Division and District	Young men and women per 10,000 persons of: General Population 1951 Persons	General Population 1951 Males	General Population 1951 Females	General Population 1941 Persons	Rural Population Males	Rural Population Females	Urban Population Males	Urban Population Females	Agricultural Classes Males	Agricultural Classes Females	Non-Agricultural Classes Males	Non-Agricultural Classes Females
(1)	(2)	(3)	(4)	(5)	(6)	(7)	(8)	(9)	(10)	(11)	(12)	(13)
Bay Islands												
Andaman & Nicobar Islands	**4,192**	**2,805**	**1,387**	..	**2,646**	**1,447**	**3,220**	**1,225**	**1,766**	**1,453**	**2,946**	**1,378**

Series VI—concld.

VI (13) Middle aged persons (aged 35-54) per 10,000 persons

Natural Division and District	Middle aged persons per 10,000 persons of: General Population 1951 Persons	1951 Males	1951 Females	1941 Persons	Rural Population Males	Rural Population Females	Urban Population Males	Urban Population Females	Agricultural Classes Males	Agricultural Classes Females	Non-Agricultural Classes Males	Non-Agricultural Classes Females
(1)	(2)	(3)	(4)	(5)	(6)	(7)	(8)	(9)	(10)	(11)	(12)	(13)
Bay Islands												
Andaman & Nicobar Islands	1,937	1,373	564	..	1,279	646	1,629	341	997	798	1,425	532

VI (14) Elderly persons (aged 55 and over) per 10,000 persons

Natural Division and District	Elderly persons per 10,000 persons of: General Population 1951 Persons	1951 Males	1951 Females	1941 Persons	Rural Population Males	Rural Population Females	Urban Population Males	Urban Population Females	Agricultural Classes Males	Agricultural Classes Females	Non-Agricultural Classes Males	Non-Agricultural Classes Females
(1)	(2)	(3)	(4)	(5)	(6)	(7)	(8)	(9)	(10)	(11)	(12)	(13)
Bay Islands												
Andaman & Nicobar Islands	420	266	154	..	295	145	189	177	427	285	245	136

CHAPTER VII

Question No. 13

The Government of India left one question in the Census questionnaire to the discretion of the State Government, this question to relate to some problem or event of local importance.

The outstanding event in the Andaman Islands during the last decade having been the Japanese occupation, (and the torture of the people by the invading troops) it was decided to ask the people of the Andamans how many of them had suffered physical ill treatment at the hands of the Japanese Forces. In the Nicobar Islands the question was not of the same importance, as fewer people had suffered at the hands of the Japanese. There the immediate topic was the epidemic of poliomyelitis that swept the islands during 1947-48; and the people there were asked if they had suffered any permanent injury as a result of this epidemic.

As the enumerators were, in almost all cases, acquainted with the people they were questioning, there is little chance of error in the figures recorded by them.

The following table gives the number of persons in the Andamans tortured by the Japanese Forces during the occupation:

	Livelihood Class Nos.															
	I		II		III		IV		V		VI		VII		VIII	
	Males	Females	Males	Females	Males	Females	Males	Females	Males	Females	Males	Females	Males	Females	Males	Females
Urban	10	3	..	..	..	..	..	..	74	2	54	1	26	4	112	3
Rural	74	6	3	..	1	..	..	..	64	..	8	..	4	..	50	2
Total	84	9	3	..	1	..	..	..	138	2	62	1	30	4	162	5

The following figures indicate the incidence of poliomyelitis in the Nicobar Islands (accurate figures are only available for Car Nicobar and the Nancowry group of islands):

Car Nicobar		Nancowry	
No. admitted in hospitals	889	Approximate number of incidence	98
Deaths in hospitals	122	Abortive cases	25
Deaths in villages	103	Total	123
Approximate number affected	992	Deaths	29

The poliomyelitis epidemic was fortunately controlled promptly by the despatch of medical assistance by air from India; it was completely stamped out within six months; and has shown no signs of breaking out again.

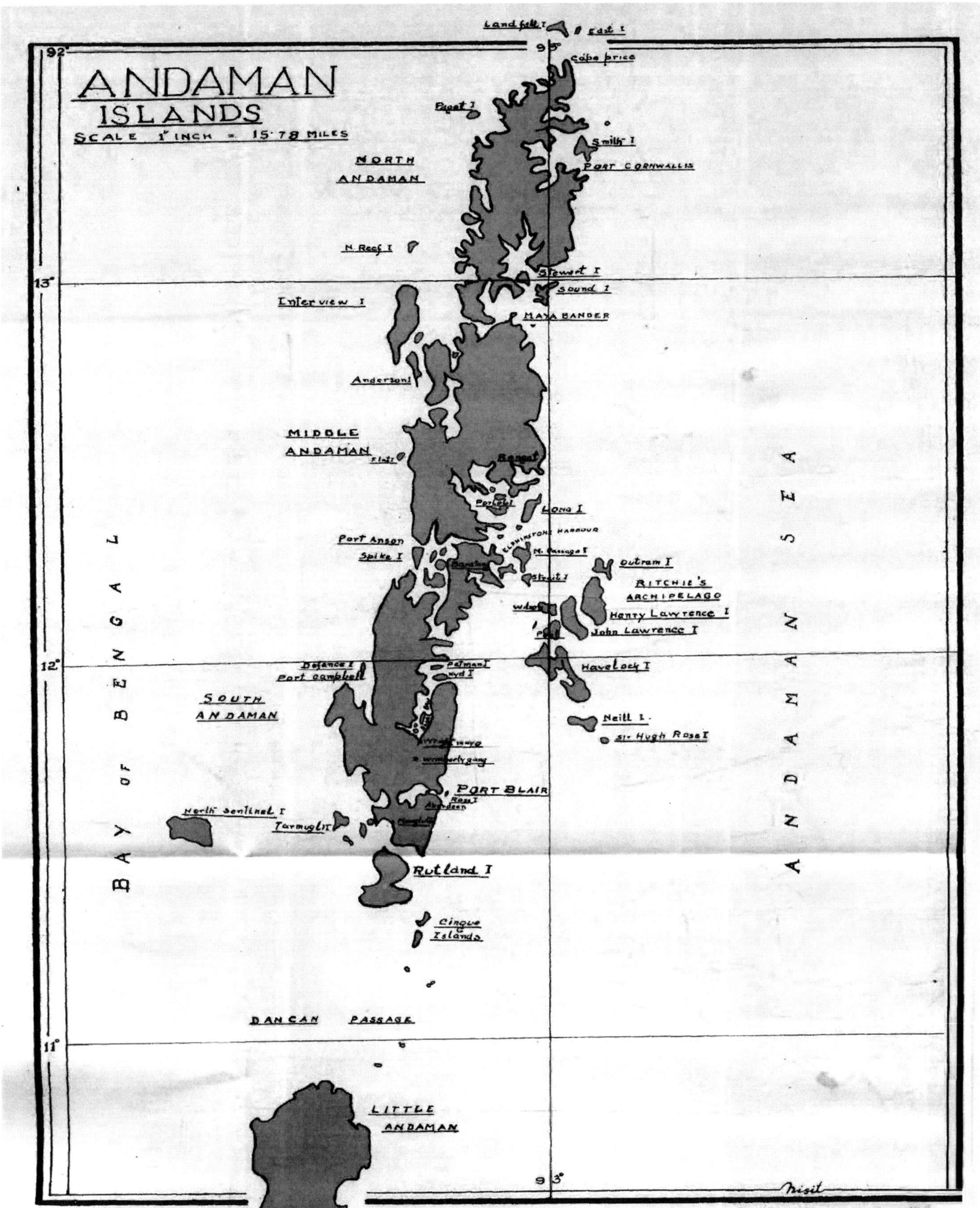

Reg. No. 2778 E' 54—1004'55.

PRINTED AT THE SURVEY OF INDIA OFFICES (P.L.O.)

Reproduced from original supplied by the Chief Commissioner and ex-officio Superintendent of Census Operations, Andaman and Nicobar Islands, and the Survey of India is not responsible for the accuracy of detail, names etc. appearing on the map.

APPENDIX A

The Andaman and Nicobar Islands

By SHRI S. K. GUPTA, I.A.S., *Deputy Commissioner and Superintendent of Census Operations*

I. Introduction

Unfortunately I have to leave these islands before the Tabulation of figures collected during the current census operations. I feel, however, that I should write up the report on the basis of provisional figures, as it would be difficult for my successor to adequately collate and interpret data gathered by me, in course of my tours spread over a period of three years, by a mere reference to notes that I may leave. The element of personal equation can hardly be ignored.

In this report I propose shifting the emphasis from historical and anthropological researches to current problems with a view to facilitate formulation of future policies. History is important only in so far as it assists in explaining the present and foreseeing the future.

In studying the aborigines of these islands I have refrained from following the time honoured procedure of using our own concepts and ideas as yardsticks for judging theirs and have attempted a sympathetic understanding of their points of view also. I only hope all future developmental schemes will be drawn up against this background and thus be correlated to the life current of the people. Otherwise they tend to be exotic and eventually infructuous.

Lack of water transport has been the main handicap during the present operations. In 1921 Mr. Lowis availed of the R.I.M.S. *Minto* and in 1931 Mr. Bonnington used the station ship. In 1951 no special craft could be obtained for the purpose and I used naval vessels as and when available for organising the operations and training of Enumerators in the Nicobars group.

Actual enumeration in this group of islands, splashed over 120 miles of the Indian Ocean, was carried out by a band of Nicobarese volunteers under the able leadership of Bishop John Richardson and the efficient guidance of Shri B. N. Sharma, the Assistant Commissioner. Thanks to Mr. Sharma's able organisation, enumeration in Car Nicobar, Nancowry, Camorta and Trinkat was done synchronously during the census period. But the other islands had to be taken up according to convenience between the 23rd of January and 12th of February, owing to lack of personnel and transport. This band of keen workers did their "island hopping" in frail canoes, often in unpropitious weather, having been dropped at central spots by the Brig. Daya, belonging to Messrs. Akoojee Jadwet & Co., the Government appointed traders for these islands. My grateful thanks are due to Bishop John Richardson and his volunteers and Mr. Yusuf Jadwet, the trader for their glorious contribution to this great national cause. This is the first time in the history of these islands that a complete enumeration in all inhabited islands of the Nicobars group (except for a very few Shom-Pens, living in inaccessible hills) has been possible.

In the Andamans group also the entire enumeration from Landfall to McPherson Strait was done on a purely voluntary basis by both official and non-official agencies. My thanks are due to all those numerous workers whose whole-hearted and sincere assistance has brought the operations to a successful conclusion, meticulously according to plan.

The writing up of the National Register of Citizens has gone on *pari passu* enumeration, thanks to the willing co-operation of the Enumerators.

The organisation is also grateful to all the employers, both State and private, for the facilities they gave to their staff engaged in the operations.

I am grateful to Shri P. Sundaramurthi, Deputy Superintendent for his assistance in organising the operations at all stages. The clerk Shri V. Gurumurthi has all through taken a very intelligent interest in the work and was of great help to me.

II. Organisation and Finances

1. For the purposes of this census, these islands have been divided into the following six tracts, each under a Charge Officer, the first two constituting one charge :—

1. Aberdeen Tahsil . . Urban area.
2. Aberdeen Tahsil . . Rural area.
3. Wimberleygunj Tahsil.
4. Wimberleygunj Forest Division.
5. Middle Andaman Forest Division.
6. Nicobars.

In thickly populated areas, each enumerator had on an average 50 houses in his block, whereas, in villages, the number was much less. The entire organisational set-up has been published in the little booklet of instructions to Enumerators.

2. I formally took over as Superintendent of Census Operations in April, 1950. But house-numbering and preparation of house-lists had started much earlier.

3. Below are the budget provisions for 1950-51 and 1951-52:—

	1950-51			1951-52		
	Rs.	A.	P.	Rs.	A.	P.
A. SUPERINTENDENCE						
A.1—Pay of Officers .	2,200	0	0	1,200	0	0
A.2—Pay of Establishments . . .	1,400	0	0	1,320	0	0
A.3—Allowances, Honoraria, etc. .	700	0	0	..	..	..
A.5—Other charges .	100	0	0	..	..	..
C.—ABSTRACTION AND COMPILATION CHARGES						
C.2—Pay of establishment	..	..	..	3,741	11	0
C.3—Allowances, Honoraria, etc. . .	..	..	..	1,748	6	0
C.4—Other charges (contingencies) . .	..	..	..	200	0	0
GRAND TOTAL .	4,400	0	0	8,210	1	0

4. Appendix B gives the complete programme of the operations up to the stage of collection of census papers in the Tabulation Office.

PART A—ANDAMANS

III. The Land

Geographically these islands lie sprawling at the mouth of the Bay of Bengal in the form, more or less, of a semi-circle tapering off on the north at a point about 120 miles from Cape Negrais in Burma and on the south about 91 miles from Pulo Brasse off Achin Head in Sumatra. Their strategic importance, therefore, to the Union of India, cannot be over-estimated. It is significant that the Japanese occupied them in the very early stages of the last Great World War.

Geologically they certainly have been flung off the main land mass of the Asian Continent in course of a big cataclysm—a Manwantar (change of epoch). Boden Kloss' theory that there has never been any surface connection with the continent does not seem to be very convincing, in view of the presence of human life specially of Jarawas in the hinterland, whose highest maritime achievement is crossing of narrow creeks in rickety rafts and who could not have, therefore, migrated into these islands from any other part of the world. It is difficult also to believe that these islands witnessed the whole process of evolution from slime to man on a miniature scale. Where then are the failures or the intermediate species?

A careful study of the navigation charts of these seas would reveal the considerable variations in the depth of the waters, proving thereby "that these islands form a continuous range of lofty submarine mountains extending from Cape Negrais in Burma to Achin Head in Sumatra."

That being so, the possibility of the presence of petroleum cannot be completely eliminated. Actually, two mud volcanoes have been discovered in the Middle Andamans. Some minerals with abrasive properties have also been found in the White Cliffs of Havelock. An intensive geological survey is indicated.

What is more important is a proper ground water survey. Lack of sources of potable water supply is one of the most effective bottle-necks in colonisation. The luxurious vegetation and the moist clayey soil of the Wandur valley, for example, would normally lead one to believe in the existence of some source of water supply in the vicinity, but no permanent spring or well could be struck there.

The terrain in all the islands, except in Car Nicobar, is hilly and any wanton denudation of forests from the slopes would result in soil erosion of the worst type, on account of excessive rains for the best part of the year. The lack of foresight displayed in the past, in clearing hills and slopes in the Andamans and planting coconuts thereon is responsible for the very poor condition of some of the plantations due to extensive soil erosion. The only way to arrest further deterioration is the costly work of cross-bunding. This lesson has to be very carefully learnt.

IV. The Climate

These islands get the full blast of both the monsoons. Navigation becomes difficult during the changeovers.

The climate is equable and the temperature varies between 85 and 95 degrees Fahrenheit all throughout the year. The average rainfall is 123" spread over the whole year, the only dry quarter being January-March.

This uniformity of temperature favours growth of all types of vegetables throughout the year, provided arrangements are made for proper drainage.

The average velocity of wind being 9·5 m.p.h. irrigation by wind-mills appears possible.

V. Flora and Fauna

Forests—Almost all the islands except a few in the Nicobars group are rich in forests. I quote below from Bonnington's Census Report of 1931:—

"The forests are divided into two main types, *i.e.*, evergreen and deciduous, the type depending entirely on the underlying soil and rock formation which determines the presence or absence of water near the surface during the dry weather, and this is probably the real factor governing the distribution of the two types of forests.

In the deciduous forests which exist mainly on the lower and more gentle slopes of the hills, the principal tree is *Pterocarpus dalbergioides* (Padauk) and associated with it are *Canarium euphyllum* (Dhup), *Sterculia campanulata* (Papita), *Albizzia lebbek* (Koko), *Bombax insigne* (Didu), *Lagerstroemia hypoleuca* (Pyinma), *Terminalia manii* (Black Chuglam), *Terminalia bialata* (White Chuglam), and *Terminalia procera* (Badam) which are the principal timber trees. Besides these there are many other species of minor importance from a timber or revenue-producing point of view.

The moist valleys along fresh water streams and also the steeper hills are taken up by evergreen forests. Various species of *Dipterocarpus* (Gurjan) are the most conspicuous and with it are associated *Sterculia campanulata, Myritsica irya* (Nutmeg), *Calophyllum spectabile* (Lalchini), *Artocarpus chaplasha* (Taungpeing) and several others of minor importance.

Mangrove forests are found on the estuaries of the many creeks in belts varying from a few yards to over a mile in width. Some of these growing near high tide limits are covered with high trees (*Bruguiera gymnorhiza*) up to 5 feet in girth which form more or less pure forests, the yield varying perhaps from 50 to 100 tons to the acre or even more.

Of the 2,508 sq. miles forming the total land area of the Andamans about 1,500 square miles are estimated to contain forests other than mangrove. Recent enumeration of all species shows that the stand of mature timber of all species varies from 8 to 30 tons per acre and averages 15 tons to the acre. It is therefore roughly estimated that the forests contain some 14 to 15 million tons of mature timber ripe for the axe".

So far a full utilisation of this excellent forest wealth has not been found possible. In this connection I reproduce an excerpt from a note recorded by me in May 1948:—

"B This desirable expansion in the working of the forests has not been possible on account of :

(a) the dented, high and inhospitable coastline with very few anchorages,

(b) the inaccessibility of the hinterland;

(*a*) is beyond, control,

(*b*) can certainly and should be attacked.

The best way to tackle this problem is to open up the country northwards by constructing a road right through the hinterland. The total length of the proposed road would be about 120 miles from Port Blair to Port Cornwallis. Of this length about 30 miles already exist.

The intervening creeks can always be crossed at suitable points by means of rafts. Incidentally the permanent way and the rolling stock of the D. H. Railway between Kisanganj (Purnea) and Siliguri (Darjeeling) which, it is understood, is going to be replaced by a metergauge line can very well be utilised in these parts as the terrain is very much similar to the Terai regions of the Himalayas through which this railway passes.

This would very considerably facilitate utilisation of the virgin forests both on the hinterland and the coastal areas and ensure colonisation of the valleys and thus eventually afford an appreciable solution of the refugee problem. Quite considerable human labour will be required for working the forest as also for bringing the valleys and cleared areas under cultivation".

Shri B. S. Changapa, Conservator, Working Plans, has kindly written a note on the present situation of these forests, based on his invaluable experience of over 30 years in these islands. This will be found at Appendix C.

Agriculture—At the moment only 5,102 acres of land are under wet cultivation, the main crop being paddy with an average yield varying between 15 to 20 maunds per acre and 3,910 acres under coconuts. No separate figures for other crops and vegetables are being given owing to the very restricted nature of such cultivation.

With the settlement of displaced persons from East Bengal, almost all the cleared area in South Andamans, excepting about 500 acres of land inundated by sea-water owing to breaches in sea-walls and leaks in sluice gates, has been brought under cultivation. The essence of agriculture in these islands is the proper maintenance of these preventive works. In their present condition they portend a definite threat of further damage to agriculture.

The present view of the administration is that the maximum area that may possibly be available for colonisation and expansion of agriculture is 300 sq. miles. No definite estimate is possible in the absence of a proper survey. But if by this is only meant lands of the 'billiard table top' type, perhaps the estimate is almost correct. But terraced cultivation is also possible and paying. The Japanese, during their occupation, had most of the hills and slopes in the settlement area burrowed up for growing tapioca, sweet potatoes, etc. Even now successful experiments in terraced paddy cultivation are going on in Protheropore, Nayashahar and other places by local people. If, therefore, the possibility of this type of cultivation is kept in view, the area available for expansion after clearing of forests should be much more than 300 sq. miles. Barring a few, almost all crops can be grown here. This year some people are experimenting in wheat. Success is, however, doubtful. Potatoes have consistently been a failure. I think the Agricultural department should now try it under controlled conditions. Sugar-cane thrives very well. The new Bengali settlers have grown excellent pulses and chillies All types of Indian vegetables also grow well. During the dry period, of course, irrigation becomes a problem. The proposed irrigation by wind-mill system is well worth a trial.

Fauna—The most extraordinary absence of animal life except of the reptile and some avian variety, forces one almost to the "isolationist" theory of Boden Kloss mentioned before. Then dense tropical forests are completely devoid of wild life, except for pigs which have constituted the main source of food of the aborigines. There is a considerable number of spotted and barking deer introduced within the last century by the administration and not native to the soil. Amongst bird life, the birds of prey are conspicuous by their absence. Even crows are rare. Is it that all the animals perished in the cataclysm and man somehow saved himself? This will, perhaps, remain a mystery.

As a compensation perhaps the waters around abound in marine life. There is a craze amongst the Singapore Chinese to fish *Trochus* and other shells. The administration had to refuse a large number of such applications. A separate note on fisheries by Shri V. Sadasivan, Assistant Fisheries Research Officer will be found at Appendix D.

VI. Population

Distribution and Movement—General

Year	Andamans			Nicobars		
	Males	Females	Total	Males	Females	Total
1901	15,158	2,980	18,138	3,537	2,974	6,511
1911	14,737	2,904	17,641	4,833	3,985	8,818
1921	15,551	2,263	17,814	5,242	4,030	9,272
1931	14,258	4,965	19,223	5,444	4,796	10,240
1941	14,872	6,444	21,316	6,586	5,866	12,452
1951	12,734	6,228	18,962	6,321	5,688	12,009

General—The previous table shows the distribution and movement of population during the last 50 years. The figures for Andamans and Nicobars have been given separately as ethnologically the inhabitants of the two groups are completely dissimilar and each should be studied singly. To the 1951 enumerated figure of Andamans should be added the estimated number of aboriginal population of 220.

Population movement in Andamans—Up to 1941 the movement of population in the Andamans was completely artificial and not at all indicative of the normal biological and economic forces which operate to cause variations in population. Being a penal settlement fluctuations depended to a large extent on existing administrative policies and convenience. The main basis of the population was the community of convicts transported from the mainland. The rest of the population largely was Government staff necessary to run the penal settlement. The variations in the former bore a direct relation to the variations in the latter.

Conditions, however, are completely different in 1951. Since re-occupation in 1945, the islands have ceased to be a penal settlement and movement of population is free and normal as in any other State of India.

This census has registered a decrease by 2,797 from the 1941 figures. But this is actually more apparent than real. During 1941, there were still 7,000 convicts and about 300 members of the armed forces. In fact, therefore, there has been a net increase and not decrease in the free population by 4,935=18,961—(21,316—7,300). This upward trend is persistently noticeable since re-occupation in 1945.

Assuming that during Japanese occupation the population remained static (which unfortunately it was not, as we have reliable information of deaths due to oppression, starvation and malnutrition—but no correct figures are available) we have on re-occupation in October, 1945, 21,316—7,300=14,016. In February, 1948, when the whole island was a rationed area the total number of ration cards issued was 15,532. Thus between October, 1945 and February, 1948 there was a net increase in the population by 1,516 or about 500 annually. February, 1951 (*i.e.,* the current census) shows a further net increase by 3,429. During the second triennial period, the increase has thus been more than double. This is definitely due to rehabilitation of 1,500 refugees from East Bengal. It follows, therefore, that the annual increase in the population due to normal causes is about 628 and it is more due to economic than to biological causes. There is a persistent demand from people from various parts of South India and West Bengal for settlement in these islands. The vital statistics for the last three years record only, on an average, an excess of 220 births over deaths.

Distribution of population by sexes—There is a remarkable preponderance of males over females during this half a century. From about 20 per cent. of the male population in 1901, the female population has risen up to about 50 per cent. in 1951. This was largely due to the presence of overwhelmingly large number of convicts who were not allowed to bring in their families. At the present moment also a considerable number of imported labour is responsible for this disparity. The seriousness of the problem will be apparent only after a complete tabulation, but evidence is not wanting of importation of females often of questionable character from the mainland for marriage with the permanent male population of the Andamans. In certain instances, this practice has degenerated into almost an illicit traffic in women by unscrupulous persons. This position is likely to be eased to a certain extent by the advent of new

Bengali settlers who do not seem to be very much opposed to exogamy.

Economic structure of the population—The economic tables under preparation will give a correct idea of the economic division of population. But from all available evidence a rough percentage amongst the main general professions can be worked out as follows:—

Labour (skilled and un-skilled)	33%
Agriculture and plantation	29%
Office work and other professions—trade and commerce	38%

This certainly reveals a lack of proper balance and top-heaviness. Agriculture is certainly being starved. There is, however, 100 per cent. employment and no economic passivity amongst the self-supporting community.

Special groups : Andaman Indians—The main basis of the population is what, in the old days, was known as "Local Borns" signifying thereby the convicts settled here and their progeny. This terminology with a rather humiliating connotation has since been changed and in this census all permanent residents of the Andamans who have made these hospitable islands their home have been recorded as Andaman Indians, be he a new settler from East Bengal, a naturalised Karen from Burma or a person born here out of convict ancestry. To ensure assistance and facilities in the matter of education and other social development for these people, the local administration has recommended the inclusion of the permanent residents of these islands in the list of backward communities. The artificial creation and nurturing of a special community as "Local Borns" were obviously due to the social disabilities to which the early convict settlers were subjected to in those days. But it certainly has created a fissiparous tendency which is very undesirable in the present political context of the country. A feeling of separateness attended with an inferiority complex has crept in, retarding the progress and development of the people. As one young graduate very aptly put it the other day "the people here are suffering from a 'backward-phobia'—although in point of fact they are on an average much better off than other Indians of comparable economic status". This youth is at the moment engaged in a random sampling of the economic life of the people, under the auspices of the Indian Statistical Institute. An impression was painfully apparent sometime ago that these islands belong to the "Local Born" people only and the new settlers are interlopers. But this is gradually dying out. In fact, the term 'settler' used to denote only displaced persons settled here is a misnomer, as all non-tribal people in the Andamans are settlers—the difference is only in the point of time of settlement.

I personally feel a sociological experiment of tremendous national importance is going on in this little community of roughly 10,000 souls who have cut across all barriers of caste, creed, community or province of origin. Free inter-marriage irrespective of caste or religion has gone on with perfect ease and without the slightest shock or violence to the general social structure.

Religion to these people is a completely personal matter and is not allowed to interfere with the secular life of the community. This process of integration of a variety of territorial and religious groups has produced a most interesting community of people with a remarkable quickness of intellect and practical sense. This great fusion has been largely facilitated by the prevalence of Hindustani as the common language of the people. These islands are witnessing perhaps the birth of the organic essence of Indian humanity. But this grand experiment will be futile if these people are treated as a separate community and subjected to social disadvantages—both here and in the mainland. It is most satisfactory to record here that the example of this unique community has been followed by other Hindus living here and no anxiety was evinced by any member of that community, whether belonging to the scheduled or non-scheduled castes, to have his caste recorded in the current census. They have all been recorded as members of one 'non-backward' community.

Displaced persons—As a 'grow more food' measure and with a view to attainment of self-sufficiency in the matter of food, I suggested colonisation of these islands early in 1948—specially as at that time about 3,000 acres of abandoned holdings were available for settlement. The idea caught and the Government of India agreed to the West Bengal Government's proposal to rehabilitate displaced persons from East Pakistan in the Andamans. The total number of such refugees enumerated in the current census is 1,500.

These may be divided in the following categories:—

(1) The batch of 171 agricultural families who came and settled down here in 1949 and were given cash doles, seeds, implements and cattle free, costing roughly Rs. 2,333 per family minus the cost of a pair of buffaloes and a milch cow. Seven artisan families also came in 1949.

(2) The batch of 49 agricultural families who came in 1950 and were given advances up to Rs. 2,000 for their maintenance, cattle, implements, etc., to be realised in six years.

In both cases 5 acres of valley and 5 acres of hills and slopes have been allotted for two years. In a few cases where the family has more than one adult 7 acres of valley land has also been given.

(3) 34 families who joined the local Labour Force in 1950 for eventual settlement on lands they would clear and reclaim. They are about to be settled on the same conditions as the 1950 batch.

(4) 47 families of businessmen and artisans who came in January this year and will be given maintenance, house-building and business advances upto Rs. 1,500 and ⅓ acre of house-site.

(5) Besides these, 43 young Bengalis, some of whom are even Matriculates, initially joined the Labour Force and are working as ordinary mazdoors in other organisations. Their performance, of course, is not up to standard but this is inevitable in the circumstances.

This unfortunate section of uprooted humanity is labouring under a very lamentable sense of defeatism and frustration. Continued existence on state charity has produced a peculiar helplessness and laziness amongst them which it took the administration a lot to dispel. Whether businessmen or artisans, middle class or cultivator, each one is evincing an almost insatiable lust for land, irrespective of his capacity to till. People reported to be good carpenters refused jobs offererd to them, just to settle down on land. This is quite understandable amongst people whose roots were dug deep in the fertile lands of East Bengal and to whom trade or business was just secondary and land was *Lakshmi*. Some of the 1950 and 1951 batch have volunteered to go to jungle areas which they will themselves clear and till. This is indeed very encouraging. It is refreshing to see the little community of Mondals at Wandur, hacking away trees and growing an excellent crop on the newly cleared lands, in the *jhum* system. While most have shown diligence and industry, a few have proved complete slackers and were employed on occasional labour during the lean period.

The largest single limiting factor to the progress and development of these people is their lack of financial staying power. They came as complete destitutes, leaving their own home and lands which gave them plenty. Future schemes, therefore, dealing with such people must provide for an insurance against distress. For example, if one of the plough animals die, the man has not the means to replace it.

On the whole, I think, they have done reasonably well, but it will at least take a couple of years or more for them to properly find their feet. It would be interesting to see what the Superintendent of Census, 1961 writes of them in his report. Much of their troubles could have been obviated if they worked on the basis of small agricultural co-operatives. But the administration's best efforts met with failure. It is extraordinary that even this dire distress has not been able to kindle the spirit of "mutual aid" latent in man. In this respect, the 12 families of repatriated Indians from Burma, settled in Shoal Bay have shown a remarkable solidarity and co-operative spirit. The displaced person needs the Government's sympathy and care undoubtedly, but undue generosity will be his ruin.

This scheme of colonisation is also designed to obviate the necessity of recruitment of labour from the mainland and absorbing the population surplus to agriculture in the various Government and private industries. A small beginning has been made in this direction but the fact should not be lost sight of.

Other homogeneous communities—Apart from these Bengali settlers from Eastern Pakistan the following other homogeneous communities have settled down here permanently:—

1. The Karens.
2. The Mapillas.
3. The Burmans.

Migrating initially in 1925 for working in the Forest Department as labourers and forest villagers, the Karens have finally settled down as agriculturists in Middle Andamans, near Steward Sound. They have named their location 'Webi' which literally means haven and are living in perfect peace and mutual amity. Did they flee a civil strife in their homeland? Tucked away a hundred miles from the head-quarters, this little christian community of 384 souls is developing completely on its own with hardly any assistance from the State, except for the pay of two school teachers. They have built a beautiful church which also accommodates the School. I shall never forget my first visit to this village, when in answer to my enquiries regarding any possible assistance they may need they told me that they want nothing more than our goodwill. How unlike other villages in India! We have just given this very industrious agricultural community another 100 acres of forest land near their village for expansion. The pressure on land was great. They also do a lot of fishing and hunting in their spare time. Recently they have all naturalised themselves as Indian Citizens and as such been recorded as Andaman Indians in this census. An integrated population is to be very much preferred to a mosaic of little communities. From 263 in 1931 their number has gone up to 384 in these two decades.

The Mapillas are the remnants of the deported rebels of Malabar and their progeny with considerable volunteer settlers thrown in. In the past two years, there was a great demand from this community to increase their number by importing from the mainland, till pressure on land became too great and the administration had to interfere by screening issue of permits to intending settlers. Only those who really needed assistance on their land or in their trade were allowed to import relations. In this census this community also is not going to be recorded separately and will be an integral part of the Andaman Indian community.

Burmans, however, are a little different. They neither want to merge nor to leave. Their contributions both past and present towards the development of these islands and the economic life of the community are remarkable. They find it difficult, however, to adopt Indian Citizenship, only a few have taken out naturalisation certificates. Non-violence is not their strong point.

Japanese occupation—Some mention of Japanese occupation of these islands is imperative for a census report of the last decade. The islands were under their occupation from the 23rd March, 1942 to the 6th October, 1945. While their relations with local people were quite amiable initially, their regime developed gradually into a veritable reign of terror, the more they suspected existence of British espionage. Against this background people tried to "feed fat their ancient grudge" as and when opportunity occurred, but their favours were fickle and fall from grace became so frequent that all sense of security was completely gone. Their only objective appeared to be "to win the War" and at the altar of that ideal they were prepared to sacrifice all finer values of life. On the slightest suspicion people were burnt alive, beaten up to death like dogs and physical tortures of fantastic types were perpetrated. But by violence and threat of violence they certainly did expand agriculture and made these islands practically self-supporting. Evidence still left of look outs and gun emplacements at many inaccessible places shows the thoroughness and efficiency of their defence arrangements. Much has been said about collaboration by the local people. Without going into the ethics of such conduct, one may say, that placed under those circumstances against the background of a reign of terror within and a complete lack of help or even hope of help from without, few communities could have reacted differently.

Economic, social and cultural—I am afraid I shall have to leave a study of these matters to my successor who will have the advantage of having the numerous tables under preparation now. But the remarkable feature about the social life of the so-called "Local Borns" is their admirable regard for law and authority which seems somewhat extraordinary in the context of their origin. Up at Phoka Dera, near Stewart Sound, live a mixed community of 100 ex-convicts and their progeny, contiguous to the Karens, without almost a single crime to their credit for the last quarter of a century. Only recently a Police outpost has been established, but no crimes have been reported so far. Owing to my other pre-occupations it was not possible for me to make any intensive criminological studies here but I am almost convinced that crime has no relation to heredity. I would even go so far as to say that a habitual criminal is not born but made by conditions favourable to the commission of crimes.

Density of population—Any attempt to work out the density of population on the basis of the entire area will be misleading. The largest concentration of population of about 17,000 is in the small settled area of about 50 to 60 sq. miles and the density comes to 280 per sq. mile. What is important is to note the pressure on the agricultural land. It is obvious that 5,000 acres cannot support 19,000 people and a considerable expansion is definitely indicated.

VII. Population—Aboriginal

Ethnology—Delving deep into the archives of anthropology to label and catalogue the aboriginal population of Andamans according to their various groups and sub-groups may be of very great academic interest but hardly useful in the present context of their appallingly dwindling number. I have had opportunities of coming into close contact with the three main tribes, *viz.*, the coastal Andamanese, the Jarawas and the Onges and am definitely of the opinion that they are just different species of the same genus. The slight cultural difference cannot obliterate the fact of their common stock and are due merely to their "isolationistic habits" caused by their fundamental calling of collection of food. For this purpose, their haunts have to be extensive and any mutual poaching is naturally resented. This sense of property and natural jealousy arising out of the fear of trespass have prevented all inter-communication and the development or lack of it of each tribe has been entirely on its own lines. Hence the difference in language, in manners and also in attainments. Essentially there are two main species, the Ereintaga, *i.e.*, the forest dwellers of whom we have only more or less indirect knowledge of the Jarawa and the Aryoto or the coastal tribes to which both the Onges and the Andamanese belong. Bonnington's assimilation of the Onge with the Jarawa is not quite understood. The Onge is a real sea-farer, even better than the Andamanese, while the Jarawa is essentially a land-lubber. The Onge settlement, seen by me, is in the coastal area of Little Andamans very similar to Andamanese settlements, except for the absence of the communal hut amongst the Andamanese. Perhaps they had it before their contact with civilisation. The over-whelming similarity of these tribes in their physical features, mode of life, food and pastimes completely out-weigh the problematic differences noticed by previous observers. The adjective 'problematic' has been used intentionally. Bennington, for example, at page 9 of the Census Report, says that the Onge basket is coarsely woven. We collected a basket from the Onges the other day which is very finely woven. In an Onge hut, right away in Little Andaman, I saw a specimen of fine weaving work in a fibre fishing trap. The Onge has perforce to make his canoe differently as he has to traverse vast distances on the sea. I thus think that these negligible differences had been over-emphasised and the fundamental unity overlooked in the past.

According to modern anthropology they are of the Negrito stock. But according to Ramayana they are *Kiratas*. These *Kiratas* have been described in our epic literature as shiny black, with a copper coloured head of hair* (Tamra-murdhaja), bulging eyes and strong teeth. The description of this tribe, recorded several thousand years ago, holds good to-day. All these tribes have copper coloured, curly short hair growing as it were in separate insulated tufts.

I think the finest description of these tribes will be found in the following couplet of the Ramayana:—

"AMAMINACANASHTATRA KIRATAH DWIPA-BASINAH"

[There (in the East) you will find is land dwelling *Kiratas* living on raw meat and fish.]

The passage of thousands of years has not changed their diet to the slightest degree.

(*a*) This is further reinforced by the fact that most of the native appellations of the Andamans tribe seem to have phonetical similarity to *Kirata*, *e.g.*, Aka-kora (da), Aka-kede (da), Aka-Kol (da).

(*b*) Still another remarkable fact is the phonetic similarity of the Onge word *Boan* with the Santhal word *Bonga*, both signifying God or a Supreme Being. Does this similarity on a fundamental concept common to all humanity point to an ethnic affinity between the two tribes?

The Santhal is also a *Kirata*.

I am, therefore, quite convinced that the aborigines of Andamans are the same people who, in the dim past, inhabited the marshes of Bengal, the uplands of Santhal Pargans or the dense forests of Burma and Malaya. They are of that race of hunters and fishers who practically ruled this part of the world, away from the ravages of the *Purusada* (cannibalistic) Rakshasas. The local tribes had either drifted away to these islands in their frail craft or saved themselves somehow during the cataclysm. It depends on whichever geological theory is accepted. But it is obvious that in their case time has had a stop. For that most ancient description of the Ramayana still holds true.

I commend this theory to the professional Anthropologists, who may consider the desirability of replacement of *Negrito* by *Kirata*—after all *Negrito* is an innovation and *Kirata* is historical.

Movement of population—The table below shows the movement of the aboriginal population during the last five decades. Only the coastal tribe of Great Andaman, now called Andamanese, was actually enumerated. The rest of the figures are just estimates based on certain data which will be discussed later:

Coast tribes of	1951	1941	1931	1921	1911	1901
Great Andaman .	23	..	90	209	455	625
Jarawas . . .	50	..	70	114	114	585 (Jarawas and Sentinelese)
Sentinelese . .	..	..	50	117	117	
Onges . . .	150	..	250	346	631	672

I can only exclaim with Hutton, Census Commissioner in 1931 that "this devastating fall in the number of the Andamanese" in less than a century's "contact with administration paralyses comment but it is impossible not to agree with Von Eickstedt's view of the 'Andaman Home' policy. The relation with the Onges prove that the method was not without alternative".

The other tribes also register a steady decrease although not to the appalling extent as that of the Andamanese. Here also the administration cannot be completely absolved of the responsibility for this sad state of affairs.

This sheer fall in the total number of these tribal people from 5,000 in 1858 (the year of permanent establishment of the penal settlement here) to 223† in 1951, *i.e.*, in less than a century's connection with civilization, is simply staggering.

Andamanese—Though, originally, the most numerous of all the tribes, their decadence has been the worst, their contact with civilization being the earliest and most thorough.

Andaman Home—Originating out of a policy of conciliation with the rather truculent coastal tribes, the Home degenerated into a sort of prison for these free nomads whose normal habits were just the opposite of what was attempted to be a foisted on them in this

* The Mahabharat describes it more precisely by saying copper coloured spiral like hair.

† NOTE—As a result of investigation carried out during 1952 and 1953, their total number to-day is estimated to be about 1,000, not 223.—A.K.G.

institution. To quote Rev. Corbyn, the pioneer in the matter, he 'daily employed them in work with native convicts clearing sites, etc., taught them to speak English and wear clothes'. In short a thorough attempt was made to domesticate this roving community, directly opposed to their ingrained habits, with devastating results. Completely devoid of pathological defences they fell an easy pray to venereal, pulmonary and bronchial diseases and got addicted to the habits of smoking, drinking, etc., most deleterious to their constitution. Their innate sense of freedom revolted against this restriction and eventually they had to be released but with innumerable disease-spreading bacilli in their organism. And these hundred years have seen the near annihilation of this erstwhile thriving community of hunters and fishers. The process was perhaps a little accelerated during 1942-45, when the Allied Intelligence Officers visited the Middle and North Andamans and, as a price of their services, gave them drinks, smoke and tinned food. *Loka,* the present headman of the Middle Andamans group, himself a half-breed, waxes eloquent of his contact with American and British Officers during this period.

In a fresh attempt to save this little community, the Forest Department collected them all and put them in Bluff Island in 1949 to act as buffer against maurading Jarawas. But restricted life apparently does not appeal to them and when I went to visit them a couple of months ago, only two males were found at Bluff, the rest having paddled away in their canoes to Havelock and Neill Islands for fishing.

Their distribution at the moment is as follows:—

	Males	Females	Children
North Andamans	3	4	0
Middle Andamans	7	8	1
TOTAL	10	12	1

The child is a male—the chances of regeneration are thus almost nil. As Anie, the old queen of North Andamans, told me that there must be a divine curse on this community, otherwise her three young sons with their three young wives should have been able to propagate the species. I am told that she is now living completely on her own at Interview island. Is it in disgust at the inefficiency of her off-spring? This applies equally well to the Middle Andaman group who also blame God for their unproductivity.

The 16 souls in Middle Andamans have all the islands up to Neill to roam about in their little canoes, while the seven, rather six now, northerners hold sway over the entire area between Landfall and Stewart Sound. They often wander overland leaving their little canoes at various centres. Reasons are obvious for the seas from Stewart Sound to Landfall are completely unsheltered and a voyage in a canoe precarious.

Cultural—It is useless to dilate on their cultural attainments. They have practically lost their pristine culture, thanks to their continued contact with foreigners. It is, however, a pleasure to see *Loka* and his band in Middle Andamans doing turtle hunting with formidable harpoons in their frail canoes swirling round and round a huge turtle trying to make its escape. It is also a sight to see them climbing up tall coconut palms without any aid. They still possess their dancing board—but dances are few and far between. Their huts which exist in Port Cornwallis and Stewart Sound only, the people in Bluff island using huts made by the Forest Department, are the ordinary lean-to type with a raised platform inside used as a bed. I have always seen them clothed, the men in shorts and the females in petticoats of sorts. Their ruin both physical and spiritual is almost complete.

Religion—I have often heard them talk about God, but I doubt very much if the idea is native to them or just borrowed from others. Bonnington has mentioned about their religious beliefs but I have no first hand information. The reported belief in the existence of a Tree on which the Heavens rest is very suggestive of the geological cataclysm when these tribes must have saved themselves by climbing up on trees. But this is far fetched. Some of them, specially females, still wear their ancestor's skulls.

Economic—Up to 1949, that is still their employment as Forest Guards, the Middle Andaman people used to collect tortoise sheels and edible birds' nests which the Administration took over in exchange of luxuries like tea, sugar, cigarettes or necessities like dahs, files, etc. But now they barter their pay and so perhaps do not bother collecting birds' nests from inaccessible caves. The North Andamanese, however, sent me a packet of edible birds' nests the other day. They have refused to work under the Forest Department and have reverted to their normal mode of life.

The Onges—The entire community is now to be found at Little Andamans. The Rutland group mentioned in previous census reports must have either perished or shifted to Little Andamans. But they regularly visit Rutland every cold weather and from there hop over to Maymyo ghat and call on us at Port Blair. They, however, failed their date this year which is a little disturbing. As to their estimated number,

(*a*) in 1948, the Anthropological Party led by Dr. B. S. Guha contacted about 28 near Bomila Creek in Little Andamans,

(*b*) in the cold weather of that year 7 pairs with three children visited Port Blair,

(*c*) in 1949, another Anthropological Party contacted about an equal number in Hut Bay,

(*d*) in 1950, 21 males came to Port Blair and went with us on a special cruise of the Maharaja. At Djugong Creek, which is a little to the South of Bomila Creek, we found the other members of the community, totalling about 50 in all inclusive of women and children. Enquiries revealed that there were 3 or 4 similar locations along the coast of Little Andamans, the farthest one being on the West coast, south of Jackson Strait. So at that time I estimated their total population at 200, although the Onge headman told me that there were "many many fifty" Onges—but his idea of many did not go beyond five—as later I discovered he could not count up to 10,

(*e*) but in my final estimate I have decreased this by 50 because an Anthropological Party led by Dr. S. Sarkar visited Djugong Creek in February, 1951 and I had great expectations that this time perhaps, we shall be able to actually enumerate Onges. But alas! not a single soul was found by this party along a seven mile coast line up to the next creek and up to three miles inside. On the contrary they saw

(1) two communal huts at a distance of a mile and a half from each other, the second one newly re-conditioned lying vacant,

(2) 7 canoes, two of which we saw in the process of being built in 1950, lying about and

(3) most suspicious of all great mounds looking like graves with several small ones thrown

in were noticed which seemed to Dr. Sarkar as evidence of mass burial.

They stayed there for about a week and put up smoke signals but not a single one appeared.

This is indeed very disheartening news. Has there been a complete annihilation of this Sept by any epidemic or was there an inter-sept war ? They could not have been on their annual voyge to Great Andamans as all available canoes were lying strewn about, nor could they have gone very far inland as inter-sept boundaries are definitely demarcated and may not be crossed with impunity. Actually their non-appearance in this cold weather had made me a little anxious and early in January I had asked the Burmans of Maymyo village, who generally bring them in, as to what could have happened. They thought that the rather unfavourable weather prevailing up to then was perhaps causing delay. Little did I know then that this friendly tribe has in all probability been effaced from the face of the earth. Lack of time and transport has not made it possible for me to check-up on this report but I hope the administration will soon start investigations. *

In any case this is the reason why I had to cut down my estimate of these Onges to 150 only, very sorrowfully indeed. The present estimate, however, is quite in keeping with the trend of the previous estimates—but I had high hopes that the community was quickening up.†

Past relations—Bonnington records the various futile and punitive attempts made by the administration before final conciliation with this tribe was attained by kind behaviour and heavy donation of presents. Although the Djugong-Bomila Creek Sept has been found to be very friendly, no definite opinion can be given as to the attitude of Septs living near Jackson Strait and beyond. In any case in the Special Cruise in which 21 Onges accompanied us, we did not find them fidgetty or nervous as Bonnington found there. They seemed to enjoy the trip immensely and had their eyes and ears always alert.

Intelligence—(a) In 1950 as the Maharaja was about to leave on Special Cruise, 21 Onges who had been to Port Blair only a few days ago returned with a request to take them to their homeland in the Maharaja. Local enquiries at Maymyo, their anchorage, revealed that the canoes they came in had become almost unserviceable. This certainly is indicative of discursive thinking.

(b) Again as the Maharaja steamed away from Djugong Creek, their the then location, this little band of abobrigines became very restive aboard and finally the headman approached the writer and explained that the ship was on a wrong course. After a discussion with Captain Gibson, the master of this vessel, the ship was diverted to Djugong Creek and in about two hours time the smoke from their village was visible. It clearly shows their keen power of maritime observation and sense of bearing. The long voyages they undertake in open seas, without any landmarks between Little Andamans and Rutland have certainly quickened their navigational instinct and the present writer does not agree with Bonnington that their canoe-culture is of a much lower standard than that of the Andamanese or that they belong to the Erantaga or the jungle dweller type. With that great pride they showed us round their canoe-building yard where two new canoes were being made—big enough to carry two dozen persons.

(c) Mrs. Ghosh, the wife of the Chief Commissioner Shri A. K. Ghosh, I.C.S., and some other ladies along with the writer collected a vocabulary of a number of words during this trip, reproduced in Appendix E. An underlying scientific basis of the language is clearly noticeable. All words relating to the body and acts connected therewith begin with the prefix *'Eni'*—thus the eye is *Enijibole*, the leg *Enichege*, going *Eniqualebe*, and coming *Enikochobe*. Is it something like Urdu "Tasrif Laiye" (be pleased to bring your body)? The most remarkable group of words is *Injobe* (water), *Inja* (Sea), *Injokabe* (Infinite). They thus have the concept of the Infinite, expressed in a term almost similar to that for the sea. I have already remarked about their word for God *'Boan'*. These words also indicate power of abstract thought. It is a little extraordinary that people without the knowledge of the numerals should have an idea of the Infinite. But perhaps their economic life does not require numerals. *'Iccheli'* for child has a remarkable similarity to Hindi *'Chelia'*.

Living in comparative isolation is their island home this community offers a vast field for researches in psychological and social anthropology.

Tribal organisation—Their organisation has almost a political tint. The writer's investigations reinforce the previous theory that organisation of society is on a septal basis, with clear cut boundaries for hunting ground for each sept near their locations. The Onge is generaly very nervous and reticent of speaking about other folk and all that information that could be obtained from the headman of the group contacted was that "there are many many fifty Onges". It is this restricted field of operations that forces them to make these long voyages to Rutland and Cinque islands as and when weather conditions become propitious. Their attempts at expansion and acquisition of more "Labensarum" have been noted by Lowis in 1921. He said that the Onges first used the Rutland as a camping ground and then gradually settled down there and shown a tendency to cross the McPherson Strait and come to South Andamans. They still do cross the McPherson Strait but not for additional territory.

The Headman certainly is respected but did not seem to hold much authority—the community seemed to be quite democratic and the economy communistic. The existence of communal huts, communal canoes, common fire, etc., points to this.

This "Septism" verging almost on political nationalism is probably leading them slowly along the path of annihilation. Some septs have most certainly vanished for want of food within their limited zone. Those that dare out perhaps still exist. In this connection some excerpts are reproduced from the writer's tour diary of March, 1950:—

"The village itself is in the clearing of a deep jungle very close to the beach about 20′ × 10′ in which there were 14 little sheds. The sheds were about 4′ high with a platform of 1½′ by about 2½′ to 3′. The roof was of leaves and there were no walls around. The fixed log at one end of the

---

* Note 1—This has been done. The people were all in the interior of the Island, collecting wild honey. —A.K.G.

† Note 2—Dr. Cipriani lived with the Onges in Little Andaman for three months in 1953, and moved all over the Island. He counted over 400 men, women and children; and estimated their total number at between 500 and 600.—A.K.G.

shed is perhaps used as a pillow. The place was filthy and flies were buzzing about. There were a large number of mangy famished dogs, which show that the people perhaps do not have sufficient food.

* * * * *

It seems a little curious to me that this 300 sq. miles of land is not adequate for their food and they have to migrate to Rutland for some part of the year in search of food. Anyhow I am definite that they do not have enough to eat from the look of things in the village.

* * * * *

While I agree that we should not try to disturb the normal conditions of life of these tribal people I feel it to be the duty of the State to see at least that they are brought to human level. It would be worth while putting some social anthropologists on the job. They would at least be able to suggest steps for improvement of their living conditions."

Social customs and religion—Girls certainly are married very early. I saw a girl wife almost below her teens and when questioned about the utility of such an union, both man and wife laughed. Marital relations seem to be very strict. The Onges will always squat in pairs—the woman in front of the man almost on his lap. In one of these visits, the writer saw a lone female lying very disconsolate away from the rest. Enquiries revealed that she had just been widowed. Obviously the widow has no place in the community. Bonnington actually speaks of widow murders, by drowning.

Some ossuary practice is noticeable, as amongst all these primitive people. This attachment for bones of the dead perhaps arises from the fact that the bone is the only part of human body with comparative permanence. Preservation of the bone of the dead might give the psychological satisfaction of close material proximity of the beloved dead. It need not have any religious significance.

People having the fundamental concept of a Supreme Being cannot be said to have no religion. Whether their religious ideas are crúde or developed is more than can be asserted. No evidence was available of religious practices.

Pastime and recreation—'Enilalabe' is their word for dance and '*Gaga*' is their word for song. There is hardly any '*Gaga*' spirit in their music though, which was indeed very plaintive. The dance is the usual 'contredance' type, males and females standing opposite each other. On the whole they do not give the impression of a cheerful crowd as their opposite numbers in Great Andamans although in state of rapid decay, do. The only physical decoration still remaining is the smearing of white clay on the body.

Technical skill—Some very beautiful weavings of fibre were noticed in their village. Their canoes are also quite strong and sea-worthy. They have learnt the use of dahs, chisels and files and are keen to acquire these in lieu of their collections. The tassel of yellow fibre used by their women in front, is quite artistic too. Their weapons are sufficiently murderous and the bow-string made of fibre is quite strong and yet resilient.

Jarawas: Population and movement—The writer's direct contact with this community is through the four captive children, at present being brought up by Bishop Richardson at Car Nicobar, and the three males captured in 1948 who finally gave the administration the slip. Naturally, therefore, his knowledge about this community is most meagre.

In estimating the present population, note was taken of the following incidents that took place during 1948-1951:—

(*a*) On 14th September, 1948 a band of Jarawas of about 15 to 20 raided a forest camp near Bajalungta in Middle Andaman and looted pots, pans and white cloth to the exclusion of *khaki* and killing a Burman boy with an arrow. A gun fire scared them away.

(*b*) On 19th October, 1948 some officers of the Forest Department sighted three adult Jarawa males and a boy in Spike island and after some dexterous manouvers Mr. Joseph and Mr. Pooviah, two Assistant Conservators of Forests and Mr. Gupta, the Accounts Officer captured them. They had bark armour and the paint on. They finally escaped from Port Blair.

(*c*) On 1st April, 1949, 2 or 3 Jarawas shot one Telugu mazdoor dead in Foster valley. The interesting fact is the Jarawas picked up both the arrows they shot. They took away two dahs too.

(*d*) On 13th April, 1949 a forest Ranger heard a cooing voice behind him almost like that of hog deer and as his dog ran that way it was stabbed. The party did not consist of many.

(*e*) On 19th April, 1949 there were definite indications of Jarawas crossing over from Baratang island in Middle Andamans to the mainland. There was buttress beating on both sides of the creek.

(*f*) On 28th December, 1949 an estimated number varying between 17 and 23 attacked a party of forest mazdoors in Porlob Jig in Middle Andamans. Two were killed on the spot and another fled with an arrow stuck on him. One of the murders was brutal, the man's skull having been cut open and nose chopped off.

(*g*) Trace of Jarawas in Lakra Lunta on 4th January 1950.

(*h*) In May-June, 1950 one Burman who strayed north of the settled area of Herbertabad in South Andamans was killed by one Jarawa.

(*i*) Burning of old forest camps at Rangat and Happy valley was noticed about November, 1950.

(*j*) A lone Jarawa was noticed by a Survey Party bush policeman in Mile Tilek in South Andaman in January, 1951.

(*k*) Two Jarawas visited a bush police camp at Lakra Lunta in the early morning of 11th January, 1951. One was shot dead. An attempt was made to exaggerate the number of Jarawas to 50 to 60 by the bush policemen, but cross examination revealed that they saw no more than two and guessed that there might be more. This incident is interesting in two ways.

(1) this is the first time that a Jarawa was shot dead.*

* NOTE—Unfortunately not one but many Jarawas have been shot dead in skirmishes during the hundred years we have been in occupation of these Islands.—A.K.G.

17 Home/54

(2) that the Jarawas did not shoot before they were shot at and came out in the open in front of the camp where there were four bush policemen. This is quite contrary to their ambushing habits.†

(l) In January, 1951 a number of Burmans from Bassein drifted away to these islands in a small boat from Bassein. Enroute, while getting a supply of drinking water in a creek on the west coast which from their description appeared to be Lowis Inlet, they saw communal huts with pigs' skulls strung on the entrance and considerable number of footprints both of adults and children.

The Lakra Lunta incident shows how the number of these raiders is apt to be exaggerated by the victims. All the evidence about these raids point to the conclusion that at the outside about 20 Jarawas are roaming about with their headquarters at Lowis Inlet, across the Middle Andaman up to Spike island to the South and the Happy Valley to the West. Besides there might be two or three (perhaps the three runways) in South Andamans moving along Chawlanga range from Mile Tilek in the east to the Bajiunta creek in the west. So at the outside there may be about 25 male adults of the tribe, some of whom are according to reports only grown-up lads. From a survey of the Onges it appears that there is a little preponderance of males over females amongst the tribal population. On this basis there would be about 20 females. The general decline of the race would warrant a caution in estimating the number of children and I would put it at 5. The story goes that there were some Japanese air-raids during the occupation on the western coast, the usual Jarawa haunts, to punish these truculent people. This might have resulted in some decrease too. In any case, the present estimate of 50 seems to indicate that the tribe is rallying round, for the rate of fall during the last two decades is much less than that between 1921-31. Thus, while between 1931 and 1951 the decrease is only one a year, between 1921-31 it is over 4 a year. But the number certainly cannot be very much more, as some people seem to think, for in that case they should have been more visible.

The continued truculence of this tribe is certainly disturbing. The 1949 incidents produced a scare amongst the forest labour. The administration must pursue a "catch 'em alive" policy. Actually the writer's own view is that if the bush policemen at Lakra Lunta had not lost their nerves in January, 1951, we might have been able to catch these two Jarawas. The fact that they came out in the open, early in the morning and walked right into the camp and did not attempt to shoot, would warrant a prèsumption that they meant a friendly visit. The reason is not far to seek. Since the string of incidents in 1949, the forest department has been very watchful and practically bottled them up between Lowis Inlet and Lakra Lunta on the west, and a zig-zag along Yeratil Jig to Rangat and Happy Valley to the east, very narrow at certain points. This restricted existence must be very galling and inconvenient to a people who held sway practically over the whole of the western coast within about 25 miles of Port Blair and might have inspired an attempt at an overture for peace. But this shooting of the Jarawa might, in all probability, stiffen them up.

Intelligence—Topsy, the captive Jarawa girl at Car Nicobar can read away Jawahar Lall Nehru's Letters to his daughter with a perfect ease and excellent accent. She and her three little brothers are doing arithmetical sums, and reading Hindi and their receptivity is amazingly good. The yougest, Chengapa, sometimes feels the lure of the jungle and escapes to the forests for days on end and Bishop Richardson has to use the birch to domesticate him.

The three captive adults, who could be studied only for a few days, gave evidence of surprising intelligence. The very fact that they gave their Captors a slip, although under day and night surveillance, by dint of a keen power of observation in learning to unfasten the bolt of a window and eventually jumping out of it shows their intellectual capabilities. In a split second they picked up the mechanism of an alarm clock and thoroughly enjoyed the repeated rings. The difference between a cushioned sofa and a hard wooden office chair was immediately grasped and preference shown for the more comfortable seat. Civilization's solicitation for their welfare in giving the wounded Jarawa a penicillin injection or making them sleep in closed doors or giving them cooked meat to eat was not at all appreciated. Soon they were found dressing up an entire pig and making a feast of it in their own way. With what dexterity was the dissection done without the aid of any instrument. The stiff bones were broken up as match sticks. They must have a thorough knowledge of animal anatomy. The lesson of this escape is that in case of future captures, the captives must be placed in surroundings normal to them under proper vigilance and must not be introduced into high class drawing-rooms and given joy-rides in automobiles, all too soon.

Weapons—The only contact with this tribe being through violence, local knowledge of them is limited to their big bows and almost spear-like arrows, bark armour, war paint, the cooing war cry and buttress beating as a signal to rally.

On the whole I think they are the most thriving of all the tribes.

Sentinelese—No information is available and no estimate of their number is possible.

PART B—NICOBARS

I. The Land

Physiography—The 10° channel with a uniform depth of 400 fathoms and an approximate width of 80 miles separates the Andamans group of islands from the Nicobars. Does the existence of this fracture indicate that the two groups are results of two distinct geological processes? There is a fundamental difference in the physiography of each. Some of the islands in the Nicobars like Chaura and Pulo Milo and the littoral fringe of Car Nicobar are essentially coral, while Katchall, Nancowry and Great Nicobar are hilly as the Andamans. This group contains the following

† This is incorrect. The men were in bark armour, and were evidently scouts. As soon as they were seen they shot arrows at the policemen, slightly injuring one of them. When the police fired, one Jarawa dropped dead, while the other ran away, injured, into the forest.—A.K.G.

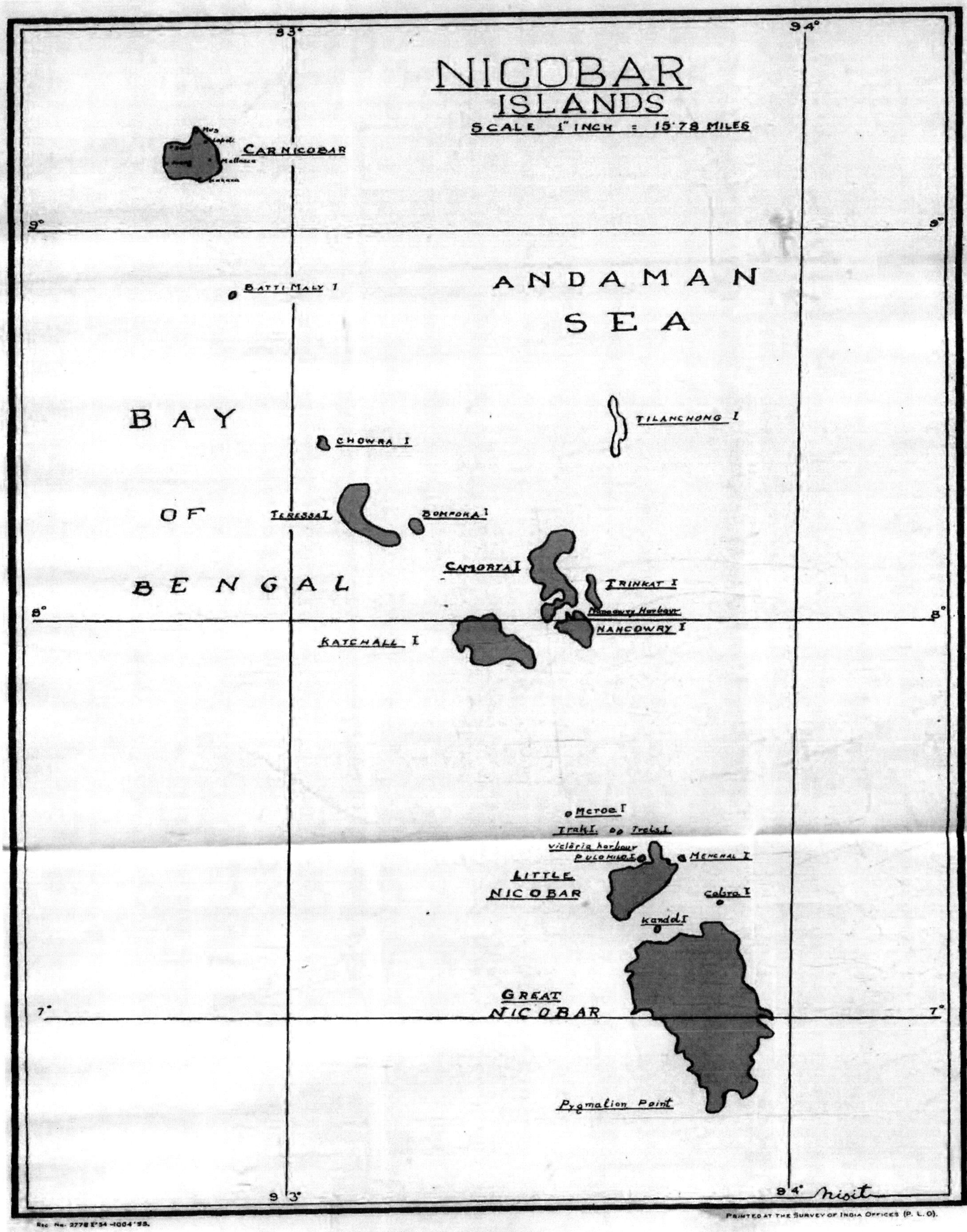

Rec. No. 2778 E'54-1004'55.

PRINTED AT THE SURVEY OF INDIA OFFICES (P. L. O).

Reproduced from original supplied by the Chief Commissioner and ex-officio Superintendent of Census Operations, Andaman and Nicobar Islands, and the Survey of India is not responsible for the accuracy of detail, names etc. appearing on the map.

islands, of which those marked with asterisk are not inhabited:

Car Nicobar	Katchall
*Batti Malv	*Meroe
Chowra	*Trak
*Tilangchong	*Treis
Teressa	*Menchal
Bompoka	Little Nicobar
Camorta	(Pulo Milo)
Trinkat	Great Nicobar
Nancowry	Kondul
	*Kabra

Flora—There is considerable difference in the flora too. Padauk and Gurjon, the pride of Andamans Forests are conspicuous by their absence, although the possibility of utilisation of some soft timber of Great Nicobar for matchwood cannot be overruled. Extensive coconut groves and areca palms constitute, however, the beauty of these islands and according to one school of thought, have given the islands their name, Nicobar being supposed to have been derived from Narikel-dwip. These fruits are the staple food of the inhabitants.

There is no agriculture in the proper sense at all, although 'yams' are grown in considerable quantities as an item of food. In one village in Camorta, it was refreshing to see villagers growing gourds, pumpkins, and other vegetables. This is, however, quite uncommon.

Large areas are under 'lalang' grass which is so useful to the people for their thatches.

Fauna—Monkeys are a nuisance in Great Nicobar and the cause of ruin of the coconut groves. As Bishop Richardson aptly put it in his report, after enumerating the inhabitants of this island during the current census, that "monkeys and malaria will, perhaps, wipe off the coastal community in course of time". Pythons have been found in Car Nicobar. There are other species of reptiles too.

Climate—Rainfall is much heavier and temperature higher specially in the southern group than the Andamans, but no correct meteorological data is available.

II. The People

Ethnology—So also with man—the Nicobarese belong to a completely different race group from the aborigines of Andamans. Unfortunately as the Nicobarese do not possess a collective memory it is very difficult to affiliate them with other extinct or extant groups of human beings through folk-lore or beliefs. Although at times quite idyllic, their folk-lore have hardly any solid basis to offer clues to their past history. They are certainly an ancient race of people identified as *Lojenke* (Naked people) of L 'Tsing (672 A.D.) or the *Lankabhalus* of the Arab mariners (851 A.D.) or Marco Polo's *Necuveram*. There is definite historical evidence of the Second Rajendra Chola's conquest of Car Nicobar (Kar Dwipa) and Great Nicobar (Nag Dwipa). Even to-day a little stream in Great Nicobar is called 'Ganga' and a village in Teressa is known as 'Lakshmi' which is suggestive of past Hindu influence. But this is only identification in isolation and not within any ethnic group.

Here again the Ramayana has not only identified them but claimed them as children of the Indian soil. When Sugriva, the king of the great race of Banaras, was ordering a mass rally of all his troops he mentioned:

"Khisirodabelanilayah
Tamalabanabasinah
Narikelacanah Chaiba
Tesam Shankhya na vidyate."

(Summon also my countless vassals who build their homes on the beach, or live in *tamala* forests, and *live on coconuts.*)

The Nicobarese are the former type of coconut-eating variety of human beings. Several thousand years have passed since and there has not been the slightest change in the mode of life of the Nicobarese.

There is also numerous other internal evidence:

(*a*) Quite frequently the Ramayana describes Banaras as golden hued—some Nicobarese still answer to that description.

(*b*) The main food of this race was "*fala and mula*" (fruits and roots) and even to-day the Nicobarese live on coconuts, yams, pandanus and bananas.

(*c*) Their muscular prowess has always been emphasised in the Ramayana. The modern Nicobarese is reputed for his brawns—"*Eyurhoracka*" (broad-chested) and "*Mahabhuja*" (long-armed).

(*d*) The Banaras did not possess any murderous weapons—and fought with rocks or stones or twigs. To-day, barring a small bow which due to its mechanised arrangements seems an innovation, the Nicobarese do not possess any instrument of killing. Their biggest weapon of offence is a quarter staff.

(*e*) Like the Banaras of Ramayana, their main sport is wrestling.

(*f*) The decorative wooden fretwork which the Nicobarese affixes to the prow of his canoe reminds one of the excellent wood carving of the bier in which the corpse of Bali was carried for cremation—it was "*drumakarmabibhusitam*", *i.e., decorated with wood carving work.*

(*g*) The Banara houses have always been described as "Guhas" (caves). This to my mind seems to refer to a particular type of house which looks like a cave. It could not have referred to caves literally as the internal fittings and furnishings described could not possibly be found in caves. Those who have seen the Nicobarese beehive type huts will at once realise how these can be aptly described as "Guhas" (caves). Standing on stilts, with just a little aperture for egress and ingress and a high dome-like thatched roof, dark and cool inside, they would always give one the impression of a "Guha".

(*h*) Mention is also appropriate perhaps of their fondness for wearing their loin-cloth with a tail at the end, which was also the Banara custom—some of them used to wear even long tails like a cow's tail (*Golangul*).

(*i*) Even the psychological traits are common to both. Hanuman scolds the army as "*Nityamasthira chittah*", *i.e.*, having a grass-hopping mind, unsteady. It is so even to-day. It is very difficult to make the Nicobarese stick to anything for a reasonable length of time.

(*j*) Again Angada, in pious rage against his sovereign and uncle Sugriva for his sins of omission and commission, preferred a fast unto death to a fight. To-day an aggrieved Nicobarese would much prefer destroying his own canoe or killing his own pig to avenging on the offender. I shall dilate on this remarkable non-violent trait in proper context.

(*k*) And last of all his ingrained addiction to spirituous liquor. The Chowra group which typifies the Nicobarese in his purest form will start drinking with day-break. And Sugriva almost failed his date with Rama on account of his heavy drinking.

There is thus an over-whelming evidence that the twentieth century Nicobarese belong to that great and most populous race of Banaras who inhabited the submontane regions of Eastern India, the uplands of Central India and the coastal regions of Burma and Malaya, a yellow coloured people but quite distinct from China and Mahachina according to Ramayana. Their civilisation was of a high order and the collection of precious metals and stones in Sugriva's court dazzled even the Aryan royal brothers Ram and Lakshman.

To hold that these Banaras were monkeys is sheer fatuity. An army of monkeys could not have defeated a mighty race of cannibals, efficiently organised and armed with a variety of lethal weapons. 'Nara' etymologically means 'cultivator' and refers to that stage of human civilisation in which agriculture is the main economic activity, while *Ba-Nara* means 'near-cultivator' that is people who do not grow 'Osadhi' (annual crops) but live on long-lived crops like fruits and roots. This referred to that stage of civilisation, which is intermediate between hunting and fishing and agriculture, between the nomadic and the settled state and is perhaps now called 'bamboo-culture'.

The complete absence of a Rama cult amongst these people does not disprove the above theory:

(*a*) having no written language, they have no means of preserving tradition, and

(*b*) the army that joined the expeditionary forces of Sugriva may not have returned to tell the tale.

How many uneducated Indians, for example, know about the battle of Piassey or Nawab Sirajuddowla—historical facts of only 3 centuries ago. How then can these people remember what must have happened several thousand years ago without the aid of written language?

It is clear, therefore, that these islanders are not just a little community falling from the blues, but formed an integral part of that great yellow race which populated the best part of South East Asia in prehistoric days. No wonder that Grierson has established a philological affinity of their language with Mon Khmer group which is also a similar variety of the human race. (My investigations, however, reveal that only a very few words of the Nicobarese language belong to the Mon Khmer group.) But whereas the Bhutanese or the Burmese or the Malayan has been twisted out of shape by the irresistible march of time, these people living in complete isolation in their island homes have retained the pristine glory of their culture. Glory, it is indeed, as will be shown in the pages that follow.

A mention is, perhaps, necessary of a legend prevailing in Car Nicobar about the canine origin of the people. As Rani Islon of Nancowry told me that "this is a figment of the intellectual brain and we illiterate people neither know nor believe it". I heard two variants of this story.

The first speaks of a cataclysmic flood in which one male could save himself by climbing upon a tree. The only other mammal saved was a bitch and from the union of these was born the race of Nicobarese.

The second depicts a Burmese princess, exiled by her father for her unnatural connection with a dog, who hit upon these shores and had a son by this dog. Before the birth of her child she killed the dog to eliminate the evidence of her shame. A desire to propagate, however, led her to marry the son and multiply.

Both are biological impossibilities so far as the canine origin is concerned, but there may be some faint trace of truth in the latter part of the second story which speaks of the maternal incest. Oedipus-complex has foundations in fact. Most likely the later progeny, having come to know of this, must have called the female ancestor a bitch.

The writer's own view, however, is that the Nicobarese habit of wearing tails and using a head-gear of areca spathe looking like dog's ears are responsible for this foist by foreigners, which these people in their simplicity have accepted as correct. None of the variants of this legend seems to be or needs to be true.

The crux of the matter may be put in the form of this query "Is there any race of human beings who live near the beach in cave, like huts and live on fruits and roots, specially coconuts?" If there is, then the Nicobarese are of that stock—but the stock itself wherever it may be found radiated from the highlands of India. The Nicobarese have thus formed an integral part of India from time immemorial, and are even to-day free citizens of the Republic of India—a fact of which they may very well be proud of.

I dwelt at some length on this to dispel any possible feelings that the Nicobarese may have—about their being separate from other inhabitants of the Indian Union. The fundamental fact remains that from Galatea Bay in Great Nicobar to the Himalayas this great country is one indivisible whole and we are all an integral part of it, whether living in Nicobar or in Bombay.

III. Shom-Pens

These are the highlanders of Great Nicobar who barter cane in exchange of coconuts, fish, tobacco and other necessities. I am not aware of the basis on which the previous estimates of their number were made, but present enquiries indicate that they come down to the coast occasionally in batches of 5 and 6 and that also towards the south. The raids in coastal villages have completely ceased. I should, therefore, think their number cannot be more than 20.

The Great Nicobarese description of them indicates that they are also of the same stock as Nicobarese except that they are a little darker and wear their hair long. Sir Richard Temple also holds the same view. Bishop Richardson who contacted a naturalised family of Shom-Pens consisting of the parents and three children says that their features are similar to those of the Car Nicobarese, Chowrites or Teressians. These two adults, of course, were picked up by Great Nicobar people as children, married and multiplied on the coast and have no connection with the main stock. Another woman of 30 who was adopted in her infancy has married a coastal man and is living happily in the village.

Hostilities between the highlanders and the coastal people have become quite infrequent. Disputes as to exchange rates of commodities only enrage them, otherwise their contacts are quiet.

They use bows and arrows† and spears made of betel nut stalks with a groove near the spear-head. The spear, after a thrust, is twisted and the lance breaks and the spear-head remains inside the body.

In the old days the cane that the coastal people collected from them found a clandestine passage to Malaya by Chinese brigs. With the opening of a branch of the local trade agents at Kondul, the people will be able to have normal trade in canes.

IV. The Movement of Population

The last half a century has registered a considerable increase in the Nicobarese population. Below is a comparative table of distribution and movement of population island by island:—

	1951	1941	1931	1921	1911	1901
Car Nicobar	8,374	..	7,182	6,087	5,550	3,451
Chowra	1,076	..	615	234	348	522
Teressa . 523, and Bompoka . 73	596	..	506	640	656	702
East Katchall 249, West Katchall 244, Camorta . 618, Trinkat . 118, Nancowry . 322	1,551	..	1,041	1,071	1,165	1,095
Little Nicobar (Pulo Milo) 197, Kondul . 47, Great Nicobar 161	405	..	245	216	272	192
Total	12,002	12,452	9,589	8,248	7,991	5,962
Less Indians	100	200				
Total	11,902	12,252	9,589	8,248	7,991	5,962
Shom-Pen (Estimated)	20	..	200	375	375	348

The Shom-Pens were never enumerated and previous reports indicate that complete enumeration of the population of the southern group and some of the central group of islands was not done. So there is an element of guess work in the previous figures. The figures for 1941 and 1951 include some non-Nicobarese. So far as 1951 is concerned their total is not likely to exceed 100 and a correct picture will be obtained after complete tabulation figure. The 1941 figures include about 200 non-Nicobarese.

(a) There has thus been an almost 100 per cent. increase in the Nicobarese population during the last 50 years. This increase, however, does not appear to be steady. It started with a spurt of 33⅓ per cent. in 1901-1911 and then slowed down during the next two decades till it reached the original rate by 1931-1941.

(b) The slight decrease in the total population during this census is due mainly to the heavy toll in life taken by poliomyelitis in 1947-1948, the total number of deaths being 225 and destruction of all English knowing youth of Car Nicobar by the Japanese during their occupation numbering about 100. Besides the 1941 figures contain an element of guess work too. It is thus very unlikely that there has been a slowing down in the process of multiplication through biological and economic forces.

(c) Chowra which Lowis in 1921 apprehended was declining rapidly in her population, has rallied round to an amazing extent, the present population being nearly 500 per cent. more than that of 1921.

(d) The central group has recorded a 50 per cent. increase while even the southern group has gone up by 200 per cent.

(e) Here also there is a slight preponderance of males over females (*vide* table at page XXV). Promiscuity of sexual intercourse is thus frequent. But such extra-marital relationship in these islands has always a sentimental basis. The humid climate and beautiful surroundings have, perhaps, made the people a little over-sexed.

Density—The density of population per island is as follows:—

Islands	Area	Population	Density
Car Nicobar	49 sq. miles	8,374	170
Chowra	3 ,,	1,076	358·7
Teressa	34 ,,	523	15
Bompoka	4 ,,	73	18
Camorta	58 ,,	618	10·7
Nancowry	19 ,,	322	17
Trinkat	6 ,,	118	19·6
Katchall	62 ,,	493	9·5
Little Nicobar (Pulo Milo)	58·5 ,,	197	0·3
Kondul	0·5 ,,	47	94
Great Nicobar	333 ,,	*161	0·48

*Excluding 20 estimated Shom-Pens.

The density of Chowra is appalling but as these people live off the rest of the country by their wits, the restriction of territory does not very much worry them. Car Nicobarese have to spread into other islands. The movement is already in progress. Normal economic forces are bound to iron out this unevenness in the distribution of population. The limiting factor according to Bonnington is the coral-line soil necessary for growth of coconut plants. The plantations in Andamans show that coral-line soil is not essential; besides, in Great Nicobar, Camorta and Katchall plenty of suitable soil is available. The writer seems to think, however, that the innate exclusiveness and aversion to outsiders of the inhabitants of the various islands of southern and central groups are responsible for the concentration of population in smaller areas. Bishop Richardson mentions in his report on enumeration in Kondul and Great Nicobar that some villagers definitely non-cooperated with the census party, although for a very brief period. Rani Islon of Nancowry did not seem to be very happy over settlement of Car Nicobarese in her supposed domain while the Rani of West Katchall seemed to relish the idea. More inter-communication and steady contact will resolve this difficulty. But a spread-out is imperative.

† Note—They have no bows or arrows; only long spears or javelins.—A.K.G.

V. General Characteristics

Fundamentally the entire population from Car Nicobar to Great Nicobar has one underlying culture and outlook on life. Continued insular existence and absence of regular inter-communication owing to inhospitable weather conditions, coupled with different types of foreign influence (*e.g.*, Chinese, Malayan down south and Indian and Western at Car Nicobar up north) have overlaid this essential cultural unity with certain seeming differences even in the spoken language. The inhabitants of Little and Great Nicobar have absorbed a Malayan tongue to such a considerable extent that they are now almost unintelligible to the Car Nicobarese. Again the people of Champi, in Nancowry evince a gaiety and cunning of port people quite contrary to the quiet happy and care-free existence of the Car Nicobarese. The Teressean with his long tuft of hair and a nervous look is a poor specimen of humanity and can be easily disowned by his tribesmen of other islands. Chowra perhaps retains the essential Nicobarese culture in its purest form, mainly due to its inhospitable coastline and aversion of the people. The superior brains, craftsmanship and industry of the people of this very congested island have given them an easy moral ascendancy over the rest. It is really the metropolis or the industrial area of Nicobars, where one would see busy people making clay pots, mending canoes, meeting visitors and treating patients. In short, it has not the sleepy atmosphere of the other islands. Within the last few years since Compton Mackenzie's visit, the Chowrites must have got rid of their dirt, disease and squalor. In 1950, we saw a very healthy and industrious community living in clean and almost picturesque surroundings. The drink evil is, however, rampant but this does not prevent Chowra's being the Holy island of Nicobars.

Mention has been made by Bonnington of the past piracies of the Nicobarese. But the complete absence of any lethal weapons and the innate non-violence of the people verging almost on timidity, make it rather difficult to believe that they adopted piracy as a profession in the past. Probably the Malayan pirates in the southern waters have been mistakenly identified as Nicobarese.

But instead of underlining or emphasising the differences an attempt should be made to discover the underlying unity of culture and heritage of this great race of Indians who in course of time are bound to take their rightful position in the body politic of the Republic.

VI. Cultural

A study of the simple and natural life of the Nicobarese from birth to death will be illuminating.

Birth—During pregnancy, both man and wife are prohibited from doing any hard work or joining up things. Such work would cause difficult labour and probably death. In Car Nicobar each village has a maternity house which is used by all expectant mothers. But in all other islands children are born in the parent's own dwelling houses. In Car Nicobar they are gradually becoming hospital-minded and deliveries in hospital are not uncommon now. In the practice of 'couvade', that is the lying in of the man at the time of his wife's confinement, Grierson finds a confirmation of his theory that the Nicobarese are of Malayan stock. It is difficult to conclude from such isolated instances. In Chowra the bride and bridegroom are made to wear saffron cloth on the eve of their marriage—a custom prevalent, perhaps, in many parts of India. But a conclusion that the Chowrites are Hindus will be just rash.

Marriage—Continued affection resulting from courtship is the determining factor for marriage in Car Nicobar, although this is done with the agreement of the parents of both sides. The future abode of the couple depends on the man power of the either family. If the bride's father is in need of a helping hand, the bridegroom goes and lives with them. No religious rites are performed although there is always a social gathering attended with feasts. Adultery has always been held as a crime against society and is now considered as a sin owing to Christian influence.

In Chowra some religious rites are performed. The couple have their heads shaved off and are kept in an enclosed space for 7 days. They are also made to wear saffron cloth during the period. The husband has to give dowries to the wife's people and guests make presents to the couple. If they desire to start on their own, parents do not object.

In Katchall, Nancowry and Camorta and other islands of the southern group, there is a sort of "companionate marriage." The couple live together for so long as they desire and find it convenient. No malaise is felt over divorce or desertions. On the contrary, it is said that the prouder a woman becomes the more numerous her husbands are. But instances are also not rare of duels having been fought with quarter staves over girls.

Domestic Life—(a) Their main vocation consists of plucking coconuts, up-rooting yams, collecting other forest produce or fishing. This they do for several days on end and when they have collected enough food for the family for some time they just give themselves away in swimming, wrestling and racing with canoes or feasting friends. Pinning down fish with a spear, attracting it by the light of flares is both a sport and an economic activity. They loathe sustained efforts. They know what leisure is and love it.

(b) The people have so far not felt the need of money and exchange of goods is still generally effected by a barter system. But I am afraid the "lure of the lucre" is gradually appearing specially in Car Nicobar and Nancowry.

(c) The population, both male and female, is very fond of dyed stuff and next to their love of precious metals is their liking for this material. A Nicobarese male will feel very proud of his red or black girdle with a flying tail and the female of her 'lungi' of the same stuff and blouses (whenever they wear one) of flowered designs. In Car Nicobar, of course, a majority of the people have taken to wear clothes but the girdled man and the bare-bodied woman are still a common sight. In Chowra and beyond, the population have still kept to their old tradition of "*Nakkambaram*" (nakedness). The females of the species are normally a little shy of foreigners and would betake themselves to their beehive huts and peep through the little door when strangers are about.

(*d*) Their staple diet consists of a cheese-like pulp made by boiling coconut-kernel, pandanus, banana and yam all together and then making it into a dough. This can be preserved for a long time. The main basis of this is, of course, the coconut. Besides, they would often have pig, chicken and fish curry. Rice is considered as a delicacy but thanks to Chinese smuggling, has become a necessity in Nancowry. The administration is taking care to see that they do not get habituated to some food which they cannot produce.

(e) Mention must be made of the regular and ceremonial dances of the Nicobarese. In Car Nicobar, the dance is confined to females (so far as the writer has seen) who arrange themselves according to size and form a ring with a little gap in the end. A bonfire of dried coconut husks and leaves is lighted in the middle and the whole party rhythmically describes this parted ring from one end to the other. There is hardly any accompaniment and the music is very soft and intermittent. The entire art is in the foot-work of the females. But in Great and Little Nicobars, males and females join hand in hand forming a complete ring and humming a moaning tune, suggestive of the sound of surf breaking on the beach. It is something like the old 'Rasa' dance of India but the rhythmic movement is confined up to the waist only.

Decked in multi-coloured but spare garments, this happy species of Home Sapiens, singing, dancing, racing, wrestling and then lazing away on the beach, perhaps intoxicated by the juice of their native trees, give one the impression of Tennyson's Lotus Eaters. Their life is not one mad rush for conquest of nature but a slow and easy movement assimilating all the good things of nature in the current of their life. Sustained labour is not undertaken as it is not needed. Nature is bountiful to them and what they can get without much effort is enough and adequate. Aldous Huxley rightly says:

> "Modern man no longer regards nature as being in any sense divine and feels perfectly free to behave towards her as an over-winning conqueror and tyrant. The spoils of recent technological imperialism have been enormous; . . . . but such acts of 'hubris' directed against nature are generally accompanied by corresponding disadvantages.
>
> Whether the net result of this elaborate debit and credit operations is a genuine progress in virtue, happiness, charity and intelligence is something we can never definitely determine."

VII. Villages

A village is ring of huts with an open space in the middle, spotlessly clean and covered with sand from the beach. This is used for village sports, meetings, etc. The huts are practically devoid of any material possessions but full of wooden statues and other works of art. A piece of wood, carved out on sides at regular intervals to be used for foot-hold, generally serves the purpose of a ladder. The surroundings of the village are generally very clean except in Teressa and some villages of Nancowry which have a rather dirty look. When this fact was pointed out to some of the villagers in Nancowry they started cleaning up and on the writer's next visit four months' later, the surroundings were quite clean. Each village in Car Nicobar has an 'Al panam' or a guest house on the beach where travellers may stay as long as they like as guests of the villagers. Chowra has a string of such 'Al panams' owing to constant pilgrimage of people of the other islands, perhaps. In a village in Car Nicobar was seen a communal kitchen, where women of every household cook in turn and the whole community mess together. This is not common in other islands, perhaps.

VIII. Production and Trade

The economic activity of this community consists in the simple vocation of attending to coconut groves and growing yams, plucking the fruits and drying coconuts in a very crude fashion (by placing the kernel on a platform over a sort of furnace without any controlled temperature) and then bartering this copra for necessities and luxuries. Both male and female take part in the process and both sexes are economically active. The necessity for a copra-drying plant has been felt and the Government have sanctioned a loan for starting one on a co-operative basis. In Car Nicobar, each village has a little co-operative trading society called "Panam Hineng" which arranges for sale of the village produce to the authorised agents and distribution of consumer goods to villagers in return. The best part of this trade is in the form of barter although now-a-days cash payment is not very uncommon. These societies, inspired by Mr. Majid, the then Chief Commissioner and nursed by Shri B. N. Sharma, Assistant Commissioner, Nicobars, have done exceptionally well in course of the last three years. The total profit of these societies during this period amounted to Rs. 1,25,231-1-0. The people are happy, the agent is saved the bother of individual collection and the administration can ensure proper control through them.

In other islands up to 1949, there was no arrangement for trade and the entire volume of trade was in the hands of the Chinese from Malaya who mercilessly exploited the people and gave them dops and drinks in lieu of their copra. But the Government Agent has now opened branches in all the islands of the central group and has just opened another in Kondul in Great Nicobar. Trade is now taking proper shape. The administration has also established two police out-posts, one at Camorta and the other at Kondul, with wireless stations to counter-act the clandestine activities of the Chinese.

Internal trade is even more interesting. The existence of suitable timber in Great Nicobar has resulted in the people of that island specialising in canoe-building. They supply big ocean-going canoes to all the islands. Finishing touches are given to these canoes by the expert builders of Chowra. Their superior spiritual knowledge is also utilised in the proper consecration of the canoe toward off evil spirits.

The pottery clay of Teressa is used by the potters of Chowra for making earthenware and the entire supply of this commodity is in their hands. The writer had the opportunity of observing the dexterity with which the Chowra potter makes his strong and durable pots, entirely without any mechanical aid like a potter's wheel.

Lowis remarked in 1921 that the manufacture of clay cooking pots is tabooed on every island except Chowra, whereas the spirits have ordained that pig and certain other forms of food may be cooked only in these earth pots. The Chowra people also insist on the deals in canoe being made through them and thus make a middleman's profit.

I would only say that if we, in the present international context, adopt such a simple division of economy according to the capability of the man and the productivity of the land, without all nations competing in a technological race to produce things which are not in their line—much of our troubles would be resolved. I don't think the Chowraman charges the others for any unproductive labour. As said before, the canoe is definitely attended to and given finishing touches. It is not a mere observance of a ritual of consecration. It is also common knowledge that cooking in earthen pots is more hygienic than in other metallic or chemical utensils which in any case could not have been available to them.

IX. Tribal Laws

Sir Richard Temple's description that "Government is in fact simple democracy bound by custom" still holds true.

> "........no name of Magistrate,
> Letters should not be known; riches, poverty
> And use of service none; contract, succession,
> Bourn, bound of land, tilth, vineyard none;
> No use of metal, corn, wine or oil;" (*Tempest*)

almost typifies the organisation of Nicobarese society.

Certain anti-social activities like theft, falsehood, adultery, homicidal proclivity, incurable disease, etc., were punishable with death according to local custom. This has been termed by foreigners as "devil murders". But these are nothing but execution of sentences passed according to customary law. One Pa-Tun Sah, however, realised the evil effects of this practice on the growth of population and replaced it by the present system of fines in pigs. This is also banned under Government orders. Two instances of so-called "devil murders" have, however, been recently reported from Chowra. Below is an extract from Tour Diary of Shri A. K. Ghosh, I.C.S., Chief Commissioner, Andaman and Nicobar Islands, regarding these incidents:—

> "Made enquiries about some so-called ritual murders reported to have taken place some months ago. The headman admitted that there had been two such cases—one man and one oldish woman. He stated that both were in the habit of stealing poultry, pigs, fruits, and coconuts from their neighbours, and were good for nothing. They were further suspected of practising witchcraft. They had therefore been done away with. I found no signs of any terror amongst the people: they certainly did not appear to be living in dread of being put to death any moment, as reported. No effort need be made to investigate these two murders, or to bring to justice the offenders, since such efforts are bound to lead to failure. And in any case elimination of parasites on society is quite understandable in a place like Chowra where the villagers have little chance of recourse to the law. From time immemorial they must have destroyed such parasites; and I fancy that they consider that they have done no wrong in killing these two people. The villagers and the headman were, however, warned not to take the law into their own hands in future. If ever they have cause to complain against their neighbour they must either send him to the Assistant Commissioner, Car Nicobar, or send information to this officer who will then visit Chowra and settle the matter on the spot. They appeared to understand what is required, and agreed to conform in future".

This simple system of fines in kind and use of the big stick has been given statutory recognition in the Andaman and Nicobar Regulation and unless the case is of a serious nature or the person concerned is a habitual offender, cases do not come to court. The Assistant Commissioner is, of course, informed of all offences committed and punishment inflicted by the community. This is going on very well. Crimes are few and far between and no change is indicated.

Civil disputes do not exist, thanks to the simple but effective land tenure system and the prevalence of barter system in trade which is directly controlled by Government. All tribal justice is in the hands of the village captains and some elders, recognised by Government and very helpful to the administration.

X. Land Tenure System

The system varies from a quasi-feudalism in Car Nicobar to communal ownership in Great Nicobar with private ownership in the Central group and Chowra.

In Car Nicobar, land is owned by a family of landlords but is never let out to others on rent. The owner allows the use of the land to the whole village for the benefit of the entire community. Each individual family will have its coconut plantation on the landlord's land, the plantation being held by the family as a unit and not by individual members. The only liability of the user is occasional contributions in kind to some feasts or other celebrations if required. No particular member of the family has a right to alienate any of the trees. It is only with the consent of the whole family and that of the landlord that trees can be sold to outsiders and that also not for cash but for pigs or other commodities for which the family may be in immediate need. Demarcation of plantations is made by a peculiar system of juxta-position of the trees or by girdling them. There has never been a dispute and the system is working very satisfactorily for all these years without State interference. Although the size of a plantation may vary from family to family, on account of lack of man power or laziness of a particular family, there is no stratification of society on an economic basis.

In Katchall and Nancowry and other islands of the central group land is held on an individual basis. Inheritance is in equal shares by all the surviving children of a deceased person, the widow living with the eldest issue. This has resulted in a good deal of fragmentation of holdings. On an average, each family now possesses about 2,000 coconut trees and that also in various areas away from the homestead. This has resulted in the reduction of assets and consequent poverty. The administration should now encourage the establishment of new plantations. There was a likelihood of some dispute about usufruct of the plantation in the uninhabited island of Telenchang. Enquiries revealed that these plantations were in the old days left in charge of the Captains of Kakana and Trinkat who allowed the use of fruits to other villages in turn. I have now ordered that this old practice should continue and only the inhabitants of Nancowry, Camorta and Trinkat should be allowed the use of the plantation in turns. This order was received very well by them.

In Great Nicobar and Kondul, all plantations are communally owned. There is considerable abandoned plantation on the slopes of this extensive island and the little community of 208 souls enjoy the usufruct on a communal basis.

The State makes no direct levy for the possession of lands in this group of islands, but the imposition of royalty on export trade acts as indirect taxation.

XI. Social Life

The pivot of social life is perhaps feasting. Apart from ossuary rites to be described later, feasts are held on various other occasions, the two most important of which are:

(1) KA-NA-HA-UN: This is done in rotation in each village of Car Nicobar where practically the whole population collect and give themselves away in a big feast on a contribution basis. This is purely a social affair and has no religious significance attached to it.

(2) CANOE FEAST: Canoes are all consecrated at Chowra and when brought to Car Nicobar offerings are given to the good spirit guiding them at regular intervals.

For some time prior to the feast, specially selected pigs are penned in a small enclosure in Dutch style, to put their mettle up, so that on the day of the feast they can put up a good fight before slaughter. After slaughter, the more important people smear their bodies with pigs' blood. Then takes place the communal dancing and singing which goes on till late hours to be followed by the actual feasts. At Little Nicobar we happened to be present on a feast day and noticed troops of people, coming in carrying their own rations in beautifully made cane baskets and other receptacles. The idea is not to burden one particular village or individual. They seem to have their tribal rationing laws. Their whole social life has a co-operative basis.

Canoe race—Very often when people have leisure in a village or something important has happened, they bring their canoes down from the beach and rig them out and have canoe races. I have often watched with great interest and pleasure their races in Car Nicobar. The two competing parties will strain their very best but as soon as they reach their destination the canoe ahead relaxes so that both arrive simultaneously. Their sport is also co-operative and not competitive. They take to it for enjoyment and not for winning. It should be mentioned in this connection that these people are excellent navigators, negotiating rough open seas without any aid and almost always with success. A Car Nicobarese youth is not considered mature till he has visited Chowra all by himself in his canoe. Their navigational ability and efficiency would make the Nicobars a good recruiting ground for our Navy.

Wrestling—The same is true of wrestling. Often one would notice pairs wrestling on the beach but never is an attempt made to lay one decisively low.

It is remarkable that their entire social life is guided by a spirit of genuine enjoyment, even the slaughter of the pig is in the nature of sport.

XII. Psychological Traits

(1) ***Non-violence***—Personal violence in revenge is almost unknown. Violence is resorted to only when the birch is used to delinquents for "putting in a little sense in him" (*thora akkal de deta*). Quite recently, a servant of a very respectable citizen committed a heinous offence against his master. Instead of chastising the servant, the master smashed up his own best canoes, killed his pigs and destroyed his other property to give vent to his feelings. It is almost like righting a wrong by self-mortification and non-attachment.

When the Japanese were in occupation, threats, coercings, severe corporal punishment, starvation and even shooting down of people could not obtain the co-operation of this little community of people. They had their bodies for forced labour but not their souls for voluntary assistance.

This amazing psychological trait must have a profound religious basis which it will be worthwhile to discover.

(2) ***Co-operation***—Co-operation and not competition informs their domestic, economic and social life. As already stated, even the land is held by the landlord for the welfare of his little rural community. The writer has seen a howling baby being fed by another wet woman, not its mother. The communal kitchen of Car Nicobar villages has already been described. No one may pass a plantation without partaking of a fruit from there and residents of an "Al Panam" are guests of the village. No wonder that the little co-operative sale societies are thriving so well.

> "All things in common nature should produce
> Without sweet or endeavour, treason, felony,
> Sword, pike, knife, gun, or need of any engine,
> Would I not have; but nature should bringforth
> Of its own kind, all foison, all abundance,
> To feed my innocent people." (*Tempest.*)

This is almost true of the Nicobars and the Nicobarese.

(3) ***Self-help***—In a bunch they do not want any free assistance from Government. If the village road is bad, they repair it on their own without waiting for the State to do it. When a suggestion was made to give Hindi Primers free to the School children, the headmen of Car Nicobar in a body refused the offer with thanks and wanted to pay for them.

(4) Although the people are not generally keen on storing material possessions they show a great passion for silver and gold—this is specially noticeable in Chowra and the southern and central group of islands. Gold and silver ornaments are worn with great pride by females. The Chowra Treasure House the writer saw must be holding within its dark interior accumulation of silver articles of ages. Silver forks, spoons, etc., are quite eagerly accepted as price of canoes the Great Nicobarese make.

(5) They are ostensibly mechanically minded. The number of trucks left by the Japanese in a state of disrepair was done up and used by the villagers. A little training makes a Nicobarese capable of running a machine.

XIII. Religion

Barring the 6,000 Christians and a few Muslims, the rest of the Nicobarese do not profess any recognised religion and in this census their religion has been recorded as "NIL"—They certainly are not "Animists" in the sense that they attribute life to inanimate things or worship stocks and stones. So far as I could gather, they believe in "MA-ALA-HA" (literally Lord of the flesh), a spirit that informs the human body. At the time of death this spirit leaves the body and goes to the Spirit World. Some spirits called "SIA" are bad and cause ills. The Nicobarese live in the way of nature and in perfect happiness and it is only when something unnatural like disease or accident takes place that they invoke the 'MA-ALA-HA' to drive away the 'SIA', the cause of all sufferings. At that time they shave their heads and attempt to drive away the 'SIA' by flares. It is thus clear that they are not 'Animists.' Although this faith of theirs cannot be called theistic, it is certainly transcendental and non-materialistic. It also reveals their conception of a life beyond though not in a very developed form.

The rapid and effective spread of Christianity is due to

(*a*) their normally Christian way of life,
(*b*) the absence of any attempt by the Mission to denationalise them; Bishop John Richardson is a Nicobarese first and a Christian afterwards.
(c) the extreme solicitude of this Nicobarese Padre (Richardson) for the welfare of the people.

But this conversion has hardly affected the normal social life of the community.

The little Muslim community lost its head a little, owing to the presence of a few half-breeds and considered themselves superior to the Nicobarese whom they called 'jungli'. But tactful handling by the Administration has effaced that complex and they are also integrated in the social structure of the people.

XIV. Taboos

In common with all societies, civilized or primitive, the Nicobarese do have some superstitions prohibiting eating of certain types of food on certain occasions, barring certain actions for certain purposes, enjoining observance of certain rites on certain occasions. But some symbols which have been described as 'taboos' are not really meant to be so. For example,

(a) placing a string of dried coconut shells on a sort of scaffold in a plantation indicates that the plantation is young and fruits should not be plucked,

(b) hanging pigs' skulls in front of a hut signifies the prosperity of the owner—the larger the number of such skulls the better is his economic condition,

(c) the large number of wooden statues found inside the dwelling house are in respectful memory of dead ancestors,

(d) the Henta Koi—often quite large wooden representations of men and animals are, as far as I could gather, only decorations. These are very common in the central and southern groups and give an idea of the excellent craftsmanship of the people. That these are not any scare-devils is apparent from the fact that in the little hamlet of Chinge in Great Nicobar was found an excellent model of an aeroplane with propellors complete made by a little boy who had seen only planes flying to Singapore. This was not certainly meant to be a scare-devil,

(e) the Hentas, also common in the central and southern islands, are artistic expression of the people's conception of the Universe, painted on areca spathe. The top third depicts the Sun, Moon and Stars, the middle third, a beehive hut, coconut palms and bananas, chicken, pigs and the lower third canoes and marine life, on and under rippling water, with a man and a woman in the centre. Almost in every house in Katchall, Nancowry and Kondul, these were in evidence. These are perhaps kept near sick-bed (although the writer has no personal experience of it). Works of art certainly do have a great psychological effect when the body is in pain.

(f) Automatic bull-roarers—Found in the central group. Dr. Hutton's description of these is very precise and is quoted below:—

"They are formed of a narrow plant to which a slight screw effect has been given by twisting and cutting so that they revolve in the wind about a central pin. At each end of the plank and facing in opposite directions is a node of bamboo the open end of which is partly blocked with rubber or wax. The result is that the revolving wood produces a very deep and loud booming noise identical with that produced by a bull-roarer".

But his impression about the significance of this is wrong. Both at Katchall and Nancowry it was reported that these are put up in the first week of November to indicate the change over from the South-west to the North-east monsoon and are a sort of warning for navigators. These, of course, are put up with certain ceremonial rites, the weather playing a most important part on the life of these maritime people. This is their greeting to the incoming monsoon and farewell to the outgoing.

Undoubtedly the Nicobarese do believe that anything that is against nature both internal and external, is evil and he makes many attempts in his simple and unsophisticated way to keep this evil off. But is not the highest moral and religious effort of the modern man inspired by the same objective? The way of life that can produce such healthy body, buoyant spirit, social fraternity, and keep away fraft and grab, falsehood and deceit, is certainly informed by something effectively spiritual. No undue criticism of the sign posts on that way is either necessary or called for. They have not certainly confused these sign posts with their destination.

XV. Witch Craft

The writer had personal contact with the head witch doctor of Chowra in March last year and below is an excerpt from his tour notes:—

"The Captain who is supposed to be the biggest wizard told me that he does not pretend to be a doctor or anything but knows certain herbs and oils which he has found useful in alleviation of human suffering. He would not certainly mind having a doctor in the island and would very much welcome the establishment of a school. This alone shows that he does not want to keep the place under the dark curtain of magic."

Again in November that year he met the lone wizard of Dring, living all by himself in a little hamlet near Expedition Harbour in Camorta Island. He said he is an ordinary man and obtained the knowledge of the curative effect of some herbs in a succession of trances he had. He practices his art out of his love for humanity and is always thinking of God. Bodily diseases are the creation of the Evil Spirit while 'MA-ALA-HA' (the soul) is God's direct concern. No cure can be effected unless Fate has decreed it. He has no illusion about the infallibility of his treatment. This almost sounds like religious experience and belief in the Karmic laws. He was a big hulk of a man, of a glowing yellow complexion, blind of one eye with a merry twinkle in the other, very proud of his red loin cloth with a big flying tail and seemed to be having the laugh over the writer and other officers of I.N.S. "AVENGER" who clicked their cameras at him.

Further enquiries revealed that a sick man is first treated with herbs and oils. If that fails he is initiated to wizardry. He is decorated with silver ornaments and people dance round him all through the night till he gets initiated. He is then taught the art of curing himself and others.

So far as I could see this is mostly a question of faith. I also had reports of how the witch doctors by sleight of their hands remove foreign matter like stones, etc., from the bodies of sick persons which, they say, cause illness. All this is done during dark nights and nobody is allowed to see. Sometimes even actual blood is drawn out but very few people have knowledge of the method adopted.

It is apparent that there is a strong element of faith involved in this but in the ultimate analysis all cures are faith cures. Patients would go on wearing garlands of banana and other leaves or certain corals and shells consecrated by the doctor and bear their suffering with good cheer and patience.

Whether spell or prayer, magic or religion, this has stood the test of centuries and the followers are none the worse for it. The writer's brief contact precludes the possibility of a precise opinion, but it seems that these 'wizards' are quite capable of psycho-analysis.

XVI. Death

This seems to be the most important event in the life of a Nicobarese. The funeral rites consist of strapping the corpse with several yards of cloth on a wooden bar to keep the body straight. A portion is kept open near the heart to allow the 'MA-ALA-HA' to go out of the body. The corpse is then put in a new coffin and buried with gifts. The size of the gift represents the degree of grief. In all other islands except Chowra, dead bodies are exhumed after 7 days while in Chowra, if the deceased is an ordinary person, after 3 days while in other cases after 7 days. It is then tied up to a bar and put on a scaffold about 4′ high near the beach to decompose. Children are not buried but taken to jungles and left on a scaffold in the same way. Very often the skulls are taken away and preserved for family worship. In one island I saw an effigy of a dead person with a skull, rigged out in trousers, a black coat and a top hat. This is always followed up by a feast. In some islands, the exhumation takes place only when the family is in a position to commemmorate the death by big feasts which may be between 2 or 3 years after the death. In Katchall, I found a recent grave most artistically decorated with an effigy fully dressed up and bunches of bananas, coconuts, etc. strung around with a decorative effect. In every house there are effigies of dead persons which are worshipped. It may safely be said that the Nicobarese are ancestor worshippers.

The idea underlying the placing of all the personal property of the deceased on the grave (a practice noticed even amongst Christians of Nancowry) is to obviate disputes amongst heirs, a very effective method of securing family tranquility indeed. This is reminiscent of the practice prevalent among the Ranas of Nepal. In Chowra, however, precious metals belonging to the deceased are kept in a treasure house, which has family collections of ages, perhaps, and which is very closely guarded.

The comparative permanence of human bones has perhaps been the occasional cause of the ossuary practices of all primitive people. Although death parts they perhaps get a psychological satisfaction by keeping a portion of the material body of the beloved deceased.

Inspite of impact of foreigners on various occasions, the main life current of this ancient little community has flowed on without any remarkable change for all these thousands of years. Here also time has had a stop. Deep down in this current must be some essential sustaining element which has kept it straight in its course, which modern mind perhaps fails to discover and brands the outer layer of their culture as ignorant superstition.

XVII. Past Relations and Present Tendencies

Indians, in the past, both in trade and Government employ, gave a very poor account of themselves exploiting these simple people under protection of the British bayonet taking unusual liberties with their womenfolk, and leaving half-breeds and deserted wives, as a burden to the native community and treating the Nicobarese with no consideration at all. To an essentially insular people with an instinctive aversion for foreigners, such conduct was loathsome and produced a strong suspicion of our bonafides.

The effort of the present administration is to show the best side of our culture and treat them as free citizens of the Republic.

The despatch of medical assistance by air when Car Nicobar was in the grip of poliomyelitis in 1947-48 by the Government has been very much appreciated by the Car Nicobarese. Although 225 lives have been lost, thanks to the prompt medical help 403 have been saved and the spread of the disease arrested.

A strict control of the export trade, periodical increase of the exchange rate of copra according to fluctuations of prices in the mainland, control of prices of consumer's goods and establishment of rural co-operative trading societies have also captured their imagination. It is refreshing to hear expressions of gratitude from these normally reticent people over this action of the State.

The efforts of the present Assistant Commissioner, Shri B. N. Sharma, in propagating Indian culture by staging stories of Indian epics by local talent, printing of Nicobarese primers in Hindi script and writing Hindi primers suited to local needs, coupled with his solicitude for their general welfare are gradually bringing them closer to us and greetings of 'Jai Hind' and singing of National Anthem in Schools have become quite common.

There is naturally a great keenness for advancement of education and medical facilities in all the islands. Even the Captain of Chowra asked for a school and dispensary in that island. The administration must arrange for this and thus forge the ties of friendship and unity.

S. K. GUPTA,

PORT BLAIR, *Superintendent of Census Operations,*
23rd March, 1951. Andaman & Nicobar Islands.

APPENDIX B

Programme

Date	Programme
12th April, 1948 .	Receipt of copy of letter No. Y/4-Census, dated the 22nd January, 1948 from M. W. W. M. Yeatts, Esquire, C.S.I., C.I.E., I.C.S., Census Commissioner for India.
From April, 1948 to December, 1948	House-numbering by revenue staff in revenue areas, by forest department officials in forests camps and by the Assistant Commissioner, Nicobars, in respect of Car Nicobar and Chowra.
July, 1949 to August, 1949 . . .	House-numbering in Teressa, West Katchall, East Katchall, Nancowry, Trinkat and Camorta by teachers of Car Nicobar Schools and Captains of Car Nicobar.
March, 1950 . .	House-numbering in Little Nicobar, Kondul and Great Nicobar by Captains of Car Nicobar. It was most refreshing to see that even a lonely hut in the farthest island of Great Nicobar was numbered.
March, 1950 to October, 1950	Receipt of certificates in respect of house-lists from the revenue staff, from forest department and the Assistant Commissioner, Nicobars.
June, 1950 . .	Compilation of instructions to the Census staff and printing cf booklet "Census, 1951—Andaman and Nicobar Islands."
July, 1950 to February, 1951	Appointment of Charge Officers, Supervisors and Enumerators for the 1951 Census Operations.
19th July, 1950 .	Personal instructions by the Superintendent of Census Operations to the Nicobar Census Staff.
10th October, 1950 .	Personal instructions by the Superintendent of Census Operations to the Charge Officers, Supervisors of the Andamans Group.
15th October, 1950 .	Personal instructions by the Superintendent of Census Operations to the Charge Officers, Supervisors and Enumerators of the Andamans Group.
31st October, 1950 .	Personal instructions by the Superintendent of Census Operations to the Car Nicobar Census Staff.
3rd November, 1950	Personal instructions by the Superintendent of Census Operations to the Enumerators of Nancowry, Camorta and Trinkat islands.
13th January, 1951 .	Personal instructions by the Superintendent of Census Operations to the Charge Officer and Enumerators of Middle Andamans group.
15th January, 1951	Distribution by Census Superintendent's Office of enumeration pads, forms for National Register of Citizens, forms for enumerator's abstracts and provisional population totals by house-lists to the Charge Officers. Proper receipts obtained. The location code in the pads should be completed up to the second element.
19th January, 1951 .	Personal instructions by the Superintendent of Census Operations to the census staff of the head-quarters area of the Andamans group.
20th January, 1951 .	Distribution by Charge Officers of enumeration pads, forms for National Register of Citizens, forms of enumerator's abstracts to the Supervisors. Proper receipts should be obtained. The location code in the pads should be completed up to the third element.
21st January, 1951 .	Personal instructions by the Superintendent of Census Operations to all the census staff of the Wimberleygunj Forest Division and some staff of the Aberdeen Tehsil.
23rd January, 1951 .	Personal instructions by the Superintendent of Census Operations to all the census staff of the Wimberleygunj Circle of the Wimberleygunj Tehsil.
25th January, 1951 .	Personal instructions by the Superintendent of Census Operations to some of the census staff of the Aberdeen Tehsil.
27th January, 1951 .	Personal instructions by the Superintendent of Census Operations to all the census staff of the Mithakhari Circle of the Wimberleygunj Tehsil.
4th February, 1951 .	Distribution by Supervisors of enumeration pads, forms for National Register of Citizens and forms for enumerator's abstracts to the enumerators. Proper receipts should be obtained.
9th February, 1951 to 28th February, 1951	Enumeration.
1st March, 1951 to 3rd March, 1951	Check by Government Officers, Supervisors, and Charge Officers.
4th March, 1951 .	Supervisors to meet the enumerators at a place and time to be fixed by them and collect the enumeration pads, National Register of Citizens and Enumerator's Abstracts. Supervisors should give proper receipts to the Enumerators and inform the circle totals to the Charge Officers concerned, collected from the enumerator's abstract.

APPENDIX B

5th March, 1951	.	Charge Officers to give their charge totals to the Superintendent. In outlying areas, the information should be sent by wireless.
6th March, 1951	.	Census Superintendent sends telegram to Delhi about the provisional totals.
8th March, 1951	.	Supervisors should arrange the enumeration pads with abstracts and National Register of Citizens village-wise, and then submit to the Charge Officer concerned. Proper receipts should be obtained from the Charge Officers.
15th March, 1951	.	Charge Officers should submit all their papers to the Deputy Superintendent—proper receipts should be obtained from the Deputy Superintendent.

APPENDIX C

The Andaman Forests and their Development

By Shri B. S. Chengapa, *Conservator, Working Plans, Port Blair, Andaman*

The Forests

Except for 50 or 60 square miles cleared for the settlement in the vicinity of Port Blair, parts of Cinque Islands, and a few hill tops, the whole area is covered with a luxuriant growth of tropical jungle rarely found elsewhere.

The main types of forests are:—

1. Mangrove forests,
2. Beach forests,
3. Low level evergreen forests,
4. Deciduous and Semi-deciduous forests.

The forest types in these Islands depend almost entirely on the underlying soil and rock formation for their distribution.

The mangrove forest type is a class distinct by itself and can be easily separated from other types.

These forests are found in nearly all areas inundated by high tide but sheltered from the force of monsoon winds and waves. They occupy usually both sides of creeks and estuaries, in belts, varying from a few yards to over a mile in width.

The species of importance in this type are *Bruguiera gymnorhiza* and *Rhizophers conjugata* and *mucronata*. The *Bruguiera* grows more or less pure and attains a height of 70 to 80 ft. and a girth of 5 ft. It is estimated that these mangrove forests can produce at least 30 to 40,000 poles per year. These are now greatly in demand as transmission poles. A few were sold recently at Re. 1 per rft. for poles 25 ft. or more in length C.I.F. Madras.

However for want of extraction equipments, even an order for 1,000 poles from Mysore Government could not be accepted.

The other two species of *Rhizophoras* do not produce poles but are excellent as firewood and is considered next best to coal by the crew of Steam launches. As firewood, it is estimated that about 160 tons of this species is available per acre.

About 200 square miles are occupied by mangrove forests.

The other three types, *viz.* (1) Beach forests, (2) Low level evergreen forests, (3) Deciduous and Semi-deciduous forests, merge into one another imperceptibly and cannot be separated easily. Some species are common to all the three types. They are, therefore, considered as one type for purposes of this note.

The most important species in this group are:—

1. Padauk . . (*Pterocarpus dalbergioides*).
2. Gurjan . . (*Dipterocarpus spp.*).
3. White Dhup . (*Canarium euphyllum*).
4. Papita . (*Sterculia campanulata*).

Others of importance and now classed as miscellaneous species are:—

1. Koko . . (*Albizzia lebbok*).
2. White Chuglam . (*Terminalia bialata*).
3. Black Chuglam . (*Terminalia manii*).
4. Pyinma . . (*Lagerstroemia hypoleuce*).
5. Badam . . (*Terminalia procera*).
6. Didu . . (*Bombax insigne*).
7. Toungpsing . (*Artocarpus chaplasha*).
8. Lakuch . . (*Arteearpus gomeziana*).
9. Thingan . . (*Hopea oderate*).
10. Ywegi . . (*Adenanthera pavonina*).
11. Lal Bombwn . (*Planchonia andmanica*).
12. Lal Dhup . . (*Parishia insignis*).
13. Marblewood . (*Diospyros marmorata*).
14. Sea Mohwa . (*Mimusops litteralis*).
15. Hill Mohwa . (*Bassia butyracea*).
16. Lambapathi . (*Sideroxylon longipetiolatum*).
17. Lalchini . . (*Amoora wallichii*).
18. Lalchini . . (*Calophyllum sectabile*).
19. Gangaw . . (*Mesua ferrea*).
20. Yenma-bin . (*Chukrasia tabularis*).

All these timber species are now greatly in demand for various purposes, *viz.*, as construction wood, Matchwood, plywood and as packing case wood. Padauk is, in fact, the only Indian wood that equals the standard timber, teak, in every respect and beats it in some respects. It is, however, slightly heavier than teak. Like teak, Padauk is one of the best general utility timbers.

These islands have some of the world's best decorative timbers in Padauk (*Pterocarpus dalbergioides*), White Chuglam—Silvergrey (*Terminalia bialata*), Yenmabin—Chickrassy (*Chukrasia tabularis*), Koko (*Albizzia lebbek*) and Marblewood (*Diospyros mermorata*).

Resources of Timber

Though these forests are very dense, the proportion of really valuable species is very small and they are found scattered as a useless crop all over the area. Recent clear fellings have shown that very rarely is the yield of merchantable timber more than 15 tons per acre.

Inspite of the poorly stocked forests, it is estimated that the sustained or perpetual yield for these forests is about 1,35,000 tons per year. But with the present method of regeneration, actually 'One of the greatest achievements in Indian Forestry,' the yield per acre in the future crop will be about 75 tons, *i.e.*, 5 times. The future yield, if the forests are wisely worked, will be 6,75,000 tons per year and with the present method of timber extraction by short elephant operated tramlines also are the greatest achievements in Indian Forestry, everything can be extracted on a profitable basis.

Roughly, the quantity of timber that will become available per year (they will vary from year to year) will be as shown below:—

	Tons
1. Padauk	7,000
2. Gurjan	28,000
3. White Dhup	21,000
4. Papita	28,000
5. Koko	500
6. White Chuglam	7,000
7. Black Chuglam	2,500
8. Pyinma	1,500
9. Badam	11,000
10. Didu	7,000
11. Others	14,000

In addition to this, there are at least 30,000 mangrove poles per year suitable for use as transmission poles.

Timber Exploitation

(i) General—These islands have a number of well sheltered harbours and numerous tidal creeks, running many miles inland, cutting up the islands into small area. These creeks serve as very useful and cheap waterways for inspections and for exploitation of timber. It is also, perhaps, one of the easiest places for timber extraction in the world. It is however important that an intimate knowledge of local conditions is absolutely essential to make timber exploitation a success.

Forest exploitation may be said to have begun by Government agency from 1858, with the establishment of the Penal settlement. Until 1870 however, Burma teak was imported for all substantial buildings, and the local timber was considered useless. In fact, until 1929 Dhup and Papita, now most valuable as Matchwood, were being thrown away after making use of them as floats to raft sinker logs. In 1883, a Forest Officer was deputed from India and a Forest Division was formed.

From the very beginning, these forests have been worked by departmental agency. A small saw-mill erected by the Public Works Department was in operation but was cutting timber mostly for their own use. Hand sawing in the forest was also done for cutting sleepers and Padauk poles for the Indian Telegraph Department. Export was about 400 to 500 tons of timber per year. Elephants and also buffaloes were dragging timber from stump site. But buffaloes were soon found unsuitable except for small timber and these are few. Therefore, elephants became the main-stay.

In 1915, this mill was closed and a new mill capable of a monthly output of 750 tons in squares and scantlings was erected by the Forest Department. A second mill, an American circular mill, was erected in Chatham in 1927.

In 1915, a new division was formed with headquarters at Mayabandar, Stewart Sound, called North Andaman Division. An American handmill was erected at this place in 1925. The mill gave endless troubles for want of expert supervision which was difficult to secure. The division itself was not a financial success for want of better sales organization which was difficult to obtain under Government Agency, greatly hampered by rules and regulations. The mill and the new division were closed down in 1931. The mill was later sold in 1941 to a timber firm in Burma (Messrs. Steel Brothers).

(ii) Past Limitations

Up to 1934 or 1935, there were two great limiting factors in the development of the Andaman Forest Department. They are:—

(1) Extraction of timber. (2) Regeneration of forests.

(*a*) Extraction of timber was by means of elephants except in the case of Padauk; it did not pay to extract timber from more than half a mile from any rafting point. Therefore, not more than 500 square miles of forests out of a total area of 2408 square miles (area of Andaman Islands) were considered accessible for economic exploitation. Costly tramlines were built, skidders and tramlines under American experts were tried and several lakhs of rupees were spent trying to solve timber extraction problems. All these proved costly failures and were abandoned. Interior area, therefore, remained inaccessible and the Working Plan prepared in 1936 prescribed an annual yield of only 57,000 tons of timber for the whole of the Andaman forests. The coastal areas were getting exhausted, and therefore, the maximum quantity of timber ever extracted rarely exceeded 35,000 tons per year though there were more than 100 elephants on the roll.

(b) Regeneration in forests until 1934-35 was mainly artificial and was costly and not always successful and the area planted was rarely more than 100 acres per year. Exploitation fellings traversed over many square miles a year. This was thus pure and simple lumbering and not scientific forestry. There was, therefore, no progress at all and the forests were fast being replaced with worthless species.

(iii) Removal of the Limiting Factors

(a) Timber extraction methods—In 1932, an experimental tramline was built in Rangat. The novel feature introduced in the construction of this line was that it was confined to a valley, avoided all big cuttings and fillings and was graded downhill. Elephants were trained to load, transport and unload a log train. As some officers called it, it proved a 'Columbus egg' and rendered all the former inaccessible areas accessible for economic exploitation. After a further careful examination it was found that these forests could yield 1,35,000 tons of timber per year against a bare 57,000 tons prescribed in the Working Plan in 1936 (the Working Plan was prepared before this tramway system was developed).

(b) Regeneration methods—The regeneration problem was also solved in 1932 though it was perfected in 1936-37. According to this method, the old crop is removed in two or more successive fellings, allowing nature to do the sowing. The resulting crop is tended for two or three years. The results are amazingly good everywhere and the cost of such operation was about Rs. 20 to Rs. 25 (prewar) against Rs. 150 to Rs. 200 (prewar) per acre for plantations of indifferent success. The areas dealt with rose to 1,500 to 2,000 acres per year against 100 acres of plantations per year and about 3,000 acres of plantations in all in 60 years.

(iv) Results of the Removal of these Limitations

Because of these limitations, the Department had many ups and downs and the financial position caused great anxiety. For 10 years, from 1919 to 1929 the period of an attempt at expansion and development, it showed continuous loss. From 1869 to 1933, *i.e.*, in 66 years, the net surplus amounted to only Rs. 36,00,000.

The results of these two innovations have revolutionized the outlook and the management of these forests. The annual yield is now 1,35,000 tons and this quantity can be taken without any fear, because the problem of regeneration is also solved. These forests can, therefore, be safely worked up to their maximum capacity, maintaining at the same time their maximum productive capacity. The productive capacity of these forests based on the results of regeneration so far obtained is about 6,75,000 tons of timber per year on a modest estimate. The area needed to maintain a perpetual yield of 1,35,000 tons per year, is only about 750 sq. miles in all. Forestry, as developed at present, will therefore make the balance of about 1,700 sq. miles of these islands available for cultivation and other purposes. However, in view of the enormous shortage of timber in India and elsewhere, and as these islands are an important reservoir of timber wealth, it has been decided to set apart 300 sq. miles only, mostly level and undulating land, for immediate cultivation.

It is gratifying to note that the Japanese did not do any damage to these forests during their occupation from 1942-45 though they did work these forests on a small scale taking out mostly softwoods. Their favourite wood was Bakota (*Endospermum malaccense*). After re-occupation, though the Department had to be built up again, because the sawmill had been completely annihilated by allied bombing, the export of timber has risen up to about 55,000 tons mostly in round logs and the surplus revenue in 6 years from 1945 to 1951 is about Rs. 25,00,000. The estimated surplus revenue for 1951-52 is about Rs. 25,000. This is for South Andaman alone.

There is one small sawmill capable of handling about 2,000 tons of timber per year. This was built of what remained of two prewar mills that were blasted by allied bombing. A new American handmill, capable of handling about 30,000 tons per year is, in the process of erection at Chatham, Port Blair.

Attempts were made in 1906, in 1914 and again in 1929, to lease these forests to private enterprise for commercial exploitation. These attempts failed mostly because of these limitations. Departmental operations have, therefore, continued up to date. Recent attempts have met with success and the North Andamans group is now under lease to Mr. Ray of Bengal for a minimum royalty of Rs. 50,00,000. This firm is expected to extract 75,00,000 tons of timber per year.

Failure to work the forests fully and its results—It is the law of nature, that increment put on in a forest crop is balanced by decrement that goes in the shape of deterioration, death and decay. In scientific forestry, it is this equivalent of such increment, that is utilized, by removing mature and overmature trees before they die and decay, paying due attention to the raising and tending of young plants of desired species. The annual increment in these forests is about 1,35,000 tons and our maximum extraction is now about 50,000 tons. Therefore, the annual waste or loss is at least 85,000 tons, because of our failure to work these forests to their full capacity. At only Rs. 50 per ton net profit, the State is losing about Rs. 30,00,000 per year. This is apart from the loss of 85,000 tons of timber that die and decay, which, otherwise, would have gone to build houses in India, and to earn dollars and sterlings from abroad. An additional loss is that there are unmistakable signs in these forests that the young crop that is replacing the dead and decaying trees is mostly useless species, very often a tangled mass of brushwood or evergreen undergrowth. Many valuable trees, especially Dhup and Papita measured and counted in 1924-34, have now disappeared, died and decayed. It is, therefore, imperative and urgent that these forests should be worked to their full capacity as early as possible if this colossal waste of national wealth should be stopped.

(v) Further Limitations

The Forest Department has now all the experience needed to tackle timber exploitation and to build up these forests. It can realise and solve all problems that may arise in the course of timber exploitation quicker and easier than any timber firm can dream of. A Working Plan aiming at an exploitation of 1,35,000 tons of timber and regeneration of 6,000 acres per year is under preparation. Three Divisions will soon be formed with Headquarters at Mayabandar, Stewart Sound, Long or Passage island, Middle Andaman and Wimberleygunj or Port Blair, South Andaman. Sales agency has also been organized on right lines by opening departmental sales Depots in Calcutta and Madras. There is, however, one problem still to be tackled, and that is, the system of control. Unless the local officers, *viz.*, the Chief Commissioner and the Chief Conservator of Forests are given more powers as regards purchase of equipment and stores and in every other way, rapid progress can never be achieved. If this is not possible, the only alternative for rapid progress is to lease the forests to private enterprise for timber exploitation, the Forest Department exercising only a control over this exploitation and attending to the proper maintenance of these forests.

The market rates for timber are now very high. If it is assumed that an average net profit of only Rs. 50 per ton can be made, these forests should give an annual net surplus of at least Rs. 65,00,000 per year, if they are worked properly and to their full capacity. It will also then become a very valuable growing asset of the Andaman Islands with the annual yield gradually rising from 1,35,000 tons to 6,75,000 tons, yielding under the present market rates, a net surplus of more than Rs. 3,37,00,000. It is today a wasting or diminishing asset.

APPENDIX D

Marine Fisheries in Andamans

By Shri V. Sadasivan, M.A., M.Sc., *Assistant Fisheries Research Officer, Port Blair*

The importance of the fishing industry in the economic development of these islands cannot be overemphasised. The rich and varied fish fauna of the Andaman seas offers great possibilities for commercial exploitation. The inexhaustible fishery resources cover a wide range of smaller and bigger forms of fish and also include such less important types as squids, octopus, trepang, turtles and sea-weeds.

The two hundred and odd islands which form the Andaman and Nicobar group present a coast line of roughly 1,200 miles with a fishable extent of nearly 18,000 square miles capable of considerable yield of fishery wealth if properly and judiciously exploited. The numerous bays and creeks afford ample protection for the fishing boats from bad weather. The shallow regions and inlets are admirably suited for fish-farming and pisciculture operations. The heavy annual rainfall of 130" is mostly derived from the South-west monsoons which usually set in by the middle of May and last till end of August. During these months, fishing operations are carried out on the east coast. Fishing on the west coast is possible during the North-east monsoon months of November and December.

Fishing industry in Andamans has not reached to any great commercial proportions. The Fisheries of *Trochus* and *Turbo* shells by the Japanese during 1930-36 and the endeavour to exploit the resources by a business concern in 1947 were the only two commercial attempts so far made. The reasons for this undeveloped state of affairs are lack of experienced fishermen and proper methods and inadequate knowledge of the local conditions. The number of men engaged in fishing, according to the licence register for 1949, is 82. The main form of fishing is by hooks and lines; cast net is extensively used in the shallow regions. Fishing by means of bamboo tatties is practiced by the Burmans. Apart from these methods no other form of net-fishing is known. Regarding the fishing methods of the aborigines Lt. Colebrook (1789-90) remarked that " men hunt fish wading in the water to shoot with their bows and arrows. They are very dextrous at this extraordinary mode of fishing which they practice also at night by the light of torch. Of their implements for fishing and other purposes, little can be said. Hand nets of different sizes are used in catching the small fry." These primitive conditions still prevail, but the more friendly tribes who receive, in addition to the various presents, fishing hooks and lines from the Chief Commissioner on his annual cruise are learning and adopting this form of fishing. The fishing crafts are primitive, inefficient and not capable of staying for longer periods on the fishing grounds. The rocky coast line descends steeply down and the sea bottom is more or less patchy with coral rocks and sand stones making net fishing risky. To make net fishing a success it is essential to have a complete knowledge of the conditions of the fishing ground—the nature of sea bottom, currents, etc.

The main fishing region is located round about Port Blair, the Headquarter area, where the fishermen find a ready market for their catch. The line fishermen, by patient trials, have located certain spots where fish are available in greater numbers. These more favourable fishing grounds are characterised by their great depths, ranging from 40 to 60 fathoms, and rocky nature of the sea bottom. The catch at these places usually consists of bottom feeding perches of *Serranus*, *Lutianus* and *Lethrinus* species. Whiffing and trolling are practiced to catch fish like seer, bonite, tuna and berracuda. The shallow and sheltered bays are productive of smaller types of fish such as Sardines, Mullets, Silver bellies, Cock up, beaked fish, etc., which are readily captured by stake nets, bamboo tatties and cast nets.

In order to assess the value of the fisheries, accurate statistics must be available and as there are no records of catches the work of collecting data of daily fish landings was taken up in January, 1950. According to this available statistics the average daily catch is about 300 lbs. which is hardly sufficient for the local needs. For an increased production, a variety of fishing gear, improved craft and more fishermen are needed. The first experimental attempt to introduce a shore-seine net satisfying the local conditions was a success and others have adopted this method resulting in increased catch. It is hoped, in the course of this year, to popularise the gill nets of set and drift varieties and to find out, by trial and error method, the suitability of different kinds of nets. The fishing curing yard, which is to be established shortly, will serve as a demonstration centre for the correct and hygenic methods of curing and preserving of fish, preparation of shark liver oil, fish manure and other by-products. Sufficient inducement are being offered to attract fishermen from the mainland for settling down here.

It is of greatest importance to gain an accurate knowledge of the habits of the commercially important fish, their movements, etc., and these biological data are of value to the fisheries. The fisheries research unit has taken up this study and work is already in progress on the life histories of Sardines, perches and mackerals and on the study of plankton in relation to fisheries.

Thus, by introducing reforms and improvements by slow degrees, encouraging large scale enterprises, establishing the by-industries of fishery products and applying scientific and modern methods, it is hoped to remedy the situation and help the industry to attain greater developments.

APPENDIX E

On the Origin of the Andamanese

By Dr. Lidio Cipriani, *formerly Professor of Anthropology at the University of Florence*

The origin of the ancient inhabitants of the Andaman Islands, so called Negritos, is still an open question in anthropology; but although nothing certain can yet be said about it, a number of facts point clearly to several conclusions, and to the rejection of several ideas put forward by some on this subject. One such idea, old and frequently repeated, is that the Andamanese are the descendants of Portuguese Negro slaves shipwrecked on these Islands. As the Portuguese first arrived into the Indian Ocean only after the circumnavigation of the Cape of Good Hope, this would mean their coming sometime after the fifteenth century, allowing not more than five hundred years for the existence of the supposed shipwrecked in the Andaman Islands.

2. The comparison of the physical characteristics of the Andaman Negritos with those of African Negroes is sufficient to reject such theory about their origin. The true Negro characteristics (thick lips, broad nose, frequent dolichocephaly, proportions of the body peculiar to them, especially the development of thorax, shoulders, arms, legs, etc.) are not to be found in the Andamanese, nor can the comparatively short period of life in the Andamanese conditions account for the fundamental differences found. Merely to have a dark skin (and the Andamanese reach the maximum blackness known for the human races) and woolly hair is not enough to classify a man as Negro. Moreover, the ebony black with a bluish tinge to be seen in many Andamanese when the sun's rays strike in a favourable direction, cannot be found in any part of Africa. In all probability these characteristics of the Andamanese are those of an extremely ancient race apart, present in Asiatic human beings that the Portuguese travellers called Negritos— a name scientifically inappropriate. Beyond their dark skin, the Andamanese have short stature, mesati—or brachycephaly, woolly hair of the peppercorn type, thin noses and lips, not very dissimilar to those of Europeans, chestnut black eyes without the light circle round its iris frequent in the black eyes of Negroes, neither mustache nor beard, pubic and armpit hair scanty in men absent in women. Their body is robust, with muscular masses well developed, especially in the thigh. Steatopygea is marked in the Andamanese women; but it is not peculiar only to them. It produces extraordinary development of the buttocks and the attached part of the thighs, together with a strong lombosacralis curvature. The buttocks project so much that a child can easily stand upright on them, keeping only his hands on the shoulders of the mother. Steatopygea is common in Africa amongst Bushmen and Hottentots, but with a different appearance and structure —mostly fat and more developed in the Africans; chiefly muscular masses and less developed in the Andamanese—in a body of different proportions and of different general appearance. Not to be forgotton is the yellowish rough folded skin of the Bushmen and Hottentots, very different from the extremely soft, smooth ebony, black skin of the Andamanese. Still considering physical characteristics, but of different physiological and anatomical explanation, is another fact. Everybody acquainted with Africans knows of the disagreeable smell of their body. Nothing of this nature is to be found in the Andamanese, even though they are in the habit of never taking a real wash. No less important are the differences on the cultural and linguistic sides. The Andamanese differ fundamentally, spiritually as well as materially, from every people to be found in Africa.

3. The theory of origin from shipwrecked Negro slaves, which means a relatively recent arrival in the Andamans, can also be rejected after a glance at the Andamanese kitchen middens, of which there are plenty in the Islands. Many of these kitchen middens are of such dimensions and stratifications as to show that they date back millenniums, that is to say long long before the arrival of the Portuguese anywhere in Asia. But more will be said on this subject of Andamanese kitchen middens later on.

4. Because of their short stature, the Andamanese have been compared with African Pigmies. But they differ very much from these also, both physically and culturally. African Pigmies are shorter, not so dark, often very hairy all over the body; and they differ much from the Andamanese in general culture, language and primitiveness. There is so little similarity that it will be a waste of time to refute a comparison supported only by suppositions, and not even by superficial resemblances.

5. Human groups physically and culturally comparable to the Andamanese exist only in Asia. They are the Semang of the Malaya Peninsula, and the Aeta of the Philippines. Important is this finding of resemblances between people so widely separated to-day, and without any contact between them now. This similarity is not a chance similarity; it arose certainly because there was contact between these peoples in ages long ago, a contact now destroyed. This similarity is the first serious indication we have for understanding the present Andamanese anthropological position. We must consider a pre-historic, I would even say a pre-lithic human stratification, formerly diffused over Asia, and perhaps also far beyond, to the East, deep into Oceania. Of this wide and probably once continuous stratification we have at present only small fragments and a few hybrid remnants—remnants of great importance for anthropological purposes. The Semangs and the Aetas resemble, as already pointed out the Andamanese in physical and cultural characteristics. Amongst cultural similarities are the hunting weapons. One of the weapons still in use by the three groups is the bow. In the Andamans the bow underwent a considerable evolution; but what was presumably its fundamental shape is still obtainable in Little as well as in Great Andamans. This shape is common to all the bows of the three widely separated human groups; and also this similarity cannot be by chance. In the Andamans it is in possession of the Onges and the Jarawas; and it seems to represent the starting shape of the Andaman bow. Such a shape has a simple curvature; shoulders at both ends on a plano-convex blade of wood; string of twisted fibre with two different terminal loops applied at the ends of the plano-convex wooden blade. There

are local indications that this shape is the ancestor of the *S* shape bow, formerly distributed amongst several tribes that used to roam along the coasts of the South, Middle and North Andamans—tribes now all extinct. Some comparisons are instructive in different ways, and especially because they show how, from what we must admit to have been the primitive Negrito bow still with the Semang and the Aeta was developed the Little Andaman bow, the very similar Jarawa bow in the South Andaman, and finally the North Andaman bow. They show differences that can be put on a continuous evolutionary series. Following this we see how from the simple Negrito bow of Little Andaman, with one curvature, has developed the *S* shaped bow of Great Andamans as a result of small but substantial modifications. These, we must suppose, took place after the separation of the Andamanese from the other Negritos. The mechanical principle remains fundamentally that of the Negrito bow; the only changes are devices to obtain the best and most complete utilisation of the elasticity of the wood forming the weapon. The peculiarity of the simplest Andamanese bow, of having two different uses for the two ends of the blade, gradually developed the changes mentioned. The Andamanese keep their bows unstrung, stringing them only when about to use the weapon. At one end the string is always near the shoulder if not completely fixed to it; the other end is free and can receive the string when the bow is properly bent, putting it vertically on the ground and then pressing it in the middle by the application of a foot. We must, therefore, distinguish the upper end from the lower end. In the Onge and Jarawa bow both ends have a shoulder of 10-13 mm. Sometimes the upper end, although not always, is decorated with fibre and ornamented with the yellow skin of the *Dendrobium*. The loops of the string are also different, the upper loop being much wider than the lower. These distinctions developed the idea of giving two curvatures instead of the original single one in the bow, at the same time enlarging it from the middle end, then tapering to a point each end, so getting the appearance of two narrow long opposite blades. A first evolution in this sense happened in the South Andaman and was subsequently improved in the North Andaman. Consequently, we had in the Andamans three types of bow: one was that of the Onges, little changed in the hands of the Jarawas; another was with the coastal tribes of the South Andaman, and a third with the people of the North Andaman. These last two kinds are no more to be found. The differences, or improvements, were aimed at producing the strongest propulsion for the arrow with the least exertion for the man. In the North Andaman bow the results obtained were the highest in comparison with the other two types. This sequence of arguments leads to the conclusion that in the Andamans the Onge type of bow is the progenitor of all the others. As we shall see later on, this supports the idea that a migratory movement took place in these Islands, and until recent times, from the South to the North, an idea that will help to explain several Andamanese phenomena.

6. Not only bows but also arrows show corresponding affinities in the Andamanese, especially the so called harpoon arrow. This consists of a barbed detachable head connected to the shaft by a string. The harpoon arrow, like its near relative and probable forefather, the harpoon spears, offers an interesting question in ethnography. Although the Andnamans are so widely separated from Malaya, and Malaya from the Philippines, the three groups of Negritos has harpoon arrows, while such weapons do not seem to be present in other regions of Asia. The nearest harpoon arrows outside Asia are in Africa, and are probably derived from an original pigmy invention, though no more to be found to-day with the Pigmies. They are now used by several Negro groups, mostly in the Congo basin. It is certain that both the harpoon arrow and the harpoon spear known to the Andamans could have been invented before the knowledge of iron. In Africa harpoon spears and harpoon arrows have detachable heads still made from hard wood. They are used to catch wild boars, antelopes, gazelles, rock rabbits and monkeys; and also buffaloes and elephants by some tribes. The harpooned animal is halted in its flight by the shaft of the arrow or the spear getting entangled in a bush; or the wound is enlarged and made deadly by a sudden and rough extraction of the harpoon through hard pulling against the shaft caught in the bushes. Buffaloes and elephants, always attacked in the abdomen from a short distance, can be disembowelled by this terribly intelligent device. Harpoon spears and arrows are also used against fish, as we see even to-day in Africa. In the Andamans, the harpoon arrow is now used only against *Sus Andamanesis*; the harpoon spear against turtle, dugong and very large fish. The invention is certainly of immense antiquity. As for the harpoon spear, it can go back to the Paleolithic age, so explaining its diffusion through the continents, and its presence to-day in widely separated areas with primitive people as the Andamanese who have remained cut off from the rest of humanity since prehistoric times. The segregation of the Andamanese from the outside world must go back to a period when the harpoon spear and the harpoon arrow were uniformally diffused at least in continental and insular South-East Asia and East Africa including Negrito areas—that is to say, a segregation to be calculated by millenniums.

7. Besides their bodily appearance and their weapons, the Andamanese show great similarity with Malaya and Philippine Negritos in the way in which they erect their shelters, temporary simple shelters, and the big communal huts to be found in the Andamans from the South to the North. The construction of the communal hut is clearly evolved from the technique of building temporary camps; and in reality the Andamanese communal huts are nothing more than temporary camps transformed into something more complete, durable and protective. In all other details they repeat the structure and respond better to the exigencies of temporary camps. For this reason we can affirm that as the apparently complicated *S* shaped bow is an Andamanese creation evolved from the original, simpler Negrito bow, so the apparently complicated Andamanese communal hut had its starting point in the simpler Negrito temporary shelter. In every Negrito area this shelter is so rudimentary that it does not deserve the name of hut. It has no walls, only a small sloping roof with an inclination of about 45 degrees, high in front and very low at the back, so low as nearly to reach the ground. This roof covers a narrow, short bed of sticks slightly raised on four strong but short poles, a bed that shelters the whole family. The Andamanese communal hut also is marked by the absence of walls, and so affords no privacy at all to the several families sheltering in it. It consists of a single circular roof of the shape and serving the functions of an umbrella for the beds under it, and distributed along its border. Like an umbrella, the roof has an inclination of about 45 degrees; and it is impossible to stand upright near the perimeter of the hut. In the middle, and in accordance with its

dimensions (which means the number of beds in it) the hut can reach a considerable height. Inside the communal hut each family follows the same practices as in the temporary shelter, having its own fire and cooking place in addition to the communal fire and cooking place at a selected spot of the ground. Under the umbrella the construction of the bed is the same as under the temporary shelter; only the roof is stronger, more accurately built, and more watertight. In all its details the Andamanese communal hut, which may reasonably be called an umbrella hut because of its structure and appearance, shows only extensions and improvements on the original Negrito shelter.

8. As regards their general habits and methods of life, the Andamanese still preserve similarity, if not identity, with other far away Negritos—or at least the habits that were their's before they fell under alien influence. No tattooing or scarification of the body is practiced by the Andamanese, but only painting. Hunting animals, catching fish, collecting roots, fruits and honey in the forests are for the Semang and the Aeta, as well as for the Andamanese, the only ways of getting food. And they follow the same methods and use the same weapons. They have no shields for defence purposes; no traps for animals or birds or fish; no poison for their arrows, or for any other purpose; no fishing hooks; no stone implements. No less significant, pottery was unknown to the original Negrito, who had only wooden pots and basketry. Iron is a recent acquisition for all Negritos; but they are unable to work it. The Andamanese simply rub it, cold, against stones, to obtain the shape they wish. And, as can be imagined, it is a very long and painful process. Another cultural superposition appears to be the use of nets, made with the so called fisherman's knot, and spread all over the continents. It is also not clear how the Andamanese learned to use canoes. We do not know about the Aeta; but certainly the Semang have no canoes, now being an inland people. They make only bamboo rafts for use on rivers, having, it seems, forgotten how to hollow trees. There is, however, little doubt that the Negritos reached the Philippines and the Andamans by sea. In the Andamans we have more than one instance of people having forgotten how to make and use canoes. The Jarawas, now jungle dwellers, are said (not without reason) to have reached Great Andaman from the South, through Little Andaman, by the sea. A line of camps, quite obviously not of recent origin and with a good supply of drinking water and of food, is spread in a chain along the islands between Little and Great Andaman, with evidence that they have been used for ages by people migrating from the South to the North. These camps, still kept in a state of use, are situated in:—

(1) South Brother, called by the Onges, Geachenaque,
(2) North Brother, to Onges, Tetale,
(3) Small Sister, to Onges, Tagiomada,
(4) Big Sister, to Onges, Taquate,
(5) Passage Island, to Onges, Chogedda,
(6) South Cinque Island, to Onges, Geataque,
(7) North Cinque Island, to Onges, Gaalu,
(8) Rutland Island, to Onges, Gaatinnenque,

and here are two camps:—

(*a*) Tequara, and
(*b*) Lambaba.

All these organizations, with geographical names, camps, places for water and food, indicate an ancient navigating experience moving from the South to the North. About a century and a half ago the Jarawas are said to have still been in possession of canoes; and the same is said of the savage inhabitants of the North Sentinel Island less than 50 years ago. In a surprisingly short period the technique of making canoes seems to have been completely forgotten as a result of the difficulties of using them. If this be so, we can understand how the Semang and the Aeta could forget the art of hollowing canoes known to their forefathers, an art that enabled the diffusion of Negritos to far away islands. In the Andamans, the more primitive type of canoe is that of the Onges; and this together with other cultural characteristics puts Little Andaman prominent in our effort to reconstruct the original Negrito ways of life.

9. To do this we need to investigate those ancient documents, the kitchen middens, that the Negritos have fortunately left in numbers all over the Andamans. As the word denotes, kitchen middens are accumulations of refuse, mostly from kitchens. Unfortunately, systematic research on the Andamanese kitchen middens has only recently begun. But because of the importance of the results in relation to the arguments here discussed, and because these results are new, they deserve ample quotation. The remarks already made about the culture and physical characteristics of the Andaman Negritos are not so important nor so conclusive as are these results of excavations of kitchen middens. In the Andamans these accumulations show much the same appearance as do those formed by primitive populations in other continents, including Europe and Africa. The results of the excavations carried out so far in the Andamans, although as yet incomplete and not solving finally the problem of the origin of the Andamanese, bring to our knowledge several facts that need to be considered with attention. Like the kitchen middens found outside Asia, those in the Andamans generally consist of empty shells, nearly all bivalve, thrown away after the contents have been eaten. These shells constitute nearly ninety per cent. of the materials of the kitchen middens, and are uniformally distributed through them. These kitchen middens are of fairly regular geometrical shape; moreover, in every cubic foot they have nearly constant average number of shells. It is, therefore, not difficult to calculate the approximate total number of shells present in one kitchen midden. Considering how many shells can be eaten every day by one person and estimating the number of persons that, through the ages, contributed to the formation of the deposit, it is possible to calculate the age of the kitchen midden. After the studies carried on the Onges we may say that every kitchen midden is formed as a result of the activities of a small group of some thirty to forty persons who frequent the same spot for forty to fifty days in a year. Their food is rarely formed of molluscs: they resort to these only when there is absolutely nothing else to eat. They prefer wild fruits, roots, honey, fish, turtle, dugong, and more than anything else, pig. This last cooked in big pieces, is always taken by the Onges with them when they go hunting in the forests, and so the bones of these pigs are mostly dispersed in the jungle. Molluscs, on the other hand, are uncomfortable to carry because of their weight, and provide little nourishment. They are, therefore, nearly always eaten during the night halts in fixed localities. For a brief period of no more than forty to fifty days every year, and then not every day, these shells are thrown on the kitchen midden, thus very slowly contributing to its growth. In this way many of the Andamanese accumulations, often huge, required a long period for their formation, a period to be calculated in thousands of years, perhaps five or six thousand years.

Even if we reduce this number to half, the resulting antiquity is not in accordance with the opinion that the Andamanese are descendants of shipwrecked Portuguese Negro slaves. There is now hope that the antiquity of the Andamanese kitchen middens will be more exactly determined by collecting charcoal from different levels and then measuring the residual radio-activity of such charcoal.

10. The lowest strata of a kitchen midden obviously marks the time when the Andamanese arrived on that spot. But this time does not necessarily correspond to the first appearance of man in these Islands. Only *extensive comparisons between many such deposits can* in the future entitle one to give an authoritative opinion on this matter. A sequence of excavations should be undertaken in order to find out which are the most ancient of these documents left by man in the Andaman Islands. At present there have been only few researches beyond the Great Andaman. But during 1952 and 1953 some work was done in Little Andaman in this line, by studying also the interior of the island completely unexplored until 1952. The first point to strike one is that Little Andaman is conspicuous for the absence of well developed kitchen middens. There is a good reason for this: Little Andaman, besides having plenty of pure drinking water, has plenty of food, including that most relished by the Andamanese—the pig. The Onges very rarely resort to the eating of molluscs, and this always without enthusiasm, because they know that they can always obtain better food. As shells are the principal constituent of the heaps of refuse, few kitchen middens are to be found in Little Andaman, and these are small. These are, however, full of significance because they are still "alive", and so show details impossible to understand from the "dead" accumulations of the Great Andamans. In other words, the kitchen middens in Little Andaman are still in the process of formation; while in the Great Andamans they are only memories of a bygone past. From the study of the Little Andaman kitchen middens we come immediately to one very important conclusion: this is, that kitchen middens were not formed, as it is generally believed, through temporary encampments. They are formed strictly in connection with communal huts. Only this can explain the shape of the kitchen midden, its peculiar stratification, and the presence in them of human graves. Moreover, the 1953 researches in Little Andaman prove that communal huts have been distributed during the long ages past all over Great Andaman. As the location of a communal hut is frequently moved, we come to understand that a group of persons and their descendants have through countless generations contributed to the formation of many kitchen middens. This explains the starting and the stopping of several accumulations at different ages. For this reason every kitchen midden cannot be expected to show the same sequence of phenomena. On the contrary, every kitchen midden must be referred to its own age, often completely different from that of nearby similar kitchen middens. The shape, always geometrical and often hemispheric of them, can only have originated through the regular shape of communal huts, and not from the hap-hazard form of temporary camps. In these temporary camps, refuse is unavoidably and irregularly dispersed. From communal huts, on the other hand, because they are more or less only an umbrella-shaped roof open all along the circumference, refuse is radially thrown out through the opening nearest to each bed, and so forms a heap corresponding to the shape of the hut, circular or elliptical. Of considerable interest is the fact that in Little Andaman the Onges still bury their dead in the communal huts. In ancient times this must have been the custom also in the Great Andaman, because to-day we find graves in what appear to be only kitchen middens, while in reality they are the former emplacements of communal huts. The growing of a kitchen midden was facilitated by the rebuilding of the communal hut on the same spot many times, the ground being flattened every time before the hut was rebuilt. Excavations in Little and Great Andaman already indicate this through the formation of the successive strata.

11. Besides shells, which as I have already said form about ninety per cent. of the refuse found in kitchen middens, abundant materials of other kinds are found, including the bones of sea and land mammals, fish, turtles, birds, points of arrows made of bone or of shell (*Tridacna gigas*) sandstone sharpeners on which to smooth the points of arrows, great numbers of tiny chips of obsidiana and of different hard stones. A serious obstacle encountered in the excavation of the Andamanese kitchen middens is the difficulty to follow each single strata and, still more, to put it in its proper age. It is evident from the colour and quality of the earth that the accumulations along the coasts were sometimes influenced, in successive periods, by changes of the sea level and of the frequently nearby mangrove swamps, probably as a result of local rising or sinking of the land. This is of great help to us, because when clear sea water went near a kitchen midden, favourable conditions of life were offered to corals. In many places we now find such corals embedded in the black stinking mud of mangrove swamps where life for corals is to-day impossible. Changes like these undoubtedly required no short period for their accomplishment. Exploring along the coast we see that the one of such changes of sea level reached up to ten feet in height, and that it affected wide areas, because it has left traces in the Great Andaman as well as in the far away Little Andaman. In connection with this problem of the origin of the people of the Andamans, it is essential to establish the right age of this important and certainly not recent movement.

12. In many kitchen middens of the Great Andaman we find objects belonging to our own age, objects like imported smoking pipes, chips of broken bottles, bullets from rifles pieces of iron, etc.; and from these we can deduce that so little as half a foot of depth from the surface takes us back at least a hundred years, to a period before the arrival of the domesticated dog on the scene. This animal must have reached the Andamans in 1858; but no bones of it have yet been found in kitchen middens. Its arrival has, however, brought a sudden increase in the bones of *Sus Andamanensis* amongst the refuse; and these are extremely common on the surface. If we go a little deeper than half a foot iron disappears, and with it also bottle glass and other objects mentioned above. But smoking pipes continue to appear; only now the imported variety replaced the original Andamanese pipe made with the chelae of big crabs transversally cut and pierced at the distal ends. Such pipes are still used by Onges and Jarawas for smoking aromatic leaves found in the jungle. This habit of smoking is very ancient in the Andamans, for we find this type of pipe still in the lowest strata. The presence of shells at all levels, generally well preserved and mixed with a little earth, often allows easy digging for many feet of depth. Below these, in many kitchen middens we notice another sudden change, the strata from being very loose becoming very hard through the

addition of ashes to the earth. Moreover, the shells are calcined, as though burned directly in fire, and have a false appearance of fossilization, which is not to be found in the shells in the upper strata. This change connotes something of ethnological importance: we must assume that when they arrived in the place, the Andamanese did not know the use of pottery. Cooking was done directly on the fire or on hot ashes, without any pots. Later cooking was done in pots, mostly by boiling. That is why in the beginning we find shells calcined on the fire, and so made very breakable, thrown in heaps mixed with ashes. At a later stage, thrown away after boiling, they are neither calcined nor dirty with ashes. No pottery is found in these ancient and cemented strata. To-day the Andamanese cook almost exclusively by boiling, and this as a result of their superstitions. The first Andamanese pottery is of good make, with clay well worked, and well burned in the fire. It underwent degeneration, as we see when we approach the upper strata. The latest pottery, which is of relatively recent age, is extremely rough, with clay mixed carelessly with small stones, and not even baked on the fire, but simply dried by exposure in the sun. The result is fragile pottery, making it necessary to prepare the pots with very thick walls. In ancient times they could be made much thinner. This Andamanese pottery always follows the technique known as " au colombin ", or by coiling.

13. Later than pottery we begin to find bones of *Sus Andamanensis* ; and always more common as we proceed towards the surface. The unavoidable conclusion seems to be that the hunting of the pig and the making of pots were unknown to the ancient Andamanese. Pottery arrived later, probably with the same people who were responsible for the introduction of a domesticated pig in the Andamans. In this connection it is to be remembered that in these Islands there is complete absence of the great land mammals. *Sus* is the biggest, next being only a *Paradoxurus* and several little rodents.

14. No less important than the aforesaid is the presence in the Great Andaman kitchen middens of graves containing human bones. Such graves, very small, are dug in the accumulations of shells and then filled with clear earth. In many kitchen-middens, remnant found in graves are only the skull with the mandible and the long bones. Other bones are missing. In these instances, all details support the supposition that burial followed only after the bones had been kept for a long time, perhaps worn on the body in memory of the dead person. Amongst the present Andamanese a similar way of preserving the skull is practised by a group of people now almost extinct, a group reduced to only twentythree individuals. Other groups like the Onges and the Jarawas preserve only the mandibles as did several Tribes of Great Andaman, now extinct. In every case the bones are painted and ornamented, and then kept hanging from the neck as a homage to the dead person. In the nearby Nicobar Islands also is to be found this habit of preserving the skull and long bones of ancestors in the huts of their descendants, the bones being thrown away at a fixed place after a long time. For the ancient inhabitants of the Great Andamans this fixed place was evidently the floor of the communal hut. This, reminds us of the habit still followed by the Onges of burying their corpses in the communal hut. Graves of this kind, showing respect for the dead, should not be considered as the remnants of cannibalistic food, as has sometimes been presumed to be the case.

15. Nicobarese connections are also indicated by the Andamanese technique for making pottery: exclusively by coiling without potter's stone. Still more, the Nicobarese seem to help us to understand the presence of pig in the Andamans. The male Nicobarese pig, at least in the past, was generally castrated to make it fat more quickly. Moreover, males and females were, as they are now, left free to roam all day in the jungle, being called back to the house in the evening by special sounds. These semi-domesticated females were fecundated by wild males. Young domesticated pigs were the descendants of wild animals, possibly derived from young individuals that before castration ceased to obey the evening calls of their former owners. The present pig of the Andamans, showing a late appearance in kitchen middens, can derive from a semi-domesticated animal as seems to have been the case with its Nicobarese relative. The situation indicated by the kitchen middens of the Great Andamans is that of a probably ancient colonisation either in the Andamans or in the Nicobars by a people that, leaving cultural residual, were overcome by Negritos in the former, while the opposite happened in the latter. In this connection I heard in the Nicobars of an ancient tradition of the existence in the past there of a people of short stature and dark skin. In Car Nicobar I was informed that they had their headquarters in a cave, which cave is still in existence in the interior of the island. Excavations in this cave may prove useful. Anyhow, it is to be expected that researches on ancient human life in the Andamans will receive light and guidance from parallel investigations in the Nicobars.

16. As a result of the excavations carried out in the Andaman during 1952 and 1953 the following points may be summarised:—

(*a*) The Andamanese did not possess pottery on their arrival in these Islands.

(*b*) The ancient pottery was of better quality than the more recent.

(*c*) The technique of making pottery by coiling followed in the Andamans is the same as that still followed in the Nicobars.

(*d*) Human burial took place in what now is for us a kitchen midden. In many cases, only the skull and long bones were put in the graves, after having been preserved in the huts of their descendants, as happens still now in in the Nicobars.

(*e*) These bones show the same physical characteristics of the present Andamanese aboriginals.

(*f*) No traces are found in the kitchen middens of the cannibalism presumed by several people in respect of the Andamanese.

(*g*) *Sus Andamanensis*, now wild, arrived in these Islands probably domesticated, and appears in the kitchen middens later than does pottery.

(*h*) Pottery transformed the method of cooking from roasting to boiling, now nearly exclusively followed in the Andamans.

(i) Arrow points of excellent workmanship and made mostly of mammal or fish bones, sometimes also of shell, are common in kitchen middens. But none of stone have so far been found.

(*j*) Obsidians and several hard stones were chipped into tiny artifacts for shaving and for ornamental cutting of the skin.

(*k*) Iron is found only on the surface of kitchen middens, together with a large number of chips of imported glass.

(*l*) Several facts, such as the size of the kitchen middens, changes of sea level during their formation, contemporary changes in the species of shells, and in the frequency of their occurrence, all point to a long period certainly to be counted by millenniums.

(*m*) The ancient Andamanese show cultural connections with the Nicobars, indicating that a common foreign influence, of unknown origin, spread in a remote past to both groups of islands.

17. Mostly through the indications obtained from kitchen middens, and from researches carried out during 1952 and 1953 amongst the aboriginals of Little Andaman, we can now interpret some of the habits of the first Negritos to arrive in the Andamans. In this connection I may be allowed to affirm that Little Andaman will explain Great Andamans. Without going into more details, I quote here only a few instances of Onge manners connected with the problem here under discussion. Except for minor modifications, Onge habits remain substantially to-day what they were in remote prehistory, and in fact in a prelithic period. Great Andamans culture evolved more, but it had its starting point in a culture similar to that of the Onges. Migratory movements from the South to the North, not *vice versa*, seem to prove this. Like the Semang and the Aeta, the Onges do not practice tattooing or scarification ; but they paint their body with ochre. They also paint the bones of deceased persons with ochre, reminding us of well known paleolithic habits. They have no chiefs ; only headmen guiding small groups of exogamous families roaming together. Nobody is above these headmen. The Onges never knew how to prepare implements from stone. Nor have they ever learned how to make fire: having got it, they have to keep it permanently going. Cooking is done mostly by boiling, but only after they received pottery from outside long after their own arrival in the Andamans. Before that, everything was cooked in hot ashes, or directly over the fire, or on hot stones. Big animals cut in pieces were cooked only on hot stones in thick packing of leaves covered afterwards by earth. Salt is completely unknown to them. Burial takes place inside inhabited huts, as paleolithic man buried inside inhabited caves. Nudity is general, except for a tassel of fibre worn in front by women. Harpoon spears and harpoon arrows were certainly used long before they had any knowledge of iron. Neither poison nor traps for ground or water animals are known to the Andamanese.

18. All this and much more shows an archaic cultural level still "enjoyed" by the Andamanese, ("Civilization is the curse of humanity"!) but no more by African Negroes who left it centuries if not millenniums ago. It gives us an organically complete, complex and typical sequence of manners of immense, if not mysterious, antiquity showing extremely clear Asiatic connections with peoples that are already a race by themselves. It is simply absurd to consider this culture to be the casual result of decadence, or of a fortuitous rebuilding accomplished in a relatively short period from a disturbed cultural situation of a heterogeneous collection of slaves thrown by storms on the shores of the Andamans! On the contrary, it represents the unspoiled inheritance of a prelithic age. The continuance of research amongst the Onges, and if possible also amongst the Sentinelese and the Jarawas, will prove this in the most convincing way. Collateral investigations on the zoology and geology of the Andaman and Nicobar Islands are needed for the better understanding of several facts—the presence of *Sus* in the Andamans, for instance. *Sus*, as we know, is the biggest of the very few mammals in these Islands. The separation of the Andamans from the mainland before the appearance in it of mammals is supposed to explain this peculiarity. But this leaves open to question at least of the presence of pig. Persistent movements in the level of the islands, still perceptible, could have brought about a temporary general subsidence, leaving not enough room for big animals, especially the big carnivores. This question, at the same time geological and zoological, can be solved only through excavations. And since man is involved in it, excavations should be mostly in caves.

APPENDIX F

On the Shom-Pen of Great Nicobar

By SHRI B. S. CHENGAPA, *Conservator, Working Plans, Port Blair, Andaman*

Their Origin and Contact with them

It was for long believed that the interior of the Great Nicobar was inhabited by a race of Negritoes similar to the wild tribes of the Andaman Islands. Their existence was first reported by Pastor Rosen, a Danish Missionery in 1831. In 1846 Admiral Steen Bille paid the first recorded visit. This was followed by three visits by Mr. De Roepstorff; and on one of these occasions, in 1881, he was accompanied by the Chief Commissioner Colonel Cadell. Mr. Man first visited them in 1884, and maintained occasional contact for sometime. In 1901 Boden-Kloss, and in 1905 C. W. B. Anderson, also visited them.

It was then found that these Shom-Pens belong to the same stock as the other inhabitants of these Islands—an isolated group of primitive Malayans—and that later some unknown causes brought about a division among them into two distinct ethnological groups—The Shom-Pen of the interior of Great Nicobar and the Coastal people or the Nicobarese. The Shom-Pens appear to have a remote admixture of Negrito blood, they are a shade darker and are also slightly smaller in stature than the Coastal people. Their hair occurs in all the grades between curly and straight, and their appearance also varies greatly from the Nicobarese.

To account for this difference in hair and for the dull brown colour of the skin two theories are advanced; the first is that possibly the Andamanese, on one of their predatory excursions to these Islands, for some reason were unable to return and were incorporated with the local inhabitants.

The people of Car Nicobar still believe that the Andamanese in the long past came down in several canoes for their periodical raids. The second and more probable theory is that these peculiarities are due to a Dravidian strain; and that some Dravidian mariners, in their trading voyages to the Eastern Archipelago, became stranded in these Islands and later got incorporated with the local people.

The Shom-Pens are divided into two divisions. The smaller have been living nearer the Coast and a few miles up the big rivers—Jubliee, Dagmar, Alexandra and Galathea. These have been friendly with the Nicobarese, and only these friendly tribes have been visited in the past explorations. These are referred to as "Mawas Shom-Pen" meaning quite or tame Shom-Pen. The larger section, who inhabit the interior, have always been hostile and have continued in their nefarious work of raiding and killing the Nicobarese and the friendly Shom-Pens. One of the Nicobarese guides in the present Expedition, Berengse, who belonged to the East Coast, told the party that when he was about 10 years old (he is about 60 now) a pitched battle was fought between the hostile Shom-Pens and the Nicobarese and others, led by a British Officer, near Campbell Bay. In this battle many on both sides were killed, including his own brother. However, eventually the wild Shom-Pens managed to wipe out all villages on the East Coast. Berengse and his people shifted to Kondul, and others to the West Coast.

It is said that in the Exploration of the Andaman Islands in 1857 under Dr. F. J. Mouat, for establishing a Colony, one of the nervous and imaginative members brought news of a lurking body of aborgines. The Doctor addressed his followers in a warlike speech and gave orders to charge. They charged immediately, and discovered that they had knocked down some burnt tree stumps which they had mistaken for the wild tribes. Subsequently they had several serious clashes and quite a few of the aborigines were killed. This apparently led to the deep rooted hostility that still prevails amongst Jarawas. Protection against these hostile tribes is now costing the Government more than Rs. 40,000 per year. The present Expedition to the Nicobar Islands was determined that such mistakes should not be repeated and that there should be no retaliation even if the party was attacked in their attempt to penetrate the interior.

The Exploration party first came in contact with the Shom-Pens in Jubliee river. They were friendly and were already known to the guide. The Headman Akanya of the Shom-Pens took the party up to very near the source of Jubliee river, stayed a night with the party in jungle and brought them back to Ganges Harbour in the north of Great Nicobar. Next, they came in contact with the Shom-Pens living about 5 miles from the mouth of the Dogmar river. They were also friendly and well known to the guides. Two of them, Lonava and a boy about 16 years, accompanied the party in their own two men canoe, stayed two nights with the party in jungle, took them about 15 to 20 miles up this river and followed them to their camping place at Pulo-Kunyi.

The third lot of the Shom-Pens were found many miles in the interior of the Alexandra river valley, 12 or 14 miles up the main stream from its mouth and then about 2 miles up a branch stream on the south. These were wild and hostile. Fortunately, Lonava, the friendly Shom-Pen from Dagmar had accompanied the party. The first sign of the presence of wild tribes in these parts was foot prints on the bank of Alexandra river. At the sight of fresh foot prints of human beings one of the party shouted, and there was a prompt reply. This was repeated three or four times before the party came in sight of a young man about 25 years old walking boldly towards the canoe that was being paddled up stream, and a young woman with three children rushing off into the jungle for safety. They were naked except for bark cloth covering their shame. The young man had about a dozen javelins ready poised to throw at the people in the canoe. The friendly Shom-Pen shouted at the top of his voice in his language that the party means no harm. There-upon, the wild man threw down his dah and came straight to the canoe. He was immediately given sweets, *beedies*, tobacco, etc. He did not know how to smoke a *beedi* until he was taught to smoke. He guided the party to their huts about 2 miles away along a branch stream. These sheds were so remote that they could never have been discovered but for the guidance of the wild Shom-Pen himself. At the camp only two men were found, all the women and children having run away to hide themselves. After the men made certain that the party meant no harm, they brought their women and children and allowed themelves to be photographed. The Expedition party was completely unarmed. On being requested, three of them including their Headman came with the party in their canoe to the camp, received cloth, Dahs, sugar, etc., as presents and parted as good friends. They however refused to go to the Coast with the party.

The fourth lot of the Shom-Pens were found many miles in the interior of Galathea river. The friendly Shom-Pen Lonava refused to accompany the party any further, and returned to his huts near the mouth of Dagmar river as he thought that the rest of the Shom-Pens were all very wild and very hostile. The Nicobar guides however followed the party, and came in contact with another lot of Shom-Pens about a mile away from the bank of the Galathea river and about 14 or 15 miles from its mouth. While approaching the Shom-Pen huts only the Nicobar guides two of the Expedition party, showed themselves first; the others were hidden close by behind trees, watching developments. The two who went forward had taken off their clothes, and were naked but for a loin cloth. At this sight two Shom-Pens, a boy of 18 or 20 and another 10 or 12 years, rushed out with all the javelins and were about to strike. The guides had instructions not to fight or to show any signs of fear but hold up their hands and show that they are unarmed. They acted their part very well; and the Shom-Pens were a little confused, and after a little hesitation threw down their javelins and came forward. The others of the party who were hiding also came out at the same time. After exchange of a few words and presents, the women and children were sent for. While waiting for women and children to return, the Headman, who apparently had gone out hunting, also returned armed with about 10 or 12 javelins and started talking to the party as though he had known them for years. After they were photographed and more presents were given, the party returned to the canoe followed by the Headman who was promised clothes, dahs and an axe at the camp. These Shom-Pens had no axe, and the dah they had was a very poor specimen, very old and worn out. The Headman, though he got into the canoe without much persuasion, became very nervous; and at every bend of the river on the downward journey he wished to get ashore and walk home. He was however persuaded to stay on. The party had not gone a mile downstream when the two boys, with all the javelins they could collect, appeared on the bank all agitated and angry, and threatened to kill everyone of the party if their man was not set ashore at once and on the spot. He had worked himself to such a pitch that his naked body showed that he was trembling in every limb from head to foot, and that he was ready to execute his threat if it is not obeyed.

The party immediately allowed the Headman to land and requested him to follow the canoe to the camp. He agreed and followed the canoe for about half a mile and shouted back whenever the party shouted from the boat. At this stage one of the Nicobar guides got ashore hoping to lead the Shom-Pens to camp. On the shore he shouted to them and there was no answer or any sign of them and he arrived at the camp alone. After two or three hours, the guides were sent again to the Shom-Pen huts with clothes, dahs and other presents, with instructions to leave all the presents in their huts if they are not there. When they arrived they found the huts deserted; they however left all the presents in the huts.

The Nicobar guides were extremely nervous in Galathea river; and when it was suggested that the Expedition will next shift to Campbell Bay and Trinkat-Champlong Bay on the east, they were vehement that the Shom-Pens will attack the party. However, these objections were over-ruled; and the first camp on the East Coast was made at Campbell Bay. At this place the party saw some recently abandoned Shom-Pen huts, evidently abandoned while the party was exploring this Bay a week previously, for making a camp for assessing the forests. In Trinkat-Champlong however, two Shom-Pens came to the Expedition camp on their own and took the members of the party to their huts, perched in a hill top, and a few miles inland. They were anxious to obtain axes, dahs and clothes. They were successfully persuaded to visit M, L 'Valdora' that was anchored in the Bay. They returned quite happy with all they wanted.

Estimate of their Number

With the exception of a few families who have friendly intercourse with the Nicobarese, these Shom-Pens have persistently been hostile to the Coastal people and to any one who dared enter their territory. Therefore, their number has always been a guess work. Boden Kloss estimated their number in 1905 at 300-400; and subsequently a large number was wiped out by influenza, and later by poliomyelitis. In Dagmar river valley there are now only 14 people in all, sickly and dying; and the Shom-Pens in Alexandra river have disappeared completely because of this scourge. The few survivors, one of them Lonava, migrated to Dagmar. Those now found in Alexandra came from the interior, and have never been friendly with the Nicobarese. Likewise, those now found in Galathea have also never been friendly in the past, the friendly ones living mostly near the mouth of these big rivers and mentioned by Boden Kloss, have either been decimated by disease or have been wiped out by the hostile Shom-Pens after they were weakened by disease. The present Expedition in its extensive exploration, both along the Coast and the interior, counted only 48 Shom-Pens—14 men, 21 women and 13 children. Even if it is reckoned that there is an equal number that escaped contact by the party, the maximum number of Shom-Pens now in Great Nicobar can not be more than 100. It is noteworthy that out of 13 children only two belong to the friendly group.

Their Appearance

The Shom-Pens of Dagmar river, both men and women, are sickly and will probably die out completely in a few years. Those found elsewhere, especially the menfolk, are fine specimens of human beings, every one with the appearance of a very good athlete. They are not so strong or so robust as the Nicobarese; but they are tough and wiry. Their women however appeared weak, and in most cases sickly. They are also darker than the Coastal Nicobarese. They have a luxuriant growth of hair on their head, but none on their face or body. The hair varies from straight to curly, but is not frizzly. The general appearance of the Shom-Pens is distinctly Malayan.

Their Houses

These wild tribes have no settled homes, but wander about from place to place living in the crudest huts possible. These huts are built on piles varying in height from 3 ft. to about 7 or 8 ft., with a rough platform and a rough roof of palm leaf. In all the explorations, only one hut of a permanent nature, of the same bee-hive form which is a common feature of the dwelling of the Coastal Nicobarese, raised about 6 ft. from the ground, was seen near Trinkat-Champlong Bay on the East Coast. Even this had been abandoned. Huts on tree tops mentioned by Boden Kloss were not seen at all. Probably they have discarded this type of hut.

Their Food and Water

Their mode of life differs but slightly from the Nicobarese. The staple food of both Nicobarese and Shom-Pens is Pandanus. They cook them in a well-made boat-shaped vessel of sheets of bark of *Trema ambionensis*, or of *Terminalia manii*, or of *Anthocephalus candamba*, or bark of similar species. The cooking pot is about 5 ft. long, 2 to 2½ ft. high and about 2 ft. wide. The strips of bark are about 9″ to 12″ wide. One strip is folded lengthwise with the rough surfaces outwards to form a large trough and the bottom of the pot. The folded ends are inserted between two sticks tied tightly together and driven to the ground. Sides are then built up with other strips, the ends being inserted between the sticks. The whole is tightly bound up with strips of cane passing round from stake to stake and along the overlapping edges as well. The stakes at the centre are driven about 2 ft. apart to cause a bulge and give it a boat shape. A number of short round canes are inserted at the bottom, and this helps easy lifting of the contents when cooked. They can make fire by striking dry sticks. But this need never arises, as they keep their home fire always burning.

They hunt pigs, catch fish and collect fresh water mussels to supplement Pandanus. Fish however is not plenty in these rivers, and pigs are rare.

They are very fond of chewing betel nuts and betel leaves. They obtain lime for this purpose by burning shells of mussels found in fresh water.

They are very particular of water supply, and never drink water from any of the big streams or their big branch streams. They drink only the crystal clear water coming in little streamlets straight from the wooded hills and in little cataracts. They usually carry their water supply in jars and jugs collected from the shores or in tubes or in troughs made of the spathes of Areca palm.

They are fond of bathing, and rarely miss a chance of a dip and a wash when they are near these rivers.

Domestic Animals

Of the domestic animals, only dogs have got into their encampment. In Dagmar, their mouth had been muzzled to prevent them from barking. The Alexandra Shom-Pens had no dogs ; but they all had one or two small wild pigs in cages below their huts. The friendly Shom-Pens have dogs, cats, domestic pigs and chickens.

Their Industry

They make small canoes with outrigger to take two or three persons, and these are used only in rivers. They make baskets of ratten and of palm spathe, and cloth from the inner bark of two species of *Ficus*. One gives whitish cloth and the other reddish. They manufacture a javelin or dart with an iron head. This is used for warfare or for hunting pigs. They are never seen outside their huts without 10 or 12 javelins, at least three or four of them with iron heads. They throw these about 50 yards and are deadly accurate. While walking in jungle they frequently throw these javelins at a target, trying to show their skill in this art.

The friendly Shom-Pens have long been used to clothes. They obtain garments, beads, knives, axes, tobacco, etc., by barter. They are very good at splitting canes. They tie up these canes into bundles, and together with bundles of betel nut and limes wrapped up in palm leaves, hang them up on small trees at the mouth of the rivers. The Nicobarese collect them periodically, and similarly leave whatever they consider is a reasonable price. They occassionally meet also.

Their Garden

They are fond of gardening, and have been practising it for generations. All along the banks of the big rivers, occasional groups of coconut trees 60 or 70 years old, groups of betel nut palm, and an occasional lime tree, all now abondoned and neglected, are still found. There are a large number of new gardens half an acre to an acre in extent, planted with very good variety of bananas, tapioca, colocasia, tobacco, yams and Pandanus. The biggest garden, about 3 acres, on a hill slope of Mount Chaturvedi, was found near Trinkat-Champlong Bay. In this area all trees big and small had been felled and their branches cut and removed. There was no burning. Colocasia, bananas, yams and toabcco were the plants raised. They do all their digging and planting with strong sticks with pointed ends. Pandanus is raised by cuttings and these produce big fruits even when the plant is only 3 to 4 ft. high, when all the natural trees produce fruits at a height of 30-40 ft. Apart from these gardens, at every encampment they plant bananas and Colocasia near their huts.

Their Dress and Ornaments

Both men and women go about naked except for a loin cloth made of bark worn by women, and a strip of cloth worn by men, in the same manner as the Nicobarese do with a tail behind. The bark cloth of a woman is about 6 ft. to 8 ft. long and about 2½ ft. wide. In the olden days, Boden Kloss found them wearing ear rings made of bamboo (Dino-chloa andamanica) with pointed ends. In this Exploration, only Akanyo, the Jubliee river Shom-Pen was seen with these rings. Evidently it is out of fashion with them now. The friendly Shom-Pens wear ordinary clothes obtained from the Nicobarese by barter ; and whether wild or not they all wear their clothes with a tail behind in the Nicobarese fashion. The wild Shom-Pens wear necklaces made of broken coral pieced together.

Customs, Manners and Language

A Shom-Pen encampment usually has 10 to 15 persons, including women and children. The oldest man is usually the Headman ; but it is not known what control he has over others.

The Shom-Pens, whether wild or friendly, were seen with only a wife each. The wife and husband with their children live separately in a little shed of their own. Any relative, even an ailing mother or father, lives in a separate shed but close-by. The maximum number of sheds seen in any one place was six in Dagmar. Men of 50 or 60 years were not found anywhere in this Exploration. Old and ailing women about 50-60 years old were found in Jubliee and Dagmar rivers and also in Trinkat-Champlong Bay, all living in separate little huts.

Boden Kloss and other observers have said that these Shom-Pens are very timid. It is unfair to call them timid. In Alexandra river, the lone Shom-Pen hearing the party shout, shouted in return, sent away his wife and children, waited until he could see who was shouting, and with all his Javelins walked straight to the party, ready poised to strike. Similarly in Galathea valley, only two boys, one about 18 years and the other 10 or 11 years old, boldly came out with all javelins they could collect, to face two strong and hefty Nicobarese who showed themselves and three more of the party hiding just close behind. They did not flinch even for a second when all the five appeared on the scene. They are therefore by no means cowards or timid. On the other hand the Nicobarese, though strong, robust and hefty, are terribly frightened of the wild Shom-Pens.

They appear to be very hospitable. They offer pan (betel leaf, betel nut and lime) liberally. While out in jungle, they collect edible roots and shoots and offer them to their guests. In Alexandra river, they allowed a very big bunch of ripe red bananas, the only bunch they had, to be taken by the Nicobarese guides. In Dagmar river, a green bunch of bananas was offered to the Expedition party which they accepted. They freely gave a number of their iron headed javelins and also their bark cloth to the members of the Expedition party.

The language of the Shom-Pens differs from that of the Nicobarese, and the language of the wild Shom-Pens differs from that of the friendly tribes. But they appear to understand each other. Their pronunciation and accents are so much alike that a non-Nicobarese sees no difference in their language.

Their Health and Condition

The friendly Shom-Pens are weak and emaciated, and everyone was found suffering from cough and cold or some lung ailment. Some women were seen with elephantiasis and poliomyelitis in Dagmar river. It is only a question of few years before these people disappear. On the other hand, the wild Shom-Pens are all strong, tough, and wiry, and also very healthy. One woman in Galathea appeared to have suffered from Poliomyelitis; she was limping. The Galathea Shom-Pens were very particular that no one Expedition party with cold or other ailment should remain in their encampment. It was gathered that influenza and poliomyelitis killed a large number of them and some are still suffering from the after effects of poliomyelitis.

Conclusion

From the numerous gardens now found abandoned all along the big rivers, and from the fact that they have been able to wipe out all Nicobarese on the East Coast, it is evident that their number must once have been large. Influenza in 1918, and poliomyelitis in 1947, have so reduced their number that they have not been able to attack the Coastal Nicobarese for many years now. It is unlikely that they will attack any more, especially after this friendly contact made by the Expedition party with the Shom-Pens living many miles in the interior of these impenetrable forests. The latest action of these hostile and much dreaded Shom-Pens near Trinkat-Champlong Bay, coming on their own and taking the party to their encampment and their garden, goes to show that word has gone forth to all the Shom-Pens in the wilds that the party of strangers is friendly and helpful, and means no harm. It is therefore hoped that these Shom-Pens will no more be hostile. They are however just on the border line of friendship and hostility, and their future behaviour depends on the next Expedition. One false step will drive them back again to hostility, just as the Jarawas in the Andamans, once friendly, have now been driven to be our implacable and ruthless enemies. There should be an Anthropological Expedition as early as possible, and for a longer period, before the effects of this friendly visit wear off.

PART II

TABLES

GENERAL POPULATION TABLES

TABLE A-I—AREA, HOUSES AND POPULATION

This table shows the area, number of villages and occupied houses and the total Rural/Urban population with break-up by sexes. The area figures are furnished by the Surveyor General of India. There are no towns in this State.

State	Area in sq. miles	Villages	Towns	Occupied Houses		
				Total	Rural	Urban
(1)	(2)	(3)	(4)	(5)	(6)	(7)
Andaman & Nicobar Islands	**3,215**	**201**	..	**5,300**	**3,408**	**1,892**
Forest Camps	..	..	..	..	..	..
Motor Launches	..	..	..	..	..	..
Ships	..	..	..	..	..	..

State	Population								
	Persons			Males			Females		
	Total	Rural	Urban	Total	Rural	Urban	Total	Rural	Urban
(1)	(8)	(9)	(10)	(11)	(12)	(13)	(14)	(15)	(16)
Andaman & Nicobar Islands	**30,971**	**22,957**	**8,014**	**19,055**	**13,815**	**5,240**	**11,916**	**9,142**	**2,774**
Forest Camps	*2,552*	*2,552*	..	*2,360*	*2,360*	..	*192*	*192*	..
Motor Launches	*96*	*22*	*74*	*96*	*22*	*74*	..	..	..
Ships	*216*	*216*	..	*216*	*216*	..	..	..	..

TABLE A-II—VARIATION IN POPULATION DURING FIFTY YEARS

This table shows the growth of population (sex-wise) in the State during the last fifty years 1901—1951.

Year	Persons	Variation	Net variation 1901—1951	Males	Variation	Females	Variation
(1)	(2)	(3)	(4)	(5)	(6)	(7)	(8)
Andaman & Nicobar Islands							
1901	24,649	..	..	18,695	..	5,954	..
1911	26,459	+1,810	..	19,570	+875	6,889	+935
1921	27,086	+627	..	20,793	+1,223	6,293	—596
1931	29,463	+2,377	..	19,702	—1,091	9,761	+3,468
1941	33,768	+4,305	..	21,458	+1,756	12,310	+2,549
1951	30,971	—2,797	+6,322	19,055	—2,403	11,916	—394

TABLE A-III—TOWNS AND VILLAGES CLASSIFIED BY POPULATION

This table gives the distribution of villages in the State according to their population (sex-wise). Villages fall under the following five groups.

State	Total No. of inhabited towns and villages	Total Population			Towns and villages with less than 2,000 population — Total		
		Persons	Males	Females	Number	Males	Females
(1)	(2)	(3)	(4)	(5)	(6)	(7)	(8)
Andaman & Nicobar Islands	**201**	**30,971**	**19,055**	**11,916**	**200**	**16,843**	**10,632**

State	Towns and villages with less than 2,000 population — Less than 500			500—1,000			1,000—2,000		
	Number	Males	Females	Number	Males	Females	Number	Males	Females
(1)	(9)	(10)	(11)	(12)	(13)	(14)	(15)	(16)	(17)
Andaman & Nicobar Islands	**189**	**12,103**	**6,973**	**9**	**3,250**	**3,004**	**2**	**1,490**	**655**

State	Towns and villages with a population of 2,000 and above — Total			2,000—5,000			5,000 and above		
	Number	Males	Females	Number	Males	Females	Number	Males	Females
(1)	(18)	(19)	(20)	(21)	(22)	(23)	(24)	(25)	(26)
Andaman & Nicobar Islands	**1**	**2,212**	**1,284**	**1**	**2,212**	**1,284**	..	..	..

N.B. —The population figures given above include the figures for the Forest Camps, Motor Launches and Ships also.

*TABLE A-IV—TOWNS CLASSIFIED BY POPULATION WITH VARIATIONS SINCE 1901

*TABLE A-V—TOWNS ARRANGED TERRITORIALLY WITH POPULATION BY LIVELIHOOD CLASSES

*Since there is no town in these Islands, Tables A-IV and A-V have not been prepared.

ECONOMIC TABLES

TABLE B-I—LIVELIHOOD CLASSES AND SUB-CLASSES

This table gives the distribution of the population with Rural/Urban break-up in the Islands according to principal means of livelihood, self-supporting persons, earning dependants and non-earning dependants. The principal means of livelihood of non-earning and earning dependants is taken to be the same as that of the self-supporting persons on whom they depend.

State	Total Population			Agricultural Classes — All Agricultural Classes — Total			Self-supporting persons		Non-earning dependants		Earning dependants	
	Persons	Males	Females	Persons	Males	Females	Males	Females	Males	Females	Males	Females
(1)	(2)	(3)	(4)	(5)	(6)	(7)	(8)	(9)	(10)	(11)	(12)	(13)
Andaman & Nicobar Islands												
Total	*30,971*	*19,055*	*11,916*	*4,411*	*2,377*	*2,034*	*1,224*	*153*	*960*	*1,861*	*193*	*20*
Rural	22,957	13,815	9,142	4,213	2,283	1,930	1,176	147	922	1,766	185	17
Urban	8,014	5,240	2,774	198	94	104	48	6	38	95	8	3

State	Agricultural Classes — I—Cultivators of land wholly or mainly owned and their dependants — Total		Self-supporting persons		Non-earning dependants		Earning dependants	
	Males	Females	Males	Females	Males	Females	Males	Females
(1)	(14)	(15)	(16)	(17)	(18)	(19)	(20)	(21)
Andaman & Nicobar Islands								
Total	*2,177*	*1,890*	*1,085*	*120*	*906*	*1,752*	*186*	*18*
Rural	2,096	1,794	1,041	115	874	1,664	181	15
Urban	81	96	44	5	32	88	5	3

State	Agricultural Classes — II—Cultivators of land wholly or mainly unowned and their dependants — Total		Self-supporting persons		Non-earning dependants		Earning dependants	
	Males	Females	Males	Females	Males	Females	Males	Females
(1)	(22)	(23)	(24)	(25)	(26)	(27)	(28)	(29)
Andaman & Nicobar Islands								
Total	*94*	*71*	*58*	*10*	*32*	*59*	*4*	*2*
Rural	89	69	57	10	28	57	4	2
Urban	5	2	1	..	4	2	..	..

State	Agricultural Classes — III—Cultivating labourers and their dependants — Total		Self-supporting persons		Non-earning dependants		Earning dependants	
	Males	Females	Males	Females	Males	Females	Males	Females
(1)	(30)	(31)	(32)	(33)	(34)	(35)	(36)	(37)
Andaman & Nicobar Islands								
Total	*85*	*46*	*71*	*10*	*14*	*36*	..	..
Rural	83	46	69	10	14	36	..	..
Urban	2	..	2	..	..	..	..	..

TABLE B-I—LIVELIHOOD CLASSES AND SUB-CLASSES—*contd.*

State	Agricultural Classes							
	IV—Non-cultivating owners of land; Agricultural rent receivers and their dependants							
	Total		Self-supporting persons		Non-earning dependants		Earning dependants	
	Males	Females	Males	Females	Males	Females	Males	Females
(1)	(38)	(39)	(40)	(41)	(42)	(43)	(44)	(45)
Andaman & Nicobar Islands								
Total	*21*	*27*	*10*	*13*	*8*	*14*	*3*	..
Rural	15	21	9	12	6	9	..	..
Urban	6	6	1	1	2	5	3	..

State	Non-Agricultural Classes								
	All Non-Agricultural Classes								
	Total			Self-supporting persons		Non-earning dependants		Earning dependants	
	Persons	Males	Females	Males	Females	Males	Females	Males	Females
(1)	(46)	(47)	(48)	(49)	(50)	(51)	(52)	(53)	(54)
Andaman & Nicobar Islands									
Total	*26,560*	*16,678*	*9,882*	*9,517*	*440*	*4,121*	*5,492*	*3,040*	*3,950*
Rural	18,744	11,532	7,212	5,845	274	2,686	3,024	3,001	3,914
Urban	7,816	5,146	2,670	3,672	166	1,435	2,468	39	26

State	Non-Agricultural Classes							
	Persons (including dependants) who derive their principal means of livelihood from							
	V—Production other than cultivation							
	Total		Self-supporting persons		Non-earning dependants		Earning dependants	
	Males	Females	Males	Females	Males	Females	Males	Females
(1)	(55)	(56)	(57)	(58)	(59)	(60)	(61)	(62)
Andaman & Nicobar Islands								
Total	*10,636*	*6,892*	*5,072*	*144*	*2,605*	*2,858*	*2,959*	*3,890*
Rural	8,874	6,164	3,682	121	2,244	2,157	2,948	3,886
Urban	1,762	728	1,390	23	361	701	11	4

State	Non-Agricultural Classes							
	Persons (including dependants) who derive their principal means of livelihood from							
	VI—Commerce							
	Total		Self-supporting persons		Non-earning dependants		Earning dependants	
	Males	Females	Males	Females	Males	Females	Males	Females
(1)	(63)	(64)	(65)	(66)	(67)	(68)	(69)	(70)
Andaman & Nicobar Islands								
Total	*935*	*502*	*651*	*49*	*262*	*447*	*22*	*6*
Rural	291	84	239	12	42	72	10	..
Urban	644	418	412	37	220	375	12	6

TABLE B-I—LIVELIHOOD CLASSES AND SUB-CLASSES—*concld.*

Non-Agricultural Classes — Persons (including dependants) who derive their principal means of livelihood from VII—Transport

State	Total		Self-supporting persons		Non-earning dependants		Earning dependants	
	Males	Females	Males	Females	Males	Females	Males	Females
(1)	(71)	(72)	(73)	(74)	(75)	(76)	(77)	(78)
Andaman & Nicobar Islands								
Total	*737*	*356*	*529*	..	*201*	*347*	*7*	*9*
Rural	368	77	333	..	30	73	5	4
Urban	369	279	196	..	171	274	2	5

Non-Agricultural Classes — Persons (including dependants) who derive their principal means of livelihood from VIII—Other services and miscellaneous sources

State	Total		Self-supporting persons		Non-earning dependants		Earning dependants	
	Males	Females	Males	Females	Males	Females	Males	Females
(1)	(79)	(80)	(81)	(82)	(83)	(84)	(85)	(86)
Andaman & Nicobar Islands								
Total	*4,370*	*2,132*	*3,265*	*247*	*1,053*	*1,840*	*52*	*45*
Rural	1,999	887	1,591	141	370	722	38	24
Urban	2,371	1,245	1,674	106	683	1,118	14	21

TABLE B-II—SECONDARY MEANS OF LIVELIHOOD

In this table self-supporting persons and earning dependants in each of the eight principal means of livelihood classes, are classified according to their secondary means of livelihood if they have any. The classification for secondary means of livelihood is the same as that for principal means of livelihood. This table furnishes only the State figures.

Principal Means of Livelihood	Number of persons deriving their Secondary Means of Livelihood from											
	Cultivation of owned land						Cultivation of unowned land					
	Total		Self-supporting persons		Earning dependants		Total		Self-supporting persons		Earning dependants	
	Males	Females	Males	Females	Males	Females	Males	Females	Males	Females	Males	Females
(1)	(2)	(3)	(4)	(5)	(6)	(7)	(8)	(9)	(10)	(11)	(12)	(13)
Andaman & Nicobar Islands												
All Agricultural Classes	*19*	*3*	..	..	*19*	*3*	*80*	..	..	..	*80*	..
I—Cultivators of land wholly or mainly owned	19	3	..	..	19	3	79	..	..	..	79	..
II—Cultivators of land wholly or mainly unowned	..	..	..	..	..	..	1	..	..	..	1	..
III—Cultivating labourers	..	..	..	..	..	..	..	..	..	..	..	..
IV—Non-cultivating owners of land; Agricultural rent receivers	..	..	..	..	..	..	..	..	..	..	..	..
All Non-Agricultural Classes	*824*	*12*	*816*	*10*	*8*	*2*	*74*	..	*71*	..	*3*	..
V—Production other than cultivation	653	8	652	8	1	..	21	..	21	..	..	..
VI—Commerce . .	16	..	15	..	1	..	6	..	6	..	..	..
VII—Transport . .	14	1	13	..	1	1	21	..	20	..	1	..
VIII—Other services and miscellaneous sources	141	3	136	2	5	1	26	..	24	..	2	..

Principal Means of Livelihood	Number of persons deriving their Secondary Means of Livelihood from											
	Employment as cultivating labourer						Rent on agricultural land					
	Total		Self-supporting persons		Earning dependants		Total		Self-supporting persons		Earning dependants	
	Males	Females	Males	Females	Males	Females	Males	Females	Males	Females	Males	Females
(1)	(14)	(15)	(16)	(17)	(18)	(19)	(20)	(21)	(22)	(23)	(24)	(25)
Andaman & Nicobar Islands												
All Agricultural Classes	*42*	*2*	..	..	*42*	*2*	*1*	*1*	*1*	..	..	*1*
I—Cultivators of land wholly or mainly owned	42	2	..	..	42	2	1	..	1	..	..	..
II—Cultivators of land wholly or mainly unowned	..	..	..	..	..	..	..	1	..	..	..	1
III—Cultivating labourers	..	..	..	..	..	..	..	..	..	..	..	..
IV—Non-cultivating owners of land; Agricultural rent receivers	..	..	..	..	..	..	..	..	..	..	..	..
All Non-Agricultural Classes	*9*	*3*	*8*	..	*1*	*3*	*78*	*5*	*77*	*2*	*1*	*3*
V—Production other than cultivation	7	3	7	..	..	3	21	..	21	..	..	..
VI—Commerce . .	..	..	..	..	..	..	6	..	6	..	..	..
VII—Transport . .	1	.	1	..	..	..	4	1	4	..	..	1
VIII—Other services and miscellaneous sources	1	..	..	..	1	..	47	4	46	2	1	2

TABLE B-II—SECONDARY MEANS OF LIVELIHOOD—*concld.*

Principal Means of Livelihood	Number of persons deriving their Secondary Means of Livelihood from: Production other than cultivation — Total		Self-supporting persons		Earning dependants		Commerce — Total		Self-supporting persons		Earning dependants	
	Males	Females	Males	Females	Males	Females	Males	Females	Males	Females	Males	Females
(1)	(26)	(27)	(28)	(29)	(30)	(31)	(32)	(33)	(34)	(35)	(36)	(37)
Andaman & Nicobar Islands												
All Agricultural Classes	*61*	*3*	*60*	*3*	*1*	..	*102*	*6*	*97*	*3*	*5*	*3*
I—Cultivators of land wholly or mainly owned	49	..	48	..	1	..	91	5	87	2	4	3
II—Cultivators of land wholly or mainly unowned	7	..	7	..	..	..	6	..	6	..	..	..
III—Cultivating labourers	3	3	3	3	..	..	4	..	4	..	..	..
IV—Non-cultivating owners of land; Agricultural rent receivers	2	..	2	..	..	..	1	1	..	1	1	..
All Non-Agricultural Classes	*3,041*	*3,892*	*129*	*9*	*2,912*	*3,883*	*110*	*23*	*72*	*6*	*38*	*17*
V—Production other than cultivation	2,917	3,881	18	1	2,899	3,880	43	1	21	1	22	..
VI—Commerce	68	3	66	3	2	..	38	6	26	3	12	3
VII—Transport	16	..	16	..	..	..	7	1	5	..	2	1
VIII—Other services and miscellaneous sources	40	8	29	5	11	3	22	15	20	2	2	13

Principal Means of Livelihood	Number of persons deriving their Secondary Means of Livelihood from: Transport — Total		Self-supporting persons		Earning dependants		Other services and miscellaneous sources — Total		Self-supporting persons		Earning dependants	
	Males	Females	Males	Females	Males	Females	Males	Females	Males	Females	Males	Females
(1)	(38)	(39)	(40)	(41)	(42)	(43)	(44)	(45)	(46)	(47)	(48)	(49)
Andaman & Nicobar Islands												
All Agricultural Classes	*4*	..	*4*	..	..	..	*152*	*19*	*106*	*8*	*46*	*11*
I—Cultivators of land wholly or mainly owned	4	..	4	..	..	..	143	15	102	5	41	10
II—Cultivators of land wholly or mainly unowned	..	..	..	..	..	..	3	1	..	..	3	1
III—Cultivating labourers	..	..	..	..	..	..	..	1	..	1	..	..
IV—Non-cultivating owners of land; Agricultural rent receivers	..	..	..	..	..	..	6	2	4	2	2	..
All Non-Agricultural Classes	*20*	..	*5*	..	*15*	..	*116*	*56*	*54*	*14*	*62*	*42*
V—Production other than cultivation	11	..	..	..	11	..	64	10	38	3	26	7
VI—Commerce	3	..	2	..	1	..	13	7	7	4	6	3
VII—Transport	3	..	2	..	1	..	4	6	2	..	2	6
VIII—Other services and miscellaneous sources	3	..	1	..	2	..	35	33	7	7	28	26

TABLE B-III—EMPLOYERS, EMPLOYEES AND INDEPENDENT WORKERS IN INDUSTRIES AND SERVICES BY DIVISIONS AND SUB-DIVISIONS

This table shows the classification of the self-supporting persons in non-agricultural classes according to their secondary economic status, namely Employers, Employees and Independent Workers and their distribution in the various divisions and sub-divisions of Industries and Services.

The Industries and Services are classified under this Scheme into 10 Divisions which are again sub-divided into 88 Sub-Divisions.

State	All Industries and Services								
	Total			Employers		Employees		Independent Workers	
	Persons	Males	Females	Males	Females	Males	Females	Males	Females
(1)	(2)	(3)	(4)	(5)	(6)	(7)	(8)	(9)	(10)
Andaman & Nicobar Islands									
Total	*9,922*	*9,482*	*440*	*48*	*2*	*7,415*	*135*	*2,019*	*303*
Rural	6,084	5,810	274	8	..	4,305	48	1,497	226
Urban	3,838	3,672	166	40	2	3,110	87	522	77

State	*Division 0—Primary Industries not elsewhere specified*							
	Total		Employers		Employees		Independent Workers	
	Males	Females	Males	Females	Males	Females	Males	Females
(1)	(11)	(12)	(13)	(14)	(15)	(16)	(17)	(18)
Andaman & Nicobar Islands								
Total	*4,155*	*126*	*5*	..	*3,011*	*22*	*1,139*	*104*
Rural	3,435	122	..	..	2,309	20	1,126	102
Urban	720	4	5	..	702	2	13	2

State	0.1—Stock Raising							
	Total		Employers		Employees		Independent Workers	
	Males	Females	Males	Females	Males	Females	Males	Females
(1)	(19)	(20)	(21)	(22)	(23)	(24)	(25)	(26)
Andaman & Nicobar Islands								
Total	*59*	..	..	..	*59*	..	..	..
Rural	59	..	..	..	59	..	..	..
Urban	..	..	..	..	..	..	..	..

TABLE B-III—EMPLOYERS, EMPLOYEES AND INDEPENDENT WORKERS IN INDUSTRIES AND SERVICES BY DIVISIONS AND SUB-DIVISIONS—*contd.*

0.2—Rearing of small animals and insects

State	Total		Employers		Employees		Independent Workers	
	Males	Females	Males	Females	Males	Females	Males	Females
(1)	(27)	(28)	(29)	(30)	(31)	(32)	(33)	(34)
Andaman & Nicobar Islands								
Total	..	*2*	..	..	..	..	..	*2*
Rural	..	2	..	..	..	..	..	2
Urban	..	..	..	..	..	..	..	..

0.3—Plantation Industries

State	Total		Employers		Employees		Independent Workers	
	Males	Females	Males	Females	Males	Females	Males	Females
(1)	(35)	(36)	(37)	(38)	(39)	(40)	(41)	(42)
Andaman & Nicobar Islands								
Total	*1,228*	*103*	*4*	..	*150*	*1*	*1,074*	*102*
Rural	1,201	101	..	..	138	1	1,063	100
Urban	27	2	4	..	12	..	11	2

0.4—Forestry and collection of products not elsewhere specified

State	Total		Employers		Employees		Independent Workers	
	Males	Females	Males	Females	Males	Females	Males	Females
(1)	(43)	(44)	(45)	(46)	(47)	(48)	(49)	(50)
Andaman & Nicobar Islands								
Total	*2,836*	*21*	*1*	..	*2,801*	*21*	*34*	..
Rural	2,144	19	..	..	2,111	19	33	..
Urban	692	2	1	..	690	2	1	..

0.5—Hunting (including trapping and Game Propagation)

State	Total		Employers		Employees		Independent Workers	
	Males	Females	Males	Females	Males	Females	Males	Females
(1)	(51)	(52)	(53)	(54)	(55)	(56)	(57)	(58)
Andaman & Nicobar Islands								
Total	*10*	..	..	..	..	..	*10*	..
Rural	10	..	..	..	..	..	10	..
Urban	..	..	..	..	..	..	..	..

TABLE B-III—EMPLOYERS, EMPLOYEES AND INDEPENDENT WORKERS IN INDUSTRIES AND SERVICES BY DIVISIONS AND SUB-DIVISIONS—*contd.*

0.6—*Fishing*

State	Total		Employers		Employees		Independent Workers	
	Males	Females	Males	Females	Males	Females	Males	Females
(1)	(59)	(60)	(61)	(62)	(63)	(64)	(65)	(66)
Andaman & Nicobar Islands								
Total	*22*	..	..	..	*1*	..	*21*	..
Rural	21	..	..	..	1	..	20	..
Urban	1	..	..	..	..	..	1	..

Division 1—Mining and Quarrying

State	Total		Employers		Employees		Independent Workers	
	Males	Females	Males	Females	Males	Females	Males	Females
(1)	(67)	(68)	(69)	(70)	(71)	(72)	(73)	(74)
Andaman & Nicobar Islands								
Total	..	..	..	..	..	..	..	..
Rural	..	..	..	..	..	..	..	..
Urban	..	..	..	..	..	..	..	..

1.0—Non-metallic mining and quarrying not otherwise classified

State	Total		Employers		Employees		Independent Workers	
	Males	Females	Males	Females	Males	Females	Males	Females
(1)	(75)	(76)	(77)	(78)	(79)	(80)	(81)	(82)
Andaman & Nicobar Islands								
Total	..	..	..	..	..	..	..	..
Rural	..	..	..	..	..	..	..	..
Urban	..	..	..	..	..	..	..	..

1.1—Coal mining

State	Total		Employers		Employees		Independent Workers	
	Males	Females	Males	Females	Males	Females	Males	Females
(1)	(83)	(84)	(85)	(86)	(87)	(88)	(89)	(90)
Andaman & Nicobar Islands								
Total	..	..	..	..	..	..	..	..
Rural	..	..	..	..	..	..	..	..
Urban	..	..	..	..	..	..	..	..

TABLE B-III—EMPLOYERS, EMPLOYEES AND INDEPENDENT WORKERS IN INDUSTRIES AND SERVICES BY DIVISIONS AND SUB-DIVISIONS—*contd.*

State	1.2—Iron ore mining							
	Total		Employers		Employees		Independent Workers	
	Males	Females	Males	Females	Males	Females	Males	Females
(1)	(91)	(92)	(93)	(94)	(95)	(96)	(97)	(98)
Andaman & Nicobar Islands								
Total	..	..	..	..	..	..	..	..
Rural	..	..	..	..	..	..	..	..
Urban	..	..	..	..	..	..	..	..

State	1.3—Metal mining except iron ore mining							
	Total		Employers		Employees		Independent Workers	
	Males	Females	Males	Females	Males	Females	Males	Females
(1)	(99)	(100)	(101)	(102)	(103)	(104)	(105)	(106)
Andaman & Nicobar Islands								
Total	..	..	..	..	..	..	..	..
Rural	..	..	..	..	..	..	..	..
Urban	..	..	..	..	..	..	..	..

State	1.4—Crude Petroleum and Natural Gas							
	Total		Employers		Employees		Independent Workers	
	Males	Females	Males	Females	Males	Females	Males	Females
(1)	(107)	(108)	(109)	(110)	(111)	(112)	(113)	(114)
Andaman & Nicobar Islands								
Total	..	..	..	..	..	..	..	..
Rural	..	..	..	..	..	..	..	..
Urban	..	..	..	..	..	..	..	..

State	1.5—Stone-quarrying, clay and sand pits							
	Total		Employers		Employees		Independent Workers	
	Males	Females	Males	Females	Males	Females	Males	Females
(1)	(115)	(116)	(117)	(118)	(119)	(120)	(121)	(122)
Andaman & Nicobar Islands								
Total	..	..	..	..	..	..	..	..
Rural	..	..	..	..	..	..	..	..
Urban	..	..	..	..	..	..	..	..

TABLE B-III—EMPLOYERS, EMPLOYEES AND INDEPENDENT WORKERS IN INDUSTRIES AND SERVICES BY DIVISIONS AND SUB-DIVISIONS—*contd.*

1.6—Mica

State	Total		Employers		Employees		Independent Workers	
	Males	Females	Males	Females	Males	Females	Males	Females
(1)	(123)	(124)	(125)	(126)	(127)	(128)	(129)	(130)
Andaman & Nicobar Islands								
Total	..	..	..	..	..	..	..	..
Rural	..	..	..	..	..	..	..	..
Urban	..	..	..	..	..	..	..	..

1.7—Salt, saltpetre and saline substances

State	Total		Employers		Employees		Independent Workers	
	Males	Females	Males	Females	Males	Females	Males	Females
(1)	(131)	(132)	(133)	(134)	(135)	(136)	(137)	(138)
Andaman & Nicobar Islands								
Total	..	..	..	..	..	..	..	..
Rural	..	..	..	..	..	..	..	..
Urban	..	..	..	..	..	..	..	..

Division 2—Processing and Manufacture—Foodstuffs, Textiles, Leather and Products thereof

State	Total		Employers		Employees		Independent Workers	
	Males	Females	Males	Females	Males	Females	Males	Females
(1)	(139)	(140)	(141)	(142)	(143)	(144)	(145)	(146)
Andaman & Nicobar Islands								
Total	*122*	*7*	*1*	..	*55*	*1*	*66*	*6*
Rural	29	..	..	..	25	..	4	..
Urban	93	7	1	..	30	1	62	6

2.0—Food Industries otherwise unclassified

State	Total		Employers		Employees		Independent Workers	
	Males	Females	Males	Females	Males	Females	Males	Females
(1)	(147)	(148)	(149)	(150)	(151)	(152)	(153)	(154)
Andaman & Nicobar Islands								
Total	*4*	..	..	..	..	..	*4*	..
Rural	..	..	..	..	..	..	..	..
Urban	4	..	..	..	..	..	4	..

TABLE B-III—EMPLOYERS, EMPLOYEES AND INDEPENDENT WORKERS IN INDUSTRIES AND SERVICES BY DIVISIONS AND SUB-DIVISIONS—*contd.*

2.1—Grains and pulses

State	Total		Employers		Employees		Independent Workers	
	Males	Females	Males	Females	Males	Females	Males	Females
(1)	(155)	(156)	(157)	(158)	(159)	(160)	(161)	(162)
Andaman & Nicobar Islands								
Total	*12*	..	*1*	..	*8*	..	*3*	..
Rural	1	..	..	..	1	..	..	..
Urban	11	..	1	..	7	..	3	..

2.2—Vegetable oil and dairy products

State	Total		Employers		Employees		Independent Workers	
	Males	Females	Males	Females	Males	Females	Males	Females
(1)	(163)	(164)	(165)	(166)	(167)	(168)	(169)	(170)
Andaman & Nicobar Islands								
Total	*16*	..	..	..	*16*	..	..	..
Rural	15	..	..	..	15	..	..	..
Urban	1	..	..	..	1	..	..	..

2.3—Sugar Industries

State	Total		Employers		Employees		Independent Workers	
	Males	Females	Males	Females	Males	Females	Males	Females
(1)	(171)	(172)	(173)	(174)	(175)	(176)	(177)	(178)
Andaman & Nicobar Islands								
Total	..	..	..	..	..	..	..	..
Rural	..	..	..	..	..	..	..	..
Urban	..	..	..	..	..	..	..	..

2.4—Beverages

State	Total		Employers		Employees		Independent Workers	
	Males	Females	Males	Females	Males	Females	Males	Females
(1)	(179)	(180)	(181)	(182)	(183)	(184)	(185)	(186)
Andaman & Nicobar Islands								
Total	*9*	..	..	..	*9*	..	..	..
Rural	2	..	..	..	2	..	..	..
Urban	7	..	..	..	7	..	..	..

TABLE B-III—EMPLOYERS, EMPLOYEES AND INDEPENDENT WORKERS IN INDUSTRIES AND SERVICES BY DIVISIONS AND SUB-DIVISIONS—*contd.*

2.5—Tobacco

State	Total		Employers		Employees		Independent Workers	
	Males	Females	Males	Females	Males	Females	Males	Females
(1)	(187)	(188)	(189)	(190)	(191)	(192)	(193)	(194)
Andaman & Nicobar Islands								
Total	..	..	..	..	..	..	..	..
Rural	..	..	..	..	..	..	..	..
Urban	..	..	..	..	..	..	..	..

2.6—Cotton textiles

State	Total		Employers		Employees		Independent Workers	
	Males	Females	Males	Females	Males	Females	Males	Females
(1)	(195)	(196)	(197)	(198)	(199)	(200)	(201)	(202)
Andaman & Nicobar Islands								
Total	*10*	..	..	..	*9*	..	*1*	..
Rural	1	..	..	..	..	..	1	..
Urban	9	..	..	..	9	..	..	..

2.7—Wearing apparel (except footwear) and made-up textile goods

State	Total		Employers		Employees		Independent Workers	
	Males	Females	Males	Females	Males	Females	Males	Females
(1)	(203)	(204)	(205)	(206)	(207)	(208)	(209)	(210)
Andaman & Nicobar Islands								
Total	*61*	*6*	..	..	*8*	*1*	*53*	*5*
Rural	5	..	..	..	2	..	3	..
Urban	56	6	..	..	6	1	50	5

2.8—Textile Industries otherwise unclassified

State	Total		Employers		Employees		Independent Workers	
	Males	Females	Males	Females	Males	Females	Males	Females
(1)	(211)	(212)	(213)	(214)	(215)	(216)	(217)	(218)
Andaman & Nicobar Islands								
Total	*5*	*1*	..	..	*5*	..	..	*1*
Rural	5	..	..	..	5	..	..	..
Urban	..	1	..	..	..	..	..	1

TABLE B-III—EMPLOYERS, EMPLOYEES AND INDEPENDENT WORKERS IN INDUSTRIES AND SERVICES BY DIVISIONS AND SUB-DIVISIONS—*contd.*

2.9—Leather, leather products and footwear

State	Total		Employers		Employees		Independent Workers	
	Males	Females	Males	Females	Males	Females	Males	Females
(1)	(219)	(220)	(221)	(222)	(223)	(224)	(225)	(226)
Andaman & Nicobar Islands								
Total	*5*	..	..	..	..	..	*5*	..
Rural	..	..	..	..	..	..	..	..
Urban	5	..	..	..	..	..	5	..

Division 3 —Processing and Manufacture—Metals, Chemicals and Products thereof

State	Total		Employers		Employees		Independent Workers	
	Males	Females	Males	Females	Males	Females	Males	Females
(1)	(227)	(228)	(229)	(230)	(231)	(232)	(233)	(234)
Andaman & Nicobar Islands								
Total	*474*	*12*	..	..	*458*	*12*	*16*	..
Rural	144	..	..	..	135	..	9	..
Urban	330	12	..	..	323	12	7	..

3.0—Manufacture of metal products otherwise unclassified

State	Total		Employers		Employees		Independent Workers	
	Males	Females	Males	Females	Males	Females	Males	Females
(1)	(235)	(236)	(237)	(238)	(239)	(240)	(241)	(242)
Andaman & Nicobar Islands								
Total	*63*	..	..	..	*52*	..	*11*	..
Rural	26	..	..	..	19	..	7	..
Urban	37	..	..	..	33	..	4	..

3.1—Iron and Steel (Basic Manufacture)

State	Total		Employers		Employees		Independent Workers	
	Males	Females	Males	Females	Males	Females	Males	Females
(1)	(243)	(244)	(245)	(246)	(247)	(248)	(249)	(250)
Andaman & Nicobar Islands								
Total	*2*	..	..	..	*2*	..	..	..
Rural	..	..	..	..	..	..	..	..
Urban	2	..	..	..	2	..	..	..

TABLE B-III—EMPLOYERS, EMPLOYEES AND INDEPENDENT WORKERS IN INDUSTRIES AND SERVICES BY DIVISIONS AND SUB-DIVISIONS—*contd.*

3.2—Non-Ferrous Metals (Basic Manufacture)

State	Total		Employers		Employees		Independent Workers	
	Males	Females	Males	Females	Males	Females	Males	Females
(1)	(251)	(252)	(253)	(254)	(255)	(256)	(257)	(258)
Andaman & Nicobar Islands								
Total	..	..	..	..	..	..	..	..
Rural	..	..	..	..	..	..	..	..
Urban	..	..	..	..	..	..	..	..

3·3—Transport Equipment

State	Total		Employers		Employees		Independent Workers	
	Males	Females	Males	Females	Males	Females	Males	Females
(1)	(259)	(260)	(261)	(262)	(263)	(264)	(265)	(266)
Andaman & Nicobar Islands								
Total	*341*	..	..	..	*336*	..	*5*	..
Rural	116	..	..	..	114	..	2	..
Urban	225	..	..	..	222	..	3	..

3.4—Electrical machinery, apparatus, appliances and supplies

State	Total		Employers		Employees		Independent Workers	
	Males	Females	Males	Females	Males	Females	Males	Females
(1)	(267)	(268)	(269)	(270)	(271)	(272)	(273)	(274)
Andaman & Nicobar Islands								
Total	..	..	..	..	..	..	..	..
Rural	..	..	..	..	..	..	..	..
Urban	..	..	..	..	..	..	..	..

3.5—Machinery (other than electrical machinery) including Engineering Workshops

State	Total		Employers		Employees		Independent Workers	
	Males	Females	Males	Females	Males	Females	Males	Females
(1)	(275)	(276)	(277)	(278)	(279)	(280)	(281)	(282)
Andaman & Nicobar Islands								
Total	..	..	..	..	..	..	..	..
Rural	..	..	..	..	..	..	..	..
Urban	..	..	..	..	..	..	..	..

TABLE B-III—EMPLOYERS, EMPLOYEES AND INDEPENDENT WORKERS IN INDUSTRIES AND SERVICES BY DIVISIONS AND SUB-DIVISIONS—*contd.*

3.6—Basic Industrial Chemicals, Fertilisers and Power Alcohol

State	Total		Employers		Employees		Independent Workers	
	Males	Females	Males	Females	Males	Females	Males	Females
(1)	(283)	(284)	(285)	(286)	(287)	(288)	(289)	(290)
Andaman & Nicobar Islands								
Total	..	..	..	..	..	..	..	..
Rural	..	..	..	..	..	..	..	..
Urban	..	..	..	..	..	..	..	..

3.7—Medical and Pharmaceutical Preparations

State	Total		Employers		Employees		Independent Workers	
	Males	Females	Males	Females	Males	Females	Males	Females
(1)	(291)	(292)	(293)	(294)	(295)	(296)	(297)	(298)
Andaman & Nicobar Islands								
Total	..	..	..	..	..	..	..	..
Rural	..	..	..	..	..	..	..	..
Urban	..	..	..	..	..	..	..	..

3.8—Manufacture of chemical products otherwise unclassified

State	Total		Employers		Employees		Independent Workers	
	Males	Females	Males	Females	Males	Females	Males	Females
(1)	(299)	(300)	(301)	(302)	(303)	(304)	(305)	(306)
Andaman & Nicobar Islands								
Total	*68*	*12*	..	..	*68*	*12*	..	..
Rural	2	..	..	..	2	..	..	..
Urban	66	12	..	..	66	12	..	..

Division 4—Processing and Manufacture—Not elsewhere specified

State	Total		Employers		Employees		Independent Workers	
	Males	Females	Males	Females	Males	Females	Males	Females
(1)	(307)	(308)	(309)	(310)	(311)	(312)	(313)	(314)
Andaman & Nicobar Islands								
Total	*321*	..	..	..	*266*	..	*55*	..
Rural	74	..	..	..	67	..	7	..
Urban	247	..	..	..	199	..	48	..

TABLE B-III—EMPLOYERS, EMPLOYEES AND INDEPENDENT WORKERS IN INDUSTRIES AND SERVICES BY DIVISIONS AND SUB-DIVISIONS—*contd.*

4.0—Manufacturing Industries otherwise unclassified

State	Total		Employers		Employees		Independent Workers	
	Males	Females	Males	Females	Males	Females	Males	Females
(1)	(315)	(316)	(317)	(318)	(319)	(320)	(321)	(322)
Andaman & Nicobar Islands								
Total	*14*	..	..	..	*1*	..	*13*	..
Rural	2	..	..	..	..	..	2	..
Urban	12	..	..	..	1	..	11	..

4.1—Products of petroleum and coal

State	Total		Employers		Employees		Independent Workers	
	Males	Females	Males	Females	Males	Females	Males	Females
(1)	(323)	(324)	(325)	(326)	(327)	(328)	(329)	(330)
Andaman & Nicobar Islands								
Total	..	..	..	..	..	..	..	..
Rural	..	..	..	..	..	..	..	..
Urban	..	..	..	..	..	..	..	..

4.2—Bricks, tiles and other structural clay products

State	Total		Employers		Employees		Independent Workers	
	Males	Females	Males	Females	Males	Females	Males	Females
(1)	(331)	(332)	(333)	(334)	(335)	(336)	(337)	(338)
Andaman & Nicobar Islands								
Total	..	..	..	..	..	..	..	..
Rural	..	..	..	..	..	..	..	..
Urban	..	..	..	..	..	..	..	..

4.3—Cement—Cement pipes and other cement products

State	Total		Employers		Employees		Independent Workers	
	Males	Females	Males	Females	Males	Females	Males	Females
(1)	(339)	(340)	(341)	(342)	(343)	(344)	(345)	(346)
Andaman & Nicobar Islands								
Total	..	..	..	..	..	..	..	..
Rural	..	..	..	..	..	..	..	..
Urban	..	..	..	..	..	..	..	..

TABLE B-III—EMPLOYERS, EMPLOYEES AND INDEPENDENT WORKERS IN INDUSTRIES AND SERVICES BY DIVISIONS AND SUB-DIVISIONS—*contd.*

4.4—Non-metallic mineral products

State	Total		Employers		Employees		Independent Workers	
	Males	Females	Males	Females	Males	Females	Males	Females
(1)	(347)	(348)	(349)	(350)	(351)	(352)	(353)	(354)
Andaman & Nicobar Islands								
Total	..	..	..	..	..	..	..	..
Rural	..	..	..	..	..	..	..	..
Urban	..	..	..	..	..	..	..	..

4.5—Rubber products

State	Total		Employers		Employees		Independent Workers	
	Males	Females	Males	Females	Males	Females	Males	Females
(1)	(355)	(356)	(357)	(358)	(359)	(360)	(361)	(362)
Andaman & Nicobar Islands								
Total	..	..	..	..	..	..	..	..
Rural	..	..	..	..	..	..	..	..
Urban	..	..	..	..	..	..	..	..

4.6—Wood and wood products other than furniture and fixtures

State	Total		Employers		Employees		Independent Workers	
	Males	Females	Males	Females	Males	Females	Males	Females
(1)	(363)	(364)	(365)	(366)	(367)	(368)	(369)	(370)
Andaman & Nicobar Islands								
Total	*301*	..	..	..	*259*	..	*42*	..
Rural	70	..	..	..	65	..	5	..
Urban	231	..	..	..	194	..	37	..

4.7—Furniture and fixtures

State	Total		Employers		Employees		Independent Workers	
	Males	Females	Males	Females	Males	Females	Males	Females
(1)	(371)	(372)	(373)	(374)	(375)	(376)	(377)	(378)
Andman & Nicobar Islands								
Total	..	..	..	..	..	..	..	..
Rural	..	..	..	..	..	..	..	..
Urban	..	..	..	..	..	..	..	..

TABLE B-III—EMPLOYERS, EMPLOYEES AND INDEPENDENT WORKERS IN INDUSTRIES AND SERVICES BY DIVISIONS AND SUB-DIVISIONS—*contd.*

4.8—Paper and paper products

State	Total		Employers		Employees		Independent Workers	
	Males	Females	Males	Females	Males	Females	Males	Females
(1)	(379)	(380)	(381)	(382)	(383)	(384)	(385)	(386)
Andaman & Nicobar Islands								
Total	..	..	..	..	..	..	..	..
Rural	..	..	..	..	..	..	..	..
Urban	..	..	..	..	..	..	..	..

4.9—Printing and Allied Industries

State	Total		Employers		Employees		Independent Workers	
	Males	Females	Males	Females	Males	Females	Males	Females
(1)	(387)	(388)	(389)	(390)	(391)	(392)	(393)	(394)
Andaman & Nicobar Islands								
Total	*6*	..	..	..	*6*	..	..	..
Rural	2	..	..	..	2	..	..	..
Urban	4	..	..	..	4	..	..	..

Division 5—Construction and Utilities

State	Total		Employers		Employees		Independent Workers	
	Males	Females	Males	Females	Males	Females	Males	Females
(1)	(395)	(396)	(397)	(398)	(399)	(400)	(401)	(402)
Andaman & Nicobar Islands								
Total	*200*	*19*	..	..	*200*	*19*	..	..
Rural	53	3	..	..	53	3	..	..
Urban	147	16	..	..	147	16	..	..

5.0—Construction and maintenance of works—otherwise unclassified

State	Total		Employers		Employees		Independent Workers	
	Males	Females	Males	Females	Males	Females	Males	Females
(1)	(403)	(404)	(405)	(406)	(407)	(408)	(409)	(410)
Andaman & Nicobar Islands								
Total	*3*	..	..	..	*3*	..	..	..
Rural	3	..	..	..	3	..	..	..
Urban	..	..	..	..	..	..	..	..

TABLE B-III—EMPLOYERS, EMPLOYEES AND INDEPENDENT WORKERS IN INDUSTRIES AND SERVICES BY DIVISIONS AND SUB-DIVISIONS—*contd.*

5.1—Construction and maintenance—Buildings

State	Total		Employers		Employees		Independent Workers	
	Males	Females	Males	Females	Males	Females	Males	Females
(1)	(411)	(412)	(413)	(414)	(415)	(416)	(417)	(418)
Andaman & Nicobar Islands								
Total	*29*	..	..	..	*29*	..	..	..
Rural	4	..	..	..	4	..	..	..
Urban	25	..	..	..	25	..	..	..

5.2—Construction and maintenance—Roads, Bridges and other Transport Works

State	Total		Employers		Employees		Independent Workers	
	Males	Females	Males	Females	Males	Females	Males	Females
(1)	(419)	(420)	(421)	(422)	(423)	(424)	(425)	(426)
Andaman & Nicobar Islands								
Total	*32*	*2*	..	..	*32*	*2*	..	..
Rural	32	2	..	..	32	2	..	..
Urban	..	..	..	..	..	..	..	..

5.3—Construction and maintenance—Telegraph and Telephone Lines

State	Total		Employers		Employees		Independent Workers	
	Males	Females	Males	Females	Males	Females	Males	Females
(1)	(427)	(428)	(429)	(430)	(431)	(432)	(433)	(434)
Andaman & Nicobar Islands								
Total	..	..	..	..	..	..	..	..
Rural	..	..	..	..	..	..	..	..
Urban	..	..	..	..	..	..	..	..

5.4—Construction and maintenance operations—Irrigation and other agricultural works

State	Total		Employers		Employees		Independent Workers	
	Males	Females	Males	Females	Males	Females	Males	Females
(1)	(435)	(436)	(437)	(438)	(439)	(440)	(441)	(442)
Andaman & Nicobar Islands								
Total	*4*	..	..	..	*4*	..	..	..
Rural	4	..	..	..	4	..	..	..
Urban	..	..	..	..	..	..	..	..

TABLE B-III—EMPLOYERS, EMPLOYEES AND INDEPENDENT WORKERS IN INDUSTRIES AND SERVICES BY DIVISIONS AND SUB-DIVISIONS—*contd.*

5.5—Works and Services—Electric Power and Gas supply

State	Total		Employers		Employees		Independent Workers	
	Males	Females	Males	Females	Males	Females	Males	Females
(1)	(443)	(444)	(445)	(446)	(447)	(448)	(449)	(450)
Andaman & Nicobar Islands								
Total	*30*	..	..	..	*30*	..	..	..
Rural	8	..	..	..	8	..	..	..
Urban	22	..	..	..	22	..	..	..

5.6—Works and Services—Domestic and Industrial water supply

State	Total		Employers		Employees		Independent Workers	
	Males	Females	Males	Females	Males	Females	Males	Females
(1)	(451)	(452)	(453)	(454)	(455)	(456)	(457)	(458)
Andaman & Nicobar Islands								
Total	..	..	..	..	..	..	..	..
Rural	..	..	..	..	..	..	..	..
Urban	..	..	..	..	..	..	..	..

5.7—Sanitary Works and Services—Including scavengers

State	Total		Employers		Employees		Independent Workers	
	Males	Females	Males	Females	Males	Females	Males	Females
(1)	(459)	(460)	(461)	(462)	(463)	(464)	(465)	(466)
Andaman & Nicobar Islands								
Total	*102*	*17*	..	..	*102*	*17*	..	..
Rural	2	1	..	..	2	1	..	..
Urban	100	16	..	..	100	16	..	..

Division 6—Commerce

State	Total		Employers		Employees		Independent Workers	
	Males	Females	Males	Females	Males	Females	Males	Females
(1)	(467)	(468)	(469)	(470)	(471)	(472)	(473)	(474)
Andaman & Nicobar Islands								
Total	*650*	*49*	*36*	*2*	*322*	*1*	*292*	*46*
Rural	239	12	5	..	184	..	50	12
Urban	411	37	31	2	138	1	242	34

TABLE B-III—EMPLOYERS, EMPLOYEES AND INDEPENDENT WORKERS IN INDUSTRIES AND SERVICES BY DIVISIONS AND SUB-DIVISIONS—*contd.*

6.0—Retail trade otherwise unclassified

State	Total		Employers		Employees		Independent Workers	
	Males	Females	Males	Females	Males	Females	Males	Females
(1)	(475)	(476)	(477)	(478)	(479)	(480)	(481)	(482)
Andaman & Nicobar Islands								
Total	*362*	*7*	*15*	..	*263*	*1*	*84*	*6*
Rural	184	..	1	..	167	..	16	..
Urban	178	7	14	..	96	1	68	6

6.1—Retail trade in foodstuffs (including beverages and narcotics)

State	Total		Employers		Employees		Independent Workers	
	Males	Females	Males	Females	Males	Females	Males	Females
(1)	(483)	(484)	(485)	(486)	(487)	(488)	(489)	(490)
Andaman & Nicobar Islands								
Total	*220*	*23*	*13*	*2*	*49*	..	*158*	*21*
Rural	36	8	2	..	8	..	26	8
Urban	184	15	11	2	41	..	132	13

6.2—Retail trade in fuel (including petrol)

State	Total		Employers		Employees		Independent Workers	
	Males	Females	Males	Females	Males	Females	Males	Females
(1)	(491)	(492)	(493)	(494)	(495)	(496)	(497)	(498)
Andaman & Nicobar Islands								
Total	*5*	..	*1*				*4*	..
Rural	3	..	1				2	..
Urban	2	..	..				2	..

6.3—Retail trade in textile and leather goods

State	Total		Employers		Employees		Independent Workers	
	Males	Females	Males	Females	Males	Females	Males	Females
(1)	(499)	(500)	(501)	(502)	(503)	(504)	(505)	(506)
Andaman & Nicobar Islands								
Total	*37*	*2*	*5*	..	..	..	*32*	*2*
Rural	3	1	..	..	..	..	3	1
Urban	34	1	5	..	..	..	29	1

TABLE B-III—EMPLOYERS, EMPLOYEES AND INDEPENDENT WORKERS IN INDUSTRIES AND SERVICES BY DIVISIONS AND SUB-DIVISIONS—*contd.*

6.4—Wholesale trade in foodstuffs

State	Total		Employers		Employees		Independent Workers	
	Males	Females	Males	Females	Males	Females	Males	Females
(1)	(507)	(508)	(509)	(510)	(511)	(512)	(513)	(514)
Andaman & Nicobar Islands								
Total	*1*	..	*1*	..	..	..	..	..
Rural	..	..	..	..	..	..	..	..
Urban	1	..	1	..	..	..	..	..

6.5—Wholesale trade in commodities other than foodstuffs

State	Total		Employers		Employees		Independent Workers	
	Males	Females	Males	Females	Males	Females	Males	Females
(1)	(515)	(516)	(517)	(518)	(519)	(520)	(521)	(522)
Andaman & Nicobar Islands								
Total	*14*	..	*1*	..	*10*	..	*3*	..
Rural	12	..	1	..	9	..	2	..
Urban	2	..	..	..	1	..	1	..

6.6—Real Estate

State	Total		Employers		Employees		Independent Workers	
	Males	Females	Males	Females	Males	Females	Males	Females
(1)	(523)	(524)	(525)	(526)	(527)	(528)	(529)	(530)
Andaman & Nicobar Islands								
Total	*10*	*14*	..	..	..	..	*10*	*14*
Rural	..	1	..	..	..	..	..	1
Urban	10	13	..	..	..	..	10	13

6.7—Insurance

State	Total		Employers		Employees		Independent Workers	
	Males	Females	Males	Females	Males	Females	Males	Females
(1)	(531)	(532)	(533)	(534)	(535)	(536)	(537)	(538)
Andaman & Nicobar Islands								
Total	..	..	..	..	..	..	..	..
Rural	..	..	..	..	..	..	..	..
Urban	..	..	..	..	..	..	..	..

TABLE B-III—EMPLOYERS, EMPLOYEES AND INDEPENDENT WORKERS IN INDUSTRIES AND SERVICES BY DIVISIONS AND SUB-DIVISIONS—*contd.*

6.8—Moneylending, banking and other financial business

State	Total		Employers		Employees		Independent Workers	
	Males	Females	Males	Females	Males	Females	Males	Females
(1)	(539)	(540)	(541)	(542)	(543)	(544)	(545)	(546)
Andaman & Nicobar Islands								
Total	*1*	*3*	..	..	..	..	*1*	*3*
Rural	1	2	..	..	..	..	1	2
Urban	..	1	..	..	..	..	..	1

Division 7—Transport, Storage and Communications

State	Total		Employers		Employees		Independent Workers	
	Males	Females	Males	Females	Males	Females	Males	Females
(1)	(547)	(548)	(549)	(550)	(551)	(552)	(553)	(554)
Andaman & Nicobar Islands								
Total	*604*	..	*2*	..	*588*	..	*14*	..
Rural	354	..	1	..	352	..	1	..
Urban	250	..	1	..	236	..	13	..

7.0—Transport and communications otherwise unclassified and incidental services

State	Total		Employers		Employees		Independent Workers	
	Males	Females	Males	Females	Males	Females	Males	Females
(1)	(555)	(556)	(557)	(558)	(559)	(560)	(561)	(562)
Andaman & Nicobar Islands								
Total	..	..	..	..	..	..	..	..
Rural	..	..	..	..	..	..	..	..
Urban	..	..	..	..	..	..	..	..

7.1—Transport by road

State	Total		Employers		Employees		Independent Workers	
	Males	Females	Males	Females	Males	Females	Males	Females
(1)	(563)	(564)	(565)	(566)	(567)	(568)	(569)	(570)
Andaman & Nicobar Islands								
Total	*97*	..	*2*	..	*90*	..	*5*	..
Rural	14	..	1	..	12	..	1	..
Urban	83	..	1	..	78	..	4	..

TABLE B-III—EMPLOYERS, EMPLOYEES AND INDEPENDENT WORKERS IN INDUSTRIES AND SERVICES BY DIVISIONS AND SUB-DIVISIONS—*contd.*

7.2—Transport by water

State	Total		Employers		Employees		Independent Workers	
	Males	Females	Males	Females	Males	Females	Males	Females
(1)	(571)	(572)	(573)	(574)	(575)	(576)	(577)	(578)
Andaman & Nicobar Islands								
Total	*390*	..	..	..	*381*	..	*9*	..
Rural	277	..	..	..	277	..	..	..
Urban	113	..	..	..	104	..	9	..

7.3—Transport by Air

State	Total		Employers		Employees		Independent Workers	
	Males	Females	Males	Females	Males	Females	Males	Females
(1)	(579)	(580)	(581)	(582)	(583)	(584)	(585)	(586)
Andaman & Nicobar Islands								
Total	*42*	..	..	..	*42*	..	..	..
Rural	42	..	..	..	42	..	..	..
Urban	..	..	..	..	..	..	..	..

7.4—Railway transport

State	Total		Employers		Employees		Independent Workers	
	Males	Females	Males	Females	Males	Females	Males	Females
(1)	(587)	(588)	(589)	(590)	(591)	(592)	(593)	(594)
Andaman & Nicobar Islands								
Total	..	..	..	..	..	..	..	..
Rural	..	..	..	..	..	..	..	..
Urban	..	..	..	..	..	..	..	..

7.5—Storage and warehousing

State	Total		Employers		Employees		Independent Workers	
	Males	Females	Males	Females	Males	Females	Males	Females
(1)	(595)	(596)	(597)	(598)	(599)	(600)	(601)	(602)
Andaman & Nicobar Islands								
Total	..	..	..	..	..	..	..	..
Rural	..	..	..	..	..	..	..	..
Urban	..	..	..	..	..	..	..	..

TABLE B-III—EMPLOYERS, EMPLOYEES AND INDEPENDENT WORKERS IN INDUSTRIES AND SERVICES BY DIVISIONS AND SUB-DIVISIONS—*contd.*

7.6—Postal Services

State	Total		Employers		Employees		Independent Workers	
	Males	Females	Males	Females	Males	Females	Males	Females
(1)	(603)	(604)	(605)	(606)	(607)	(608)	(609)	(610)
Andaman & Nicobar Islands								
Total	*13*	..	..	..	*13*	..	..	..
Rural	1	..	..	..	1	..	..	..
Urban	12	..	..	..	12	..	..	..

7.7—Telegraph Services

State	Total		Employers		Employees		Independent Workers	
	Males	Females	Males	Females	Males	Females	Males	Females
(1)	(611)	(612)	(613)	(614)	(615)	(616)	(617)	(618)
Andaman & Nicobar Islands								
Total	..	..	..	..	..	..	..	..
Rural	..	..	.	..	..	..	..	..
Urban	..	..	..	..	..	..	..	..

7.8—Telephone Services

State	Total		Employers		Employees		Independent Workers	
	Males	Females	Males	Females	Males	Females	Males	Females
(1)	(619)	(620)	(621)	(622)	(623)	(624)	(625)	(626)
Andaman & Nicobar Islands								
Total	*6*	..	..	..	*6*	..	..	..
Rural	1	..	..	..	1	..	..	..
Urban	5	..	..	..	5	..	..	..

7.9—Wireless Services

State	Total		Employers		Employees		Independent Workers	
	Males	Females	Males	Females	Males	Females	Males	Females
(1)	(627)	(628)	(629)	(630)	(631)	(632)	(633)	(634)
Andaman & Nicobar Islands								
Total	*56*	..	..	..	*56*	..	..	..
Rural	19	..	..	..	19	..	..	..
Urban	37	..	..	..	37	..	..	..

TABLE B-III—EMPLOYERS, EMPLOYEES AND INDEPENDENT WORKERS IN INDUSTRIES AND SERVICES BY DIVISIONS AND SUB-DIVISIONS—*contd.*

Division 8—Health, Education and Public Administration

State	Total		Employers		Employees		Independent Workers	
	Males	Females	Males	Females	Males	Females	Males	Females
(1)	(635)	(636)	(637)	(638)	(639)	(640)	(641)	(642)
Andaman & Nicobar Islands								
Total	*1,176*	*42*	..	..	*1,174*	*41*	*2*	*1*
Rural	379	5	..	..	379	5	..	..
Urban	797	37	..	..	795	36	2	1

8.1—Medical and other Health Services

State	Total		Employers		Employees		Independent Workers	
	Males	Females	Males	Females	Males	Females	Males	Females
(1)	(643)	(644)	(645)	(646)	(647)	(648)	(649)	(650)
Andaman & Nicobar Islands								
Total	*105*	*27*	..	..	*104*	*26*	*1*	*1*
Rural	34	5	..	..	34	5	..	..
Urban	71	22	..	..	70	21	1	1

8.2—Educational Services and Research

State	Total		Employers		Employees		Independent Workers	
	Males	Females	Males	Females	Males	Females	Males	Females
(1)	(651)	(652)	(653)	(654)	(655)	(656)	(657)	(658)
Andaman & Nicobar Islands								
Total	*48*	*14*	..	..	*47*	*14*	*1*	..
Rural	27	..	..	..	27	..	..	..
Urban	21	14	..	..	20	14	1	..

8.3—Army, Navy and Air Force*

State	Total		Employers		Employees		Independent Workers	
	Males	Females	Males	Females	Males	Females	Males	Females
(1)	(659)	(660)	(661)	(662)	(663)	(664)	(665)	(666)
Andaman & Nicobar Islands								
Total	..	..	..	..	..	..	..	..
Rural	..	..	..	..	..	..	..	..
Urban	..	..	..	..	..	..	..	..

**Figures included in Sub-division 8.8*

TABLE B-III—EMPLOYERS, EMPLOYEES AND INDEPENDENT WORKERS IN INDUSTRIES AND SERVICES BY DIVISIONS AND SUB-DIVISIONS—*contd.*

8.4—Police (other than village watchmen)

State	Total		Employers		Employees		Independent Workers	
	Males	Females	Males	Females	Males	Females	Males	Females
(1)	(667)	(668)	(669)	(670)	(671)	(672)	(673)	(674)
Andaman & Nicobar Islands								
Total	*437*	..	..	..	*437*	..	..	..
Rural	142	..	..	..	142	..	..	..
Urban	295	..	..	..	295	..	..	..

8.5—Village officers and servants including village watchmen

State	Total		Employers		Employees		Independent Workers	
	Males	Females	Males	Females	Males	Females	Males	Females
(1)	(675)	(676)	(677)	(678)	(679)	(680)	(681)	(682)
Andaman & Nicobar Islands								
Total	*46*	..	..	..	*46*	..	..	..
Rural	7	..	..	..	7	..	..	..
Urban	39	..	..	..	39	..	..	..

8.6—Employees of Municipalities and Local Boards (but not including persons classifiable under any other division or sub-division)

State	Total		Employers		Employees		Independent Workers	
	Males	Females	Males	Females	Males	Females	Males	Females
(1)	(683)	(684)	(685)	(686)	(687)	(688)	(689)	(690)
Andaman & Nicobar Islands								
Total	..	..	..	..	..	..	..	..
Rural	..	..	..	..	..	..	..	..
Urban	..	..	..	..	..	..	..	..

8.7—Employees of State Governments (but not including persons classifiable under any other division or sub-division)

State	Total		Employers		Employees		Independent Workers	
	Males	Females	Males	Females	Males	Females	Males	Females
(1)	(691)	(692)	(693)	(694)	(695)	(696)	(697)	(698)
Andaman & Niocbar Islands								
Total	*539*	*1*	..	..	*539*	*1*	..	..
Rural	168	..	..	..	168	..	..	..
Urban	371	1	..	..	371	1	..	..

TABLE B-III—EMPLOYERS, EMPLOYEES AND INDEPENDENT WORKERS IN INDUSTRIES AND SERVICES BY DIVISIONS AND SUB-DIVISIONS—*contd.*

8.8—Employees of the Union Government (but not including persons classifiable under any other division or sub-dvision)

State	Total		Employers		Employees		Independent Workers	
	Males	Females	Males	Females	Males	Females	Males	Females
(1)	(699)	(700)	(701)	(702)	(703)	(704)	(705)	(706)
Andaman & Nicobar Islands								
Total	..	..	..	..	..	..	..	..
Rural	..	..	..	..	..	..	..	..
Urban	..	..	..	..	..	..	..	..

8.9—Employees of Non-Indian Governments

State	Total		Employers		Employees		Independent Workers	
	Males	Females	Males	Females	Males	Females	Males	Females
(1)	(707)	(708)	(709)	(710)	(711)	(712)	(713)	(714)
Andaman & Nicobar Islands								
Total	*1*	..	..	..	*1*	..	..	..
Rural	1	..	..	..	1	..	..	..
Urban	..	..	..	..	..	..	..	..

Division 9—Services not elsewhere specified

State	Total		Employers		Employees		Independent Workers	
	Males	Females	Males	Females	Males	Females	Males	Females
(1)	(715)	(716)	(717)	(718)	(719)	(720)	(721)	(722)
Andaman & Nicobar Islands								
Total	*1,780*	*185*	*4*	..	*1,341*	*39*	*435*	*146*
Rural	1,103	132	2	..	801	20	300	112
Urban	677	53	2	..	540	19	135	34

9.0—Services otherwise unclassified

State	Total		Employers		Employees		Independent Workers	
	Males	Females	Males	Females	Males	Females	Males	Females
(1)	(723)	(724)	(725)	(726)	(727)	(728)	(729)	(730)
Andaman & Nicobar Islands								
Total	*1,537*	*171*	*2*	..	*1,170*	*31*	*365*	*140*
Rural	1,040	130	2	..	750	18	288	112
Urban	497	41	..	..	420	13	77	28

TABLE B-III—EMPLOYERS, EMPLOYEES AND INDEPENDENT WORKERS IN INDUSTRIES AND SERVICES BY DIVISIONS AND SUB-DIVISIONS—*contd.*

9.1—Domestic services (but not including services rendered by members of family households to one another)

State	Total		Employers		Employees		Independent Workers	
	Males	Females	Males	Females	Males	Females	Males	Females
(1)	(731)	(732)	(733)	(734)	(735)	(736)	(737)	(738)
Andaman & Nicobar Islands								
Total	*137*	*8*	..	..	*126*	*7*	*11*	*1*
Rural	44	2	..	..	43	2	1	..
Urban	93	6	..	..	83	5	10	1

9.2—Barbers and beauty shops

State	Total		Employers		Employees		Independent Workers	
	Males	Females	Males	Females	Males	Females	Males	Females
(1)	(739)	(740)	(741)	(742)	(743)	(744)	(745)	(746)
Andaman & Nicobar Islands								
Total	*26*	..	*1*	..	*2*	..	*23*	..
Rural	7	..	..	..	..	..	7	..
Urban	19	..	1	..	2	..	16	..

9.3—Laundries and Laundry services

State	Total		Employers		Employees		Independent Workers	
	Males	Females	Males	Females	Males	Females	Males	Females
(1)	(747)	(748)	(749)	(750)	(751)	(752)	(753)	(754)
Andaman & Nicobar Islands								
Total	*28*	*6*	*1*	..	*6*	*1*	*21*	*5*
Rural	1	..	..	..	..	..	1	..
Urban	27	6	1	..	6	1	20	5

9.4—Hotels, restaurants and eating houses

State	Total		Employers		Employees		Independent Workers	
	Males	Females	Males	Females	Males	Females	Males	Females
(1)	(755)	(756)	(757)	(758)	(759)	(760)	(761)	(762)
Andaman & Nicobar Islands								
Total	..	..	..	..	..	..	..	..
Rural	..	..	..	..	..	..	..	..
Urban	..	..	..	..	..	..	..	..

TABLE B-III—EMPLOYERS, EMPLOYEES AND INDEPENDENT WORKERS IN INDUSTRIES AND SERVICES BY DIVISIONS AND SUB-DIVISIONS—*contd.*

State	9.5—Recreation services							
	Total		Employers		Employees		Independent Workers	
	Males	Females	Males	Females	Males	Females	Males	Females
(1)	(763)	(764)	(765)	(766)	(767)	(768)	(769)	(770)
Andaman & Nicobar Islands								
Total	*3*	..	..	..	*3*	..	..	..
Rural	..	..	..	..	..	..	..	..
Urban	3	..	..	..	3	..	..	..

State	9.6—Legal and business services							
	Total		Employers		Employees		Independent Workers	
	Males	Females	Males	Females	Males	Females	Males	Females
(1)	(771)	(772)	(773)	(774)	(775)	(776)	(777)	(778)
Andaman & Nicobar Islands								
Total	*13*	..	..	..	*11*	..	*2*	..
Rural	..	..	..	..	..	..	..	..
Urban	13	..	..	..	11	..	2	..

State	9.7—Arts, letters and journalism							
	Total		Employers		Employees		Independent Workers	
	Males	Females	Males	Females	Males	Females	Males	Females
(1)	(779)	(780)	(781)	(782)	(783)	(784)	(785)	(786)
Andaman & Nicobar Islands								
Total	*14*	..	..	..	*10*	..	*4*	..
Rural	2	..	..	..	2	..	..	..
Urban	12	..	..	..	8	..	4	..

State	9.8—Religious, Charitable and Welfare Services							
	Total		Employers		Employees		Independent Workers	
	Males	Females	Males	Females	Males	Females	Males	Females
(1)	(787)	(788)	(789)	(790)	(791)	(792)	(793)	(794)
Andaman & Nicobar Islands								
Total	*22*	..	..	..	*13*	..	*9*	..
Rural	9	..	..	..	6	..	3	..
Urban	13	..	..	..	7	..	6	..

TABLE B-III—*concld.*

Details of Persons Deriving their Means of Livelihood from Non-Productive Occupations

State	Total			Unclassifiable: Persons living principally on income from non-agricultural property		Unclassifiable: Persons living principally on pensions, remittances, scholarships and funds	
	Persons	Males	Females	Males	Females	Males	Females
(1)	(2)	(3)	(4)	(5)	(6)	(7)	(8)
Andaman & Nicobar Islands*							
Total	*35*	*35*	..	..	..	..	..
Rural	35	35	..	..	..	..	..
Urban	..	..	..	..	..	..	..

State	Unclassifiable: Inmates of jails, asylums, alms houses & recipients of doles		Unclassifiable: Beggars and Vargrants		Unclassifiable: All other persons living principally on income derived from non-productive activity	
	Males	Females	Males	Females	Males	Females
(1)	(9)	(10)	(11)	(12)	(13)	(14)
Andaman & Nicobar Islands*						
Total	..	..	..	..	..	..
Rural	..	..	..	..	..	..
Urban	..	..	..	..	..	..

**Means of livelihood not specified.*

HOUSEHOLD AND AGE (SAMPLE) TABLES

TABLE C-I—HOUSEHOLD (SIZE AND COMPOSITION)

This table shows the distribution of the sample households by size and composition with reference to family relationship and age group (infants, non-adults and adults) in the State for Rural/Urban areas.

"Household" includes all persons living together in the same house and having a common mess.

One Household in every thousand was taken as a sample. The samples were selected from the National Registers of Citizens. The first sample was obtained by dividing the number of households in each tract by 1,000 and adding 1 to the remainder. Every 1,000th households thereafter was taken as sample.

State	Total No. of Households	Total Household Population: Persons	Total Household Population: Males	Total Household Population: Females	Total number of sample households	Sample Household Population: Persons	Sample Household Population: Males	Sample Household Population: Females
(1)	(2)	(3)	(4)	(5)	(6)	(7)	(8)	(9)
Andaman & Nicobar Islands								
Total	*7,640*	*28,107*	*16,383*	*11,724*	*272*	*928*	*543*	*385*
Rural	4,068	20,167	11,217	8,950	137	600	335	265
Urban	3,572	7,940	5,166	2,774	135	328	208	120

Sample Households — Size of Households

State	Small (3 members or less): Number	Small: Persons	Medium (4—6 Members): Number	Medium: Persons	Large (7—9 Members): Number	Large: Persons	Very large (10 members or above): Number	Very large: Persons
(1)	(10)	(11)	(12)	(13)	(14)	(15)	(16)	(17)
Andaman & Nicobar Islands								
Total	*177*	*261*	*63*	*318*	*21*	*173*	*11*	*176*
Rural	74	112	37	187	16	135	10	166
Urban	103	149	26	131	5	38	1	10

Sample Households — Composition of Households

State	Heads of Households and their wives: Males	Heads of Households and their wives: Females	Sons of heads of households	Daughter of heads of households	Other male relations of heads of households	Other female relations of heads of households	Infants (age less than one year): Males	Infants (age less than one year): Females
(1)	(18)	(19)	(20)	(21)	(22)	(23)	(24)	(25)
Andaman & Nicobar Islands								
Total	*260*	*132*	*151*	*132*	*105*	*100*	*13*	*25*
Rural	129	80	93	80	89	85	3	5
Urban	131	52	58	52	16	15	10	20

(Columns 20–23: Family Structure; columns 24–25: Infants, non-adults and adults in households)

Sample Households — Composition of Households

State	Non-adults (age 1—20 years): Males	Non-adults: Females	Adults (age 21 years and over): Males	Adults: Females	Unmarried: Males	Unmarried: Females	Married: Males	Married: Females	Widowed or Divorced: Males	Widowed or Divorced: Females
(1)	(26)	(27)	(28)	(29)	(30)	(31)	(32)	(33)	(34)	(35)
Andaman & Nicobar Islands										
Total	*369*	*244*	*161*	*116*	*306*	*188*	*212*	*159*	*25*	*38*
Rural	215	221	117	39	107	125	124	106	14	34
Urban	154	23	44	77	109	63	88	53	11	4

(Columns 26–29: Infants, non-adults and adults in households; columns 30–35: Civil Condition)

TABLE C-II—LIVELIHOOD CLASSES BY AGE GROUPS FOR SAMPLE POPULATION

This table shows the distribution of each Livelihood Class by Age Group with Rural/Urban break-up.

This table furnishes the number of unmarried, married and widowed or divorced males and females by Age Groups with Rural/Urban break-up. Figures for widowed and divorced have been clubbed together in this table. Figures for divorced persons are shown separately in the fly-leaf to this table.

Age Groups	Total			Livelihood Classes — Agricultural Classes: I—Cultivators of land wholly or mainly owned and their dependants		II—Cultivators of land wholly or mainly unowned and their dependants		III—Cultivating labourers and their dependants		IV—Non-cultivating owners of land; Agricultural rent receivers and their dependants	
	Persons	Males	Females	Males	Females	Males	Females	Males	Females	Males	Females
(1)	(2)	(3)	(4)	(5)	(6)	(7)	(8)	(9)	(10)	(11)	(12)
Andaman & Nicobar Islands (Total)											
All Ages	**2,927**	**1,840**	**1,087**	**162**	**154**	**14**	**3**	**7**	**5**	**2**	**4**
0	107	43	64	6	8	..	..	..	1	..	..
1—4	315	186	129	18	19	..	..	..	1	..	..
5—14	588	310	278	44	46	5	..	..	..	..	2
15—24	664	461	203	32	22	4	2	3	1	..	..
25—34	563	360	203	16	24	3	1	4	..	..	1
35—44	375	255	120	19	18	2	..	..	1	1	1
45—54	192	147	45	12	7	..	..	..	1	1	..
55—64	76	49	27	9	9	..	..	..	..	..	..
65—74	32	19	13	4	1	..	..	..	..	..	..
75 & over	15	10	5	2	..	..	..	..	..	..	..

Age Groups	Livelihood Classes — Non-Agricultural Classes — Persons (including dependants) who derive their principal means of livelihood from: V—Production other than cultivation		VI—Commerce		VII—Transport		VIII—Other services and miscellaneous sources	
	Males	Females	Males	Females	Males	Females	Males	Females
(1)	(13)	(14)	(15)	(16)	(17)	(18)	(19)	(20)
Andaman & Nicobar Islands (Total)								
All Ages	**1,056**	**660**	**100**	**47**	**78**	**48**	**421**	**166**
0	24	36	5	3	2	1	6	15
1—4	110	67	9	8	5	12	44	22
5—14	190	173	14	8	8	11	49	38
15—24	268	120	23	10	15	13	116	35
25—34	192	137	19	7	20	8	106	25
35—44	146	75	18	5	15	1	54	10
45—54	87	29	8	3	9	1	30	4
55—64	25	16	2	..	4	..	9	2
65—74	8	5	2	2	..	..	5	5
75 & over	6	2	..	1	..	1	2	1

TABLE C-II—LIVELIHOOD CLASSES BY AGE GROUPS FOR SAMPLE POPULATION—*contd.*

Age Groups	Total			Livelihood Classes — Agricultural Classes: I—Cultivators of land wholly or mainly owned and their dependants		II—Cultivators of land wholly or mainly unowned and their dependants		III—Cultivating labourers and their dependants		IV—Non-cultivating owners of land; Agricultural rent receivers and their dependants	
	Persons	Males	Females	Males	Females	Males	Females	Males	Females	Males	Females
(1)	(2)	(3)	(4)	(5)	(6)	(7)	(8)	(9)	(10)	(11)	(12)
Andaman & Nicobar Islands (Rural)											
All Ages	**2,135**	**1,301**	**834**	**155**	**147**	**12**	**3**	**6**	**5**	**1**	**4**
0	75	30	45	6	7	..	..	..	1	..	..
1—4	210	121	89	18	19	..	..	..	1	..	..
5—14	471	249	222	42	43	4	..	..	..	..	2
15—24	479	328	151	31	22	3	2	3	1	..	..
25—34	395	237	158	15	22	3	1	3	..	..	1
35—44	273	169	104	19	18	2	..	..	1	..	1
45—54	138	104	34	10	6	..	..	..	1	1	..
55—64	63	39	24	8	9	..	..	..	..	..	..
65—74	19	14	5	4	1	..	..	..	..	..	..
75 & over	12	10	2	2	..	..	..	..	..	..	..

Age Groups	Livelihood Classes — Non-Agricultural Classes — Persons (including dependants) who derive their principal means of livelihood from: V—Production other than cultivation		VI—Commerce		VII—Transport		VIII—Other services and miscellaneous sources	
	Males	Females	Males	Females	Males	Females	Males	Females
(1)	(13)	(14)	(15)	(16)	(17)	(18)	(19)	(20)
Andaman & Nicobar Islands (Rural)								
All Ages	**882**	**591**	**30**	**7**	**37**	**8**	**178**	**69**
0	22	31	..	..	1	..	1	6
1—4	91	54	2	1	..	3	10	11
5—14	178	160	2	2	..	4	23	11
15—24	220	108	10	1	8	1	53	16
25—34	148	124	8	1	10	..	50	9
35—44	116	70	6	2	8	..	18	12
45—54	73	25	1	..	7	..	12	2
55—64	22	14	..	..	3	..	6	1
65—74	6	3	1	..	..	..	3	1
75 & over	6	2	..	..	..	..	2	..

TABLE C-II—LIVELIHOOD CLASSES BY AGE GROUPS FOR SAMPLE POPULATION—*concld.*

Age Groups	Total			Livelihood Classes — Agricultural Classes: I—Cultivators of land wholly or mainly owned and their dependants		II—Cultivators of land wholly or mainly unowned and their dependants		III—Cultivating labourers and their dependants		IV—Non-cultivating owners of land; Agricultural rent receivers and their dependants	
	Persons	Males	Females	Males	Females	Males	Females	Males	Females	Males	Females
(1)	(2)	(3)	(4)	(5)	(6)	(7)	(8)	(9)	(10)	(11)	(12)
Andaman & Nicobar Islands (Urban)											
All Ages	**792**	**539**	**253**	**7**	**7**	**2**	..	**1**	..	**1**	..
0	32	13	19	..	1	..	..	..	..	..	..
1—4	105	65	40	..	..	..	..	..	..	..	..
5—14	117	61	56	2	3	1	..	..	..	..	..
15—24	185	133	52	1	..	1	..	..	..	..	..
25—34	168	123	45	1	2	..	..	1	..	..	..
35—44	102	86	16	..	..	..	..	..	..	1	..
45—54	54	43	11	2	1	..	..	..	..	..	..
55—64	13	10	3	1	..	..	..	..	..	..	..
65—74	13	5	8	..	..	..	..	..	..	..	..
75 & over	3	..	3	..	..	..	..	..	..	..	..

Age Groups	Livelihood Classes — Non-Agricultural Classes — Persons (including dependants) who derive their principal means of livelihood from: V—Production other than cultivation		VI—Commerce		VII—Transport		VIII—Other services and miscellaneous sources	
	Males	Females	Males	Females	Males	Females	Males	Females
(1)	(13)	(14)	(15)	(16)	(17)	(18)	(19)	(20)
Andaman & Nicobar Islands (Urban)								
All Ages	**174**	**69**	**70**	**40**	**41**	**40**	**243**	**97**
0	2	5	5	3	1	1	5	9
1—4	19	13	7	7	5	9	34	11
5—14	12	13	12	6	8	7	26	27
15—24	48	12	13	9	7	12	63	19
25—34	44	13	11	6	10	8	56	16
35—44	30	5	12	3	7	1	36	7
45—54	14	4	7	3	2	1	18	2
55—64	3	2	2	..	1	..	3	1
65—74	2	2	1	2	..	..	2	4
75 & over	..	..	..	1	..	1	..	1

TABLE C-III—AGE AND CIVIL CONDITION FOR SAMPLE POPULATION

State (1)	All Ages: Total: Persons (2)	Total: Males (3)	Total: Females (4)	Unmarried: Males (5)	Unmarried: Females (6)	Married: Males (7)	Married: Females (8)	Widowed or Divorced: Males (9)	Widowed or Divorced: Females (10)
Andaman & Nicobar Islands									
Total	*2,927*	*1,840*	*1,087*	*1,038*	*557*	*728*	*428*	*74*	*102*
Rural	2,135	1,301	834	733	429	514	325	54	80
Urban	792	539	253	305	128	214	103	20	22

State (1)	Age 0: Total: Males (11)	Age 0: Total: Females (12)	Age 1—4: Total: Males (13)	Age 1—4: Total: Females (14)	Age 5—14: Total: Males (15)	Total: Females (16)	Unmarried: Males (17)	Unmarried: Females (18)	Married: Males (19)	Married: Females (20)	Widowed or Divorced: Males (21)	Widowed or Divorced: Females (22)
Andaman & Nicobar Islands												
Total	*43*	*64*	*186*	*129*	*310*	*278*	*310*	*277*	..	*1*	..	..
Rural	30	45	121	89	249	222	249	221	..	1	..	..
Urban	13	19	65	40	61	56	61	56	..	..	..	..

State (1)	Age 15—24: Total: Males (23)	Total: Females (24)	Unmarried: Males (25)	Unmarried: Females (26)	Married: Males (27)	Married: Females (28)	Widowed or Divorced: Males (29)	Widowed or Divorced: Females (30)
Andaman & Nicobar Islands								
Total	*461*	*203*	*335*	*73*	*122*	*126*	*4*	*4*
Rural	328	151	235	61	90	86	3	4
Urban	133	52	100	12	32	40	1	..

State (1)	Age 25—34: Total: Males (31)	Total: Females (32)	Unmarried: Males (33)	Unmarried: Females (34)	Married: Males (35)	Married: Females (36)	Widowed or Divorced: Males (37)	Widowed or Divorced: Females (38)
Andaman & Nicobar Islands								
Total	*360*	*203*	*121*	*8*	*228*	*164*	*11*	*31*
Rural	237	158	73	8	154	123	10	27
Urban	123	45	48	..	74	41	1	4

State (1)	Age 35—44: Total: Males (39)	Total: Females (40)	Unmarried: Males (41)	Unmarried: Females (42)	Married: Males (43)	Married: Females (44)	Widowed or Divorced: Males (45)	Widowed or Divorced: Females (46)
Andaman & Nicobar Islands								
Total	*255*	*120*	*25*	*6*	*214*	*93*	*16*	*21*
Rural	169	104	15	5	145	82	9	17
Urban	86	16	10	1	69	11	7	4

TABLE C-III—AGE AND CIVIL CONDITION FOR SAMPLE POPULATION—*concld.*

State (1)	Age 45—54 Total Males (47)	Total Females (48)	Unmarried Males (49)	Unmarried Females (50)	Married Males (51)	Married Females (52)	Widowed or Divorced Males (53)	Widowed or Divorced Females (54)
Andaman & Nicobar Islands								
Total	*147*	*45*	*12*	..	*117*	*31*	*18*	*14*
Rural	104	34	7	..	86	21	11	13
Urban	43	11	5	..	31	10	7	1

State (1)	Age 55—64 Total Males (55)	Total Females (56)	Unmarried Males (57)	Unmarried Females (58)	Married Males (59)	Married Females (60)	Widowed or Divorced Males (61)	Widowed or Divorced Females (62)
Andaman & Nicobar Islands								
Total	*49*	*27*	*5*	..	*31*	*10*	*13*	*17*
Rural	39	24	2	..	27	10	10	14
Urban	10	3	3	..	4	..	3	3

State (1)	Age 65—74 Total Males (63)	Total Females (64)	Unmarried Males (65)	Unmarried Females (66)	Married Males (67)	Married Females (68)	Widowed or Divorced Males (69)	Widowed or Divorced Females (70)
Andaman & Nicobar Islands								
Total	*19*	*13*	*1*	..	*11*	*3*	*7*	*10*
Rural	14	5	1	..	7	2	6	3
Urban	5	8	..	..	4	1	1	7

State (1)	Age 75 and over Total Males (71)	Total Females (72)	Unmarried Males (73)	Unmarried Females (74)	Married Males (75)	Married Females (76)	Widowed or Divorced Males (77)	Widowed or Divorced Females (78)
Andaman & Nicobar Islands								
Total	*10*	*5*	..	..	*5*	..	*5*	*5*
Rural	10	2	..	..	5	..	5	2
Urban	..	3	..	..	..	..	..	3

Classified Abstract of Divorced Persons

State (1)	All Ages Persons (2)	All Ages Males (3)	All Ages Females (4)	Age 0 Males (5)	Age 0 Females (6)	Age 1-4 Males (7)	Age 1-4 Females (8)	Age 5-14 Males (9)	Age 5-14 Females (10)	Age 15-24 Males (11)	Age 15-24 Females (12)
Andaman & Nicobar Islands											
Total	*32*	*11*	*21*	..	..	..	..	..	..	*2*	*2*
Rural	30	11	19	..	..	..	..	..	..	2	2
Urban	2	..	2	..	..	..	..	..	..	..	..

State (1)	Age 25-34 Males (13)	Age 25-34 Females (14)	Age 35-44 Males (15)	Age 35-44 Females (16)	Age 45-54 Males (17)	Age 45-54 Females (18)	Age 55-64 Males (19)	Age 55-64 Females (20)	Age 65-74 Males (21)	Age 65-74 Females (22)
Andaman & Nicobar Islands										
Total	*2*	*12*	*2*	*3*	*3*	*2*	*1*	..	*1*	*2*
Rural	2	11	2	3	3	2	1	..	1	1
Urban	..	1	..	..	..	..	..	..	..	1

TABLE C-IV—AGE AND LITERACY FOR SAMPLE POPULATION

This table shows the number of literate and illiterate males and females by age groups with Rural/Urban break-up. Persons who can write and read a simple letter have been treated as 'Literate.'

The number of persons (who can read only but cannot write) are given in the abstract after the table.

State	All Ages						Age 0—4		Age 5—9					
	Total		Literate		Illiterate				Total		Literate		Illiterate	
	Males	Females	Males	Females	Males	Females	Males	Females	Males	Females	Males	Females	Males	Females
(1)	(2)	(3)	(4)	(5)	(6)	(7)	(8)	(9)	(10)	(11)	(12)	(13)	(14)	(15)
Andaman & Nicobar Islands														
Total	*1,840*	*1,087*	*635*	*124*	*1,205*	*963*	*229*	*193*	*143*	*133*	*16*	*5*	*127*	*128*
Rural	1,301	834	342	61	959	773	151	134	115	107	10	2	105	105
Urban	539	253	293	63	246	190	78	59	28	26	6	3	22	23

State	Age 10-14						Age 15-24					
	Total		Literate		Illiterate		Total		Literate		Illiterate	
	Males	Females	Males	Females	Males	Females	Males	Females	Males	Females	Males	Females
(1)	(16)	(17)	(18)	(19)	(20)	(21)	(22)	(23)	(24)	(25)	(26)	(27)
Andaman & Nicobar Islands												
Total	*167*	*145*	*54*	*27*	*113*	*118*	*461*	*203*	*197*	*37*	*264*	*166*
Rural	134	115	32	11	102	104	328	151	112	19	216	132
Urban	33	30	22	16	11	14	133	52	85	18	48	34

State	Age 25—34						Age 35—44					
	Total		Literate		Illiterate		Total		Literate		Illiterate	
	Males	Females	Males	Females	Males	Females	Males	Females	Males	Females	Males	Females
(1)	(28)	(29)	(30)	(31)	(32)	(33)	(34)	(35)	(36)	(37)	(38)	(39)
Andaman & Nicobar Islands												
Total	*360*	*203*	*170*	*32*	*190*	*171*	*255*	*120*	*117*	*15*	*138*	*105*
Rural	237	158	84	13	153	145	169	104	62	9	107	95
Urban	123	45	86	19	37	26	86	16	55	6	31	10

State	Age 45—54						Age 55—64					
	Total		Literate		Illiterate		Total		Literate		Illiterate	
	Males	Females	Males	Females	Males	Females	Males	Females	Males	Females	Males	Females
(1)	(40)	(41)	(42)	(43)	(44)	(45)	(46)	(47)	(48)	(49)	(50)	(51)
Andaman & Nicobar Islands												
Total	*147*	*45*	*54*	*4*	*93*	*41*	*49*	*27*	*17*	*4*	*32*	*23*
Rural	104	34	26	3	78	31	39	24	10	4	29	20
Urban	43	11	28	1	15	10	10	3	7	..	3	3

TABLE C-IV—AGE AND LITERACY FOR SAMPLE POPULATION—*concld.*

State (1)	Age 65—74 Total Males (52)	Females (53)	Literate Males (54)	Females (55)	Illiterate Males (56)	Females (57)	Age 75 and over Total Males (58)	Females (59)	Literate Males (60)	Females (61)	Illiterate Males (62)	Females (63)
Andaman & Nicobar Islands												
Total	*19*	*13*	*8*	..	*11*	*13*	*10*	*5*	*2*	..	*8*	*5*
Rural	14	5	4	..	10	5	10	2	2	..	8	2
Urban	5	8	4	..	1	8	..	3	..	..	..	3

Abstract Classifying those 'Able to Read' in Age Groups

(In the Table C-IV—Those 'Able to Read' have been included in the column for Illiterate.)

State (1)	Able to read only: Total Males (2)	Females (3)	Age 5—9 Males (4)	Females (5)	Age 10—14 Males (6)	Females (7)	Age 15—24 Males (8)	Females (9)	Age 25—34 Males (10)	Females (11)
Andaman & Nicobar Islands										
Total	*15*	*11*	..	*2*	*1*	*1*	*4*	*4*	*5*	..
Rural	6	7	..	..	1	1	3	4	1	..
Urban	9	4	..	2	..	..	1	..	4	..

State (1)	Able to read only: Age 35-44 Males (12)	Females (13)	Age 45—54 Males (14)	Females (15)	Age 55—64 Males (16)	Females (17)	Age 65—74 Males (18)	Females (19)	Age 75 & over Males (20)	Females (21)
Andaman & Nicobar Islands										
Total	*4*	*2*	*1*	..	..	*1*	..	*1*	..	..
Rural	..	2	1	..	..	..	..	..	..	..
Urban	4	..	..	..	..	1	..	1	..	..

TABLE C-V—SINGLE YEAR AGE RETURNS FOR SAMPLE POPULATION

This table gives the distribution of persons with Rural/Urban break-up according to their age.

The instructions for Enumerators to record age were as follows:

"Write age at last 'birthday' *i.e.* the actual number of completed years of age. Write '0' for infants below one year."

Age Returns (1)	Males Total (2)	Rural (3)	Urban (4)	Females Total (5)	Rural (6)	Urban (7)
Andaman & Nicobar Islands						
All Ages	*1,840*	*1,301*	*539*	*1,087*	*834*	*253*
0	43	30	13	64	45	19
1	45	27	18	37	28	9
2	54	35	19	28	22	6
3	44	29	15	41	24	17
4	43	30	13	23	15	8

TABLE C-V—SINGLE YEAR AGE RETURNS FOR SAMPLE POPULATION—*contd.*

Age Returns	Males			Females		
	Total	Rural	Urban	Total	Rural	Urban
(1)	(1)	(3)	(4)	(5)	(6)	(7)
Andaman & Nicobar Islands						
5	33	24	9	28	22	6
6	18	15	3	28	24	4
7	23	20	3	26	18	8
8	37	32	5	25	24	1
9	32	24	8	26	19	7
10	36	29	7	32	26	6
11	26	20	6	25	20	5
12	44	37	7	37	28	9
13	33	25	8	27	21	6
14	28	23	5	24	20	4
15	27	22	5	28	20	8
16	28	21	7	21	16	5
17	22	15	7	17	12	5
18	47	36	11	32	26	6
19	30	22	8	22	16	6
20	88	61	27	29	17	12
21	44	28	16	13	12	1
22	89	65	24	9	7	2
23	33	20	13	16	12	4
24	53	38	15	16	13	3
25	99	68	31	43	29	14
26	46	34	12	20	14	6
27	28	24	4	14	13	1
28	44	26	18	22	18	4
29	23	14	9	23	22	1
30	72	44	28	40	29	11
31	8	2	6	4	4	..
32	18	9	9	18	12	6
33	11	8	3	8	6	2
34	11	8	3	11	11	..
35	61	37	24	29	26	3
36	27	16	11	8	8	..
37	23	14	9	12	12	..
38	25	16	9	16	14	2
39	18	17	1	13	12	1
40	61	45	16	26	16	10
41	8	6	2	2	2	..
42	12	5	7	7	7	..
43	11	7	4	3	3	..
44	9	6	3	4	4	..
45	41	24	17	17	11	6
46	10	6	4	3	3	..
47	7	6	1	3	3	..
48	15	8	7	3	3	..
49	16	15	1	2	2	..
50	30	23	7	10	7	3
51	7	5	2	2	1	1
52	13	12	1	2	2	..
53	3	2	1	1	..	1
54	5	3	2	2	2	..
55	15	10	5	5	4	1
56	6	5	1	2	2	..
57	2	2	..	1	1	..
58	3	3	..	4	4	..
59	4	4	..	2	2	..
60	11	8	3	10	8	2
61	3	3	..	2	2	..
62	3	2	1	..	..	..
63	2	2	..	1	1	..
64	..	..	..	..	..	..
65	7	6	1	3	1	2
66	1	1	..	1	1	..
67	..	..	..	..	..	..
68	2	..	2	1	..	1
69	3	3	..	..	..	..
70	4	4	..	7	3	4
71	..	..	..	..	..	..
72	1	..	1	..	..	..

TABLE C-V—SINGLE YEAR AGE RETURNS FOR SAMPLE POPULATION—*concld.*

Age Returns (1)	Males Total (2)	Males Rural (3)	Males Urban (4)	Females Total (5)	Females Rural (6)	Females Urban (7)
Andaman & Nicobar Islands						
73	..	..	..	1	..	1
74	1	..	1	..	..	..
75	3	3	..	1	..	1
76	1	1	..	..	..	..
77	..	..	..	..	..	..
78	2	2	..	1	1	..
79	..	..	..	1	1	..
80	2	2	..	2	..	2
81	..	..	..	..	..	..
82	..	..	..	..	..	..
83	..	..	..	..	..	..
84	..	..	..	..	..	..
85	1	1	..	..	..	..
86	..	..	..	..	..	..
87	..	..	..	..	..	..
88	..	..	..	..	..	..
89	1	1	..	..	..	..
90	..	..	..	..	..	..
91	..	..	..	..	..	..
92	..	..	..	..	..	..
93	..	..	..	..	..	..
94	..	..	..	..	..	..
95	..	..	..	..	..	..
96	..	..	..	..	..	..
97	..	..	..	..	..	..
98	..	..	..	..	..	..
99	..	..	..	..	..	..
100	..	..	..	..	..	..

SOCIAL AND CULTURAL TABLES

TABLE D-I—LANGUAGES

(i) Mother Tongue

This table gives the distribution of the population of the State according to returns for Mother Tongue at the 1951 Census and the number of persons speaking each one of them. Mother Tongue is defined at this Census as the language spoken from the cradle. The Mother Tongue of infants and deaf mutes has been taken to be the same as that of their mothers.

Serial No.	Mother Tongue — Language and State from which returned	Males	Females
	(1)	(2)	(3)
	Andaman & Nicobar Islands		
	All Languages	*19,055*	*11,916*
1	Andamanese	12	15
2	Androse	2	..
3	Assamese	12	..
4	Bengali	1,438	925
5	Burmese	956	628
6	Barochi	1	..
7	Badani	1	..
8	Chinese	16	7
9	Coorgee	34	23
10	Dogri	1	..
11	English	75	39
12	French	2	..
13	Gujarati	123	2
14	Garhwali	32	..
15	Gurkhali	43	15
16	German	2	..
17	Gosain	1	..
18	Hindustani	2,344	1,795
19	Hindi	684	291
20	Italian	1	..
21	Kanarese	26	8
22	Kharia	218	..
23	Khadia	110	..
24	Konkani	23	6
25	Karnatic	3	4
26	Karen	149	201
27	Khas	8	..
28	Kashmiri	..	1
29	Kannada	1	1
30	Laccadive	27	..
31	Malayalam	1,703	1,112
32	Marathi	57	8
33	Munda	245	2
34	Marwari	2	..
35	Mudari	65	21
36	Malaya	1	..
37	Nepali	53	12
38	Nagri	13	..
39	Nicobari	6,116	5,676
40	Oria	93	16
41	Odia	4	..
42	Oroan	64	..
43	Punjabi	164	60
44	Portuguese	1	..
45	Polish	1	..
46	Pushto	15	..
47	Parsi	2	..
48	Ranchi	159	16
49	Rantra	1	..
50	Sadri	397	1
51	Santhali	7	1
52	Sindhi	1	..
53	Siamese	1	..
54	Samalpuri	1	..
55	Swedish	1	1
56	Singhalese	3	2
57	Savera	1	..
58	Shan	2	..
59	Tamil	1,173	401
60	Telugu	893	151
61	Thailang	1	..
62	Urdu	428	434
63	Uraon	1,024	41
64	Uria	10	..
65	Uaro	8	..

(ii) Bi-lingualism

This table shows the number of persons commonly speaking any Indian Language or dialect other than his own Mother Tongue as a subsidiary language, *i.e.*, the second language most commonly used by them.

Serial No.	Mother Tongue — Language and State from which returned	Totals Speakers	Total persons returned as speaking a language subsidiary to that shown in column 1	Subsidiary Languages — Hindustani	Hindi	Urdu	Tamil	Telugu	Bengali	Punjabi	Malayalam	Marathi
	(1)	(2)	(3)	(4)	(5)	(6)	(7)	(8)	(9)	(10)	(11)	(12)
	Andaman & Nicobar Islands											
	All Languages	*30,971*	*11,781*	*6,938*	*3,700*	*731*	*106*	*110*	*41*	*15*	*6*	*7*
1	Andamanese	27	20	..	20	..	..	..	..	..	..	..
2	Androse	2	2	2	..	..	..	..	..	..	..	..
3	Assamese	12	11	7	4	..	..	..	..	..	..	..
4	Bengali	2,363	962	678	231	51	..	..	..	..	..	..
5	Burmese	1,584	1,005	916	85	1	2	1	..	..	..	..
6	Barochi	1	1	..	..	..	..	..	..	1	..	..
7	Badani	1	1	..	1	..	..	..	..	..	..	..
8	Chinese	23	12	12	..	..	..	..	..	..	..	..
9	Coorgee	57	46	29	9	..	2	..	..	..	..	..

TABLE D-I—LANGUAGES—*contd.*

(ii) Bi-lingualism—*contd.*

Serial No.	Mother Tongue: Language and State from which returned	Total Speakers	Total persons returned as speaking a language subsidiary to that shown in column 1	Subsidiary Languages: Hindustani	Hindi	Urdu	Tamil	Telugu	Bengali	Punjabi	Malayalam	Marathi
	(1)	(2)	(3)	(4)	(5)	(6)	(7)	(8)	(9)	(10)	(11)	(12)
	Andaman & Nicobar Islands											
10	Dogri	1	..	..	..	..	..	..	..	..	..	..
11	English	114	72	50	8	1	12	1	..	..	..	..
12	French	2	1	..	1	..	..	..	..	..	..	..
13	Gujarati	125	116	42	58	16	..	..	..	..	..	..
14	Garhwali	32	32	32	..	..	..	..	..	..	..	..
15	Gurkhali	58	44	22	22	..	..	..	..	..	..	..
16	German	2	..	..	..	..	..	..	..	..	..	..
17	Gosain	1	1	..	1	..	..	..	..	..	..	..
18	Hindustani	4,139	554	..	116	369	8	11	28	4	..	6
19	Hindi	975	498	296	..	168	3	1	8	9	..	..
20	Italian	1	..	..	..	..	..	..	..	..	..	..
21	Kanarese	34	27	13	7	1	5	1	..	..	..	..
22	Kharia	218	207	79	122	..	..	..	..	..	..	..
23	Khadia	110	105	29	58	..	..	..	..	..	..	..
24	Konkani	29	26	21	2	2	1	..	..	..	..	..
25	Karantic	7	6	6	..	..	..	..	..	..	..	..
26	Karen	350	160	93	62	..	..	..	..	..	..	..
27	Khas	8	7	7	..	..	..	..	..	..	..	..
28	Kashmiri	1	1	1	..	..	..	..	..	..	..	..
29	Kannada	2	2	2	..	..	..	..	..	..	..	..
30	Laccadive	27	26	24	2	..	..	..	..	..	..	..
31	Malayalam	2,815	1,869	1,621	136	83	28	1	..	..	..	..
32	Marathi	65	61	54	6	1	..	..	..	..	..	..
33	Munda	247	243	89	138	..	..	..	..	..	..	..
34	Marwari	2	1	1	..	..	..	..	..	..	..	..
35	Mundari	86	78	43	33	..	..	..	1	..	..	..
36	Malaya	1	..	..	..	..	..	..	..	..	..	..
37	Nepali	65	59	45	14	..	..	..	..	..	..	..
38	Nagri	13	7	..	7	..	..	..	..	..	..	..
39	Nicobari	11,792	1,552	1	1,551	..	..	..	..	..	..	..
40	Oria	109	103	83	11	2	..	7	..	..	..	..
41	Odia	4	4	3	1	..	..	..	..	..	..	..
42	Oroan	64	63	52	11	..	..	..	..	..	..	..
43	Punjabi	224	197	136	43	17	1	..	..	..	..	..
44	Portuguese	1	1	1	..	..	..	..	..	..	..	..
45	Polish	1	..	..	..	..	..	..	..	..	..	..
46	Pushto	15	11	9	..	1	..	..	..	..	..	..
47	Parsi	2	2	2	..	..	..	..	..	..	..	..
48	Ranchi	175	169	165	4	..	..	..	..	..	..	..
49	Rantra	1	1	1	..	..	..	..	..	..	..	..
50	Sadri	398	337	197	139	..	..	..	1	..	..	..
51	Santhali	8	8	6	2	..	..	..	..	..	..	..
52	Sindhi	1	1	1	..	..	..	..	..	..	..	..
53	Siamese	1	1	..	1	..	..	..	..	..	..	..
54	Samalpuri	1	1	1	..	..	..	..	..	..	..	..
55	Swedish	2	2	1	1	..	..	..	..	..	..	
56	Singhalese	5	4	1	1	..	2	..	..	..	..	..
57	Savera	1	1	1	..	..	..	..	..	..	..	..
58	Shan	2	2	2	..	..	..	..	..	..	..	..
59	Tamil	1,574	1,006	818	93	5	..	82	..	..	6	..
60	Telugu	1,044	733	457	216	13	41	..	..	..	..	..
61	Thailang	1	1	..	1	..	..	..	..	..	..	..
62	Urdu	862	290	199	74	..	1	5	3	1	..	1
63	Uraon	1,065	1,011	581	397	..	..	..	..	..	..	..
64	Uria	10	9	6	3	..	..	..	..	..	..	..
65	Uaro	8	8	..	8	..	..	..	..	..	..	..

TABLE D-I—LANGUAGES—*concld.*

(ii) Bi-lingualism—*concld.*

Serial No.	Mother Tongue: Language and State from which returned (1)	Subsidiary Languages: Sadri (13)	Munda (14)	Gujarati (15)	Burmese (16)	Nepali (17)	Kanarese (18)	Karnatic (19)	Oria (20)	Assamese (21)
	Andaman & Nicobar Islands									
	All Languages	*75*	*13*	*11*	*17*	*1*	*7*	*1*	*1*	*1*
1	Andamanese	..	..	..	..	..	..	..	..	..
2	Androse	..	..	..	..	..	..	..	..	..
3	Assamese	..	..	..	..	..	..	..	..	..
4	Bengali	..	..	..	..	1	..	..	..	1
5	Burmese	..	..	..	..	..	..	..	..	..
6	Barochi	..	..	..	..	..	..	..	..	..
7	Badani	..	..	..	..	..	..	..	..	..
8	Chinese	..	..	..	..	..	..	..	..	..
9	Coorgee	..	..	..	..	..	6	..	..	..
10	Dogri	..	..	..	..	..	..	..	..	..
11	English	..	..	..	..	..	..	..	..	..
12	French	..	..	..	..	..	..	..	..	..
13	Gujarati	..	..	..	..	..	..	..	..	..
14	Garhwali	..	..	..	..	..	..	..	..	..
15	Gurkhali	..	..	..	..	..	..	..	..	..
16	German	..	..	..	..	..	..	..	..	..
17	Gosain	..	..	..	..	..	..	..	..	..
18	Hindustani	..	..	4	7	..	..	1	..	..
19	Hindi	2	11	..	..	..	..	..	..	..
20	Italian	..	..	..	..	..	..	..	..	..
21	Kanarese	..	..	..	..	..	..	..	..	..
22	Kharia	4	2	..	..	..	..	..	..	..
23	Khadia	18	..	..	..	..	..	..	..	..
24	Konkani	..	..	..	..	..	..	..	..	..
25	Karnatic	..	..	..	..	..	..	..	..	..
26	Karen	..	..	..	5	..	..	..	..	..
27	Khas	..	..	..	..	..	..	..	..	..
28	Kashmiri	..	..	..	..	..	..	..	..	..
29	Kannada	..	..	..	..	..	..	..	..	..
30	Laccadive	..	..	..	..	..	..	..	..	..
31	Malayalam	..	..	..	..	..	..	..	..	..
32	Marathi	..	..	..	..	..	..	..	..	..
33	Munda	16	..	..	..	..	..	..	..	..
34	Marwari	..	..	..	..	..	..	..	..	..
35	Mundari	1	..	..	..	..	..	..	..	..
36	Malaya	..	..	..	..	..	..	..	..	..
37	Nepali	..	..	..	..	..	..	..	..	..
38	Nagri	..	..	..	..	..	..	..	..	..
39	Nicobari	..	..	..	..	..	..	..	..	..
40	Oria	..	..	..	..	..	..	..	..	..
41	Odia	..	..	..	..	..	..	..	..	..
42	Oroan	..	..	..	..	..	..	..	..	..
43	Punjabi	..	..	..	..	..	..	..	..	..
44	Portuguese	..	..	..	..	..	..	..	..	..
45	Polish	..	..	..	..	..	..	..	..	..
46	Pushto	..	..	1	..	..	..	..	..	..
47	Parsi	..	..	..	..	..	..	..	..	..
48	Ranchi	..	..	..	..	..	..	..	..	..
49	Rantra	..	..	..	..	..	..	..	..	..
50	Sadri	..	..	..	..	..	..	..	..	..
51	Santhali	..	..	..	..	..	..	..	..	..
52	Sindhi	..	..	..	..	..	..	..	..	..
53	Siamese	..	..	..	..	..	..	..	..	..
54	Samalpuri	..	..	..	..	..	..	..	..	..
55	Swedish	..	..	..	..	..	..	..	..	..
56	Singhalese	..	..	..	..	..	..	..	..	..
57	Savera	..	..	..	..	..	..	..	..	..
58	Shan	..	..	..	..	..	..	..	..	..
59	Tamil	..	..	..	2	..	..	..	..	..
60	Telugu	1	..	..	3	..	1	..	1	..
61	Thailang	..	..	..	..	..	..	..	..	..
62	Urdu	..	..	6	..	..	..	..	..	..
63	Uraon	33	..	..	..	..	..	..	..	..
64	Uria	..	..	..	..	..	..	..	..	..
65	Uaro	..	..	..	..	..	..	..	..	..

TABLE D-II—RELIGION

This table shows the number of males and females under different religions in the State.

State	Total Population			Hindus		Sikhs		Jains		Buddhists	
	Persons	Males	Females	Males	Females	Males	Females	Males	Females	Males	Females
(1)	(2)	(3)	(4)	(5)	(6)	(7)	(8)	(9)	(10)	(11)	(12)
Andaman & Nicobar Islands	**30,971**	**19,055**	**11,916**	**6,138**	**3,156**	**89**	**37**	**1**	..	**982**	**622**

State	Muslims		Christians		Jews		Zoroastrians		Other Religions: Tribal		Other Religions: Non-Tribal	
	Males	Females	Males	Females	Males	Females	Males	Females	Males	Females	Males	Females
(1)	(13)	(14)	(15)	(16)	(17)	(18)	(19)	(20)	(21)	(22)	(23)	(24)
Andaman & Nicobar Islands	**2,874**	**1,909**	**6,090**	**3,404**	**1**	..	**2**	..	**13**	**7**	**2,865**	**2,781**

* TABLE D-III—SCHEDULED CASTES AND SCHEDULED TRIBES

* *This table has not been prepared as there are no Scheduled Castes and Scheduled Tribes in these Islands.*

TABLE D-IV—MIGRANTS

This table gives the distribution of population enumerated in the State according to their places of birth.

District, State or Country where born	Persons	Males	Females
(1)	(2)	(3)	(4)
Andaman & Nicobar Islands			
TOTAL POPULATION	**30,971**	**19,055**	**11,916**
A. Born in India	**27,765**	**16,691**	**11,074**
I. Born within the State of enumeration	19,323	9,964	9,359
(i) District of enumeration	19,323	9,964	9,359
(ii) Other Districts	..	..	..
II. States in India beyond the State of enumeration	8,442	6,727	1,715
(i) States adjacent to the State of enumeration	..	..	..
(ii) Other States	8,424	6,716	1,708
Assam	56	48	8
Bihar	1,934	1,842	92
Bombay	113	95	18
Madhya Pradesh	380	286	94
Madras	3,919	2,978	941
Orissa	107	78	29
Punjab	254	162	92
Uttar Pradesh	479	312	167
West Bengal	424	332	92
Hyderabad	24	19	5
Madhya Bharat	293	229	64
Mysore	18	16	2
Patiala & East Punjab States Union	6	4	2
Saurashtra	9	3	6
Travancore-Cochin	268	238	30
Jammu & Kashmir	10	9	1
Coorg	48	30	18
Delhi	10	4	6
Manipur	4	3	1
Tripura	44	5	39
Rajasthan	24	23	1
(iii) Elsewhere in India	18	11	7

TABLE D-IV—MIGRANTS—*concld.*

District, State or Country where born	Persons	Males	Females
(1)	(2)	(3)	(4)
Andaman & Nicobar Islands			
B. Countries in Asia beyond India (including U. S. S. R.)	**3,156**	**2,318**	**838**
Afghanistan	3	2	1
Burma	1,213	813	400
Ceylon	4	3	1
China	12	10	2
Nepal	64	50	14
Pakistan	1,850	1,434	416
Elsewhere in Asia	10	6	4
C. Countries in Europe (excluding U. S. S. R.)	**34**	**32**	**2**
United Kingdom & Northern Ireland	32	31	1
Elsewhere in Europe (excluding U. S. S. R.)	2	1	1
D. Countries in Africa	**1**	**1**	..
Union of South Africa	1	1	..
E. Countries in America	**10**	**10**	..
United States	10	10	..
F. Countries in Australasia	**5**	**3**	**2**
Australia	1	..	1
Elsewhere in Australasia	4	3	1
G. Born at Sea	..	..	..
H. Birth Place not returned	..	..	..

TABLE D-V—DISPLACED PERSONS FROM PAKISTAN

Part (i) Origin in Pakistan and Year of arrival in India

This table gives the details of place of origin and time of arrival in India of Displaced Persons.

State	Total population of Displaced Persons			Displaced Persons from West Pakistan											
				1946		1947		1948		1949		1950		1951	
	Persons	Males	Females	Males	Females	Males	Females	Males	Females	Males	Females	Males	Females	Males	Females
(1)	(2)	(3)	(4)	(5)	(6)	(7)	(8)	(9)	(10)	(11)	(12)	(13)	(14)	(15)	(16)
Andaman & Nicobar Islands	**1,500**	**845**	**655**	..	..	**24**	**12**	..	..	..	..	**1**	..	..	..

State	Displaced Persons from East Pakistan											
	1946		1947		1948		1949		1950		1951	
	Males	Females	Males	Females	Males	Females	Males	Females	Males	Females	Males	Females
(1)	(17)	(18)	(19)	(20)	(21)	(22)	(23)	(24)	(25)	(26)	(27)	(28)
Andaman & Nicobar Islands	**36**	**28**	**168**	**113**	**230**	**185**	**92**	**77**	**290**	**238**	**4**	**2**

TABLE D-V—DISPLACED PERSONS FROM PAKISTAN—*concld.*

Part (ii) Displaced Persons by Livelihood Classes

This table gives the distribution of Displaced Persons by Livelihood Classes.

State	Total			Agricultural Classes: I—Cultivators of land wholly or mainly owned and their dependants		II—Cultivators of land wholly or mainly unowned and their dependants		III—Cultivating labourers and their dependants		IV—Non-cultivating owners of land; Agricultural rent receivers and their dependants	
	Persons	Males	Females	Males	Females	Males	Females	Males	Females	Males	Females
(1)	(2)	(3)	(4)	(5)	(6)	(7)	(8)	(9)	(10)	(11)	(12)
Andaman & Nicobar Islands	1,500	845	655	473	417	..	1	..	3	4	..

State	Non-Agricultural Classes — Persons (including dependants) who derive their principal means of livelihood from: V—Production other than cultivation		VI—Commerce		VII—Transport		VIII—Other services and miscellaneous sources	
	Males	Females	Males	Females	Males	Females	Males	Females
(1)	(13)	(14)	(15)	(16)	(17)	(18)	(19)	(20)
Andaman & Nicobar Islands	42	12	12	8	3	..	311	214

TABLE D-VI—NON-INDIAN NATIONALS

The figures for Non-Indian Nationals enumerated in these Islands are given in this table.

State	Total			Pakistani		Burmese		Chinese		British	
	Persons	Males	Females	Males	Females	Males	Females	Males	Females	Males	Females
(1)	(2)	(3)	(4)	(5)	(6)	(7)	(8)	(9)	(10)	(11)	(12)
Andaman & Nicobar Islands	1,131	720	411	39	1	582	388	4	2	29	2

State	Nepali		Swedish		Ceylonese		German		Italian		Belgian	
	Males	Females	Males	Females	Males	Females	Males	Females	Males	Females	Males	Females
(1)	(13)	(14)	(15)	(16)	(17)	(18)	(19)	(20)	(21)	(22)	(23)	(24)
Andaman & Nicobar Islands	58	16	1	1	3	1	2	..	1	..	1	..

TABLE D-VII—LIVELIHOOD CLASSES BY EDUCATIONAL STANDARDS

This table gives the distribution of population in each Livelihood Class according to Educational Standards. Persons who do not come up to any of the Standards specified in the table but are literate are classified under the first category, 'Literate'.

Educational Standard	Total			Agricultural Classes							
				I—Cultivators of land wholly or mainly owned and their dependants		II—Cultivators of land wholly or mainly unowned and their dependants		III—Cultivating labourers and their dependants		IV—Non-cultivating owners of land; Agricultural rent receivers and their dependants	
	Persons	Males	Females	Males	Females	Males	Females	Males	Females	Males	Females
(1)	(2)	(3)	(4)	(5)	(6)	(7)	(8)	(9)	(10)	(11)	(12)
Andaman & Nicobar Islands											
All Standards	**7,980**	**6,513**	**1,467**	**762**	**249**	**30**	**9**	**33**	**9**	**13**	**4**
Literate	7,492	6,064	1,428	753	248	30	9	33	9	12	4
Middle School	28	27	1	..	..	..	..	..	..	..	..
Matriculate or S. L. C. Higher Secondary	324	301	23	8	1	..	..	..	..	1	..
Intermediate in Arts or Science	48	40	8	1	..	..	..	..	..	..	..
All Degrees or Diplomas	*88*	*81*	*7*	..	..	..	..	..	..	..	..
Graduate in Arts or Science	42	39	3	..	..	..	..	..	..	..	..
Post Graduate in Arts or Science	12	10	2	..	..	..	..	..	..	..	..
Teaching	..	..	..	..	..	..	..	..	..	..	..
Engineering	9	9	..	..	..	..	..	..	..	..	..
Agriculture	..	..	..	..	..	..	..	..	..	..	..
Veterinary	4	4	..	..	..	..	..	..	..	..	..
Commerce	1	1	..	..	..	..	..	..	..	..	..
Legal	..	..	..	..	..	..	..	..	..	..	..
Medical	9	7	2	..	..	..	..	..	..	..	..
Others	11	11	..	..	..	..	..	..	..	..	..

Educational Standard	Non-Agricultural Classes — Persons (including dependants) who derive their principal means of livelihood from							
	V—Production other than cultivation		VI—Commerce		VII—Transport		VIII—Other services and miscellaneous sources	
	Males	Females	Males	Females	Males	Females	Males	Females
(1)	(13)	(14)	(15)	(16)	(17)	(18)	(19)	(20)
Andaman & Nicobar Islands								
All Standards	**2,401**	**414**	**547**	**117**	**433**	**84**	**2,294**	**581**
Literate	2,310	410	521	117	374	84	2,031	547
Middle School	21	1	..	..	2	..	4	..
Matriculate or S.L.C. Higher Secondary	53	3	14	..	39	..	186	19
Intermediate in Arts or Science	8	..	9	..	6	..	16	8
All Degrees or Diplomas	*9*	..	*3*	..	*12*	..	*57*	*7*
Graduate in Arts or Science	4	..	2	..	3	..	30	3
Post Graduate in Arts or Science	3	..	..	..	..	..	7	2
Teaching	..	..	..	..	..	..	..	..
Engineering	..	..	..	..	2	..	7	..
Agriculture	..	..	..	..	..	..	..	..
Veterinary	2	..	..	..	..	..	2	..
Commerce	..	..	1	..	..	..	..	..
Legal	..	..	..	..	..	..	..	..
Medical	..	..	..	..	1	..	6	2
Others	..	..	..	..	6	..	5	..

SUMMARY FIGURES FOR DISTRICTS

TABLE E—SUMMARY FIGURES BY DISTRICTS

In this table area, percentage variation, density of population and distribution of the population by Livelihood Classes are shown for these Islands with Rural/Urban break-up. Rural/Urban figures for area, percentage variation and density of population are not available.

State and Locality	Area in sq. miles	Population 1951			Population 1941	Percentage Variation		Density		Livelihood Classes — Agricultural Classes: I—Cultivators of land wholly or mainly owned and their dependants		II—Cultivators of land wholly or mainly unowned and their dependants	
		Persons	Males	Females	Persons	1941 to 1951	1931 to 1941	1951	1941	Males	Females	Males	Females
(1)	(2)	(3)	(4)	(5)	(6)	(7)	(8)	(9)	(10)	(11)	(12)	(13)	(14)
Andaman & Nicobar Islands	**3,215**	**30,971**	**19,055**	**11,916**	**33,768**	**—8·3**	**+14·6**	**10**	**11**	**2,177**	**1,890**	**94**	**71**
RURAL		22,957	13,815	9,142						2,096	1,794	89	69
URBAN		8,014	5,240	2,774						81	96	5	2
Aberdeen—													
Rural		4,617	2,921	1,696						1,058	872	45	35
Urban		8,014	5,240	2,774						81	96	5	2
Wimberleygunj—(Rural)		3,931	2,362	1,569						1,034	921	44	34
Wimberleygunj, Forest Division—(Rural)		1,110	1,040	70						2	1	..	..
Middle Andaman, Forest Division—(Rural)		1,290	1,171	119						1	..	..	..
Nicobars—(Rural)		12,009	6,321	5,688						1	..	..	..

State and Locality	Livelihood Classes — Agricultural Classes: III—Cultivating labourers and their dependants		IV—Non-cultivating owners of land; Agricultural rent receivers and their dependants		Non-Agricultural Classes — Persons (including dependants) who derive their principal means of livelihood from: V—Production other than cultivation		VI—Commerce		VII—Transport		VIII—Other services and miscellaneous sources	
	Males	Females	Males	Females	Males	Females	Males	Females	Males	Females	Males	Females
(1)	(15)	(16)	(17)	(18)	(19)	(20)	(21)	(22)	(23)	(24)	(25)	(26)
Andaman & Nicobar Islands	**85**	**46**	**21**	**27**	**10,636**	**6,892**	**935**	**502**	**737**	**356**	**4,370**	**2,132**
RURAL	83	46	15	21	8,874	6,164	291	84	368	77	1,999	887
URBAN	2	..	6	6	1,762	728	644	418	369	279	2,371	1,245
Aberdeen—												
Rural	21	28	10	18	376	159	54	36	288	67	1,069	481
Urban	2	..	6	6	1,762	728	644	418	369	279	2,371	1,245
Wimberleygunj—(Rural)	62	18	..	1	471	185	56	37	6	10	689	363
Wimberleygunj, Forest Division—(Rural)	..	..	3	..	987	52	4	2	..	..	44	15
Middle Andaman, Forest Division—(Rural)	..	..	2	2	1,056	94	18	9	..	..	94	14
Nicobars—(Rural)	..	..	..	..	5,984	5,674	159	..	74	..	103	14

List of Agents in India from whom Government of India Publications are available as on 31-12-54.

AGRA
English Book Depot, Taj Road.
Modern Book Depot, 4, Taj Road.
National Book House, Joonimandi.
Wadhawa & Co., Raja Mandi.
AHMEDABAD
Chandrakant Chimanlal Vora, Gandhi Road.
Hari Har Book & Stationery Mart.
Indradhanu Book House Ltd., Mission Road, Bhadra.
New Order Book Co., Ellis Bridge.
AJMER
Bookland, 663, Madargate.
Rajputana Book House.
Oxford Book Centre, Beawar Road.
AKOLA
Bakshi, M.G.
ALLAHABAD
Central Book Depot, 44, Johnston Ganj.
Kitabistan, 17A, Kamla Nehru Road.
Law Book Co., P.B. No. 4, Albert Road.
Ram Narain Lal, 1, Bank Road.
Students Friends, 224, Hewett Road.
Supdt., Printing & Sty., U.P.
Universal Book Company.
University Book Agency (of Lahore), P.B. No. 63.
Wheeler & Co., A.H.
ALWAR
Jaina General Stores, Bazaza Bazar.
AMBALA CANTT.
English Book Depot.
Sohan Lal Publications.
ANAND
Charoter Book Stall, Station Road.
AMRITSAR
Sikh Publishing House Ltd., Court Road.
BANARAS
Students Friends, University Gate.
Banaras Book Corporation, University Road, P.O. Lanka.
BANGALORE
Bangalore Book Centre, Subeder Chitram Road.
Curator, Govt. Book Depot (Director of Ptg. & Sty. & Pubns.).
Standard Book Depot, Avenue Road.
States Business Syndicate, P.B. No. 10.
The Bangalore Press, Lake View, Mysore, P.O.B. No. 7.
Vichar Sahitya Ltd., Balepet.
Book Emporium M/s. S.S., 118, Mount Jay Road, Basvengudi P.O.
BAREILLY
National Book Depot, Biharipura.
BARODA
Good Companions.
BHAGALPUR
Dealers Welfare Syndicate, 13, Anant Ram Lane, Bhagalpur-2 (Bihar).
BHOPAL
Supdt., State Govt. Press.
BOMBAY
B. M. Santilal & Co., 93, Narayan Dhuru Street.
Charles Lambert & Co., P.O. Box No. 1032.
Co-operators Book Depot, 9, Bake House Lane, Mahatma Gandhi Road.
Current Book House, Hornby Road.
Current Technical Literature Co., Ltd., 133, Mahatma Gandhi Road.
International Book House Ltd., Ash Lane, Mahatma Gandhi Road.
Lakhani Book Depot, Bombay-4.
New Book Co., Kitab Mahal, 188-190, Hornby Road.
Popular Book Depot, Lamington Road.
Raj Kamal Publications, Himalaya House, Hornby Road.
Taraporevala Sons & Co., M/s. D.B.
Thacker & Co.
Tripathi & Co., N.M., Princes Street.
Wheeler & Co., A.H., 249, Hornby Road.
Sunder Das Gian Chand, 163, Samuel Street.
Supdt., Ptg. & Sty., Queens Road.
CALCUTTA
Chakravarty Chatterjee & Co., Ltd., 15, College Square.
Chatterjee & Co., 3, Bacha Ram Chatterjee Lane.
Hindu Library, 69-A, Bolaram De Street.
Lahiri & Co., Ltd., S.K.
M. C. Sarkar & Sons Ltd., 14, Bankim Chatterjee Street.
Newman & Co.
Oxford Book & Sty. Co., 17, Park Street.
R. Cambray & Co., Ltd., Kent House, P-33, Mission Road Extn.
Roy Choudhury & Co., N.M., 72, Harrison Road.
Sarkar & Sons Ltd., B.C., 1/1/1c, College Square.
Thacker Spink & Co. (1933) Ltd.
Wheeler & Co., A.H., 18, Netaji Subhas Road.
Zoological Society of India, 34, Chittaranjan Avenue.
CHANDAUSI
Madan Mohan.
CHANDIGARH
Supdt., Ptg. & Sty., Punjab.
COCHIN
Saraswat Corporation Ltd., Main Bazar Road.
CUTTACK
Cuttack Law Times.
Prabhat K. Mahapatra, Chandni Chowk.
Press Officer, Orissa Sectt.
Utkal Stores, Balm Bazar.
DEHRA DUN
Jugal Kishore & Co.
DELHI
Atma Ram & Sons, Kashmere Gate.
* Bahri Bros., 188, Lajpat Rai Market.
Bawa Harkishan Dass Bedi (Vijay General Agencies), 9-E, Sadar Thana Road, G.P.O. Box 2027.
Federal Law Book Depot, Kashmere Gate.
General Book Depot, 538/39, Egerton Road, P.O. Box No. 220.
Imperial Publishing Co., 3, Faiz Bazar, Darya Ganj.
Indian Army Book Depot, 3, Daryaganj.
Jaina & Bros., J.M., Mori Gate.
Metropolitan Book Co., Delhi Gate.
N. C. Kansil & Co., Delhi Gate.
New Stationery House, Subzimandi.
Youngman & Co. (Regd.), Egerton Road.
DHANBAD
Ismg Co-operative Stores Ltd.
Indian School of Mines & Applied Geology.
DHUBRI
The Students Library, D.K. Road.
ERNAKULAM
Bharat Stores.
FEROZEPORE
English Book Depot.
GAUHATI
Kitab Ghar.
GIRIDIH
Popular Traders.
GORAKHPUR
Halchal Sahitya Mandir.
GWALIOR
Jain & Brothers, M.B., Sarafa Road.
Saraswati Sadan (Loyal Book Depot). Supdt., Ptg. & Sty., M.B.
HARDWAR
Shri Sewa Kunj, Booksellers.
HOSHIARPUR
Parkash News Agency.
Universal Book Stores.
HYDERABAD (Dn.)
Hyderabad Book Depot.
Swaraj Book Depot, 1368, Lakri Ka Pul.
Director, Govt. Press (Publications).
INDORE
Literature Palace, 31, Sanyogitaganj.
Rupayana, Rampurwala Buildings.
Shri Indore Book Depot, 33, Mahatma Gandhi Road.

* Has a branch at Khan Market in name of Bahri Sons.

List of Agents in India from whom Government of India Publications are available as on 31-12-54—*contd.*

JAIPUR CITY
Garg Book Co., Tripolla Bazar.
Upper India Publishing House.
Vani Mandir. Swai Man Singh Highway.
Supdt., Ptg. & Sty. Deptt., Rajasthan.

JAMMU (Tawi)
Krishna General Stores, Raghunath Bazar.

JAM NAGAR
Swadeshi Vastu Bhandar.

JHANSI
Bhatia Book Depot, Sadar Bazar.
English Book Depot.

JODHPUR
Dwarka Das Pathi.
Kitab Ghar, Sojati Gate.

JUBBULPORE
Modern Book House, Jawaherganj.

JULLUNDUR CITY
Excelsior Book Depot.
Hazooria & Sons, Mai Hiran Gate.
Jain General House.
University Publishers.

KANPUR
Advani & Co.
Sahitya Niketan.
Universal Book Stall, The Mall.

KARNAL
Malhotra & Co.

KODARMA
The Bhagwati Press, P.O. Thumsitelaiya.

KHURJA
Bharati Mandir, 31-C, Nai Basti.

KOLHAPUR
Maharashtra Grantha Bhandar.

KOZHIKODE
K. R. Brothers.

KUMTA
S. V. Kamat, Booksellers, Kumta N.K.

LUCKNOW
Balkrishna Book House.
British Book Depot, 84, Hazratganj.
Law Book Agency, 29A, Kachery Road.
Ram Advani, Hazratganj.
Universal Publishers Ltd., Plaza Building.
Upper India Publishing House Ltd.
Literature Place, Aminabad Park.

LUDHIANA
Lyall Book Depot.
Mohindra Brothers, Katchery Road.

MADRAS
Accounts Test Institute, P.O. 760, Egmore.
C. Subbash Chetty & Co., Triplicane.
Devine Trading Co., 22, Namasivaya Mudali Street, Triplicane.
Higginbothams.
K. Krishnamurty, Mount Road.
Presidency Book Supplies, 8, Pycrofts, Triplicane.
Supdt., Govt. Press, Mount Road.
Varadachary & Co.

MADURAI
Vivekananda Press, 48, West Masi Street.

MANGALORE
U. R. Shenoy & Sons, Car Street.

MASULIPATAM
M. Sheshachalam & Co.
Trivani Publishers.

MEERUT
Hind Chitra Press.
Prakash Educations Stores, Near Tehsil.
University Book Depot.
Loyal Book Depot, Chhipi Tank.

MYSORE
H. Venkataramiah & Sons.
Vedyanidhi Book Depot, Hundred Feet Road.
J. Nanumal & Sons, Lansdowne Buildings.

NAGIANA
Goyal Brothers, Booksellers, etc.

NAGPUR
Supdt., Govt. Printing (M.P.).
Western Book Depot.
New Book Depot, Moch No. 3, Sitabuldi.

NAINITAL
Consul Book Depot.

NEW DELHI
Amrit Book Co., Connaught Circus.
Bhawani & Sons, Connaught Place.
Bod Raj Marwah, Shop No. 65, Pusa Road Market, Karol Bagh.
Central News Agency, Connaught Place.
Empire Book Depot, 278, Aliganj, Lodhi Road.
English Book Stores, G. Block, Connaught Circus.
Faqir Chand Marwa & Sons, Khan Market.
Jain Book Agency, Connaught Place.
Navyug Traders, Original Road, Karol Bagh.
Oxford Book & Stationery Co., Scindia House.
Rama Krishna & Sons (of Lahore) 13/13, Connaught Place.
Saraswati Book Depot, 15, Lady Harding Road.
Sikh Publishing House Ltd., 70-C, Connaught Place.
Suneja Book Centre, 24-90, Connaught Circus.
Taneja Books & Stationery Mart, Raisina Road.

PATIALA
Jain Co., Booksellers, etc. Bazar Shaha Nashin.
Supdt., Bhupendra State Press, PEPSU.

PATNA
Shukla Book Depot, Bankipur.
Supdt., Govt. Printing, Bihar, P.O. Gulzar Bagh, Patna.

PATNA CITY
Lakshmi Trading Co., Padri-ki-Haveli.
Moti Lal Banarsi Dass, Bankipore.

POONA
Deccan Book Stall, Ferguson College Road.
Imperial Book Depot, 266, Main Street.
International Book Service, Deccan Gymkhana.
N. R. Bhalerao, 602, Shanwar Peth.
Raka Book Agency.

RAJKOT
Mohan Lal Dossabhai Shah.

RANCHI
Ideal Book Store, Near Parsthan Theatre, Main Road.

REWA
Supdt., State Govt. Emporium, U.P.

ROORKEE
Cambridge Book Depot.

SAGAR
Students Book Depot.

SECUNDERABAD (Dn.)
Hindustan Diary Publishers.

SHILLONG
Supdt., Assam Secretariat Press.
Chapala Book Stall.

SIMLA
Azad Kitab Mahal, Stall No. 13.
J. Ray & Sons (India), Ltd.
Minerva Book Shop, The Mall.
Sunder Dass & Sons, 141, Lower Bazar.
Supdt., Himachal Pradesh Govt. Press.

SIROHI
National Trading Co.

SONIPAT
United Book Agency.

SURAT
Popular Book Stores, Tower Road.
Shree Gajanan Pustakalaya, Tower Road.

TRICHINOPOLY FORT
Krishnaswami & Co., S. S., Teppakulam.

TRIVENDRUM
International Book Depot, Main Road.

UJJAIN
Manakchand Book Depot, Patni Bazar.

VELLORE
Venkatasubhan, S., Law Booksellers.

VIJAYAWADA
Hindustan Diary Publishers.
The Commercial Links, Governorpet.